Diary of a
Fox-hunting Man

Diary of a Fox-hunting Man

TERENCE CARROLL

Futura

For Yvonne

A Futura Book

© 1984 by Terence Carroll

First published in Great Britain 1984
by Hamish Hamilton Ltd

First Futura edition 1985

ISBN 0 7088 2884 1

Set in IBM 11pt Journal by 𝍐 Tek-Art, Croydon, Surrey
Printed and bound in Great Britain by
Hunt Barnard, Aylesbury

A Futura Publication
A Division of
Macdonald & Co (Publishers) Ltd
Maxwell House
74 Worship St
London EC2A 2EN

A BPCC plc Company

Contents

Foreword

While writing this book I have spoken to hundreds of fox-hunters, nearly all of whom have asked whether it is 'for' or 'against' their sport. My reply has been that it is neither; that, as impartially and thoroughly as I am able, it is simply 'about' fox-hunting in the 1980s — an account for those who know that hunting takes place, but are not aware how, or why, or how deeply important the sport is to rural Britain. There is nothing more to say — it is all in the pages that follow — but I must express my gratitude for the courtesy shown me by fox-hunters wherever I have travelled in pursuit of them, particularly those of the Hampshire Hunt and its Supporters Club, who have been unfailingly kind, patient and helpful.

Wolfhanger
Bramdean
Hampshire

Summer, 1984

Boxing Day

The Boxing Day Meet is one of Britain's great and quaint rural rituals. At 11 a.m., all over the land, upwards of half a million people gather outside country pubs, on village greens and in market squares to witness a spectacle that's just like the colourful olde worlde pictures on the cards, calendars and table mats they've given each other for Christmas — horses, hounds, red coats, top hats, white breeches, hearty stirrup-cups, and sometimes even snow to add seasonal flavour to the Dickensian scene.

It's pleasing to look at; one of the traditional ingredients of the Christmas holiday. Then, after about 20 minutes, the scarlet-clad Huntsman blows his horn, calls 'hounds, please' and the 100 or more riders clatter off.

The spectators, who may be two or three thousand strong, then climb back into their heated cars and go home to eat cold turkey and watch lukewarm television. The show is over for another year. They've shifted their yule-tide bulging bodies a bit, tried out their stiff new 'ideal gift' gloves and sheepskin coats, had a spot of fresh air, and attended an event that is strangely reassuring, oddly anachronistic, mildly entertaining and somewhat mystifying — not unlike the pantomime they may be going to see later in the day.

But what happens when a Hunt moves off? Where do all those people on horseback go to? What do they do when they get there? Who are they? What are they? Bloodthirsty aristocrats? Sanguinary snobs? Rich idiots? Sadists? Do they actually catch foxes? Kill them? How? Attack them with those long whips they carry? Why do they do whatever it is they do?

There can be few such utterly British sporting activities so widely known about, yet so little understood. Fox-hunting is part of our heritage. We have thousands of pubs called the Fox, the Fox and Hounds and the Fox and Duck; their walls are covered in old hunting prints; men in top hats and red coats gallop across curtains, cushion covers, carpets, cruets, cake-tins and tea-caddies — you could get trampled to death just making a cuppa — yet most of us associate all this charging about only with the past, vaguely equating it with copper bed-warmers, candlesticks, coaching horns, coal-scuttles and the many other comfortingly curious artefacts which nourish national nostalgia and enrich antique dealers.

Fox-hunting is of the past, of course. But it is also of the present. There are over 200 packs of foxhounds in Britain today, and although hunting has been modified by agricultural and social changes, it remains a sport so popular that it engages perhaps a quarter of a million people and is gaining more followers every season — on horseback, on foot, and on wheels.

Any winter Saturday — and on a good many mid-week days — a photographer could go out and take pictures similar to those old hunting prints, right down to the red coats and top hats flying over fences and streams — and falling into them.

The men wearing this strange attire have changed over the years. Where there used to be the titled, the privileged, wealthy landowners, rich farmers, influential politicians, successful industrialists and the like, there is now a levelling leavening of accountants, dentists, shopkeepers, journalists, actors, airline pilots and a hundred other kinds of men who seek to escape an increasingly dull, computerised existence through the outdoor joy and risk of getting on a horse and following hounds. So, very often, do their wives. And their children.

Fox-hunting has changed. Yet, paradoxically, it has remained the same.

*

Put simply, a modern Hunt is a kind of club, most of the running expenses of which are met by its members' subscriptions. The main costs are associated with the Hunt's pack of hounds, its horses, and the staff employed to look after them.

The Hunt operates in a clearly defined area called its 'country', under the overall control of its Masters. There are usually two or more Masters (known then as Joint-Masters) whose expenses are met by the Hunt Committee, but who may still dig fairly deeply into their own pockets.

Masters are elected annually, and come under the jurisdiction of the Masters of Foxhounds Association, the governing body of the sport. There are variations of this structure, but they are not really significant.

A key figure in every Hunt is its Huntsman (the Hunt's man, as it used to be) who is more often than not a paid professional working on a year's contract renewable every May the First. It is the Huntsman who is responsible for the hounds — their well-being, training and hunting. In a few Hunts a Master actually controls the hounds in the field and is referred to as an amateur Huntsman. In that case he will usually have a professional Kennel Huntsman to look after the hounds in the kennels and occasionally deputise in the field. Amateur or professional, only the Huntsman carries and uses the hunting horn. He normally has one, or sometimes two assistants called 'Whippers-in'.

The mounted field are known as 'followers', or 'the field', and are controlled by the Field-Master, who is often a Master in his own right. Although hunting has become far less class-conscious than it used to be, the sport nevertheless differentiates between those who pay to hunt and those who are employed to do so. The employees are known as Hunt servants and call people 'Sir' or 'Madam' in the field without any embarrassment to anybody — themselves, least of all.

Above all, the Master really *is* the Master. In the field he (or sometimes she) is treated with courteous deference and obeyed without question. The Master dictates the strategy of the day, can deploy riders as he pleases, and order them to leave the field — 'go home' — if they misbehave. Many Masters of old were extremely autocratic and some notoriously bad-tempered. One in the 1850s entered hunting legend when he dealt with an MP who was riding too close to hounds.

Master: Damn you, sir — where are you going?

MP: I did not come out to be damned.

Master: Then go home and be damned!

The letters MFH (Master of Foxhounds) after a man's name are no longer as grand as they were when there was a more tangible 'county set'. At one time an MFH was considered just below a Lord Lieutenant and a cut above an MP or a JP. Even today, to the fox-hunting fraternity, an MFH is certainly a VIP.

The pattern of a day's fox-hunting has remained virtually unchanged for about two centuries. Hounds and foxes are counted in twos — hounds by the 'couple' and foxes by the 'brace'. Thus it would be quite usual to talk of 19½ couple (39) of hounds killing 2½ brace (five) foxes in a day. That wouldn't be a bad day, either.

Although there are dog hounds and bitch hounds, they are *all* hounds. To describe them as dogs is to be guilty of the gravest solecism. Dogs — however immaculate their pedigrees — which are not foxhounds are called 'cur-dogs'.

A Meet is normally at 11 in the morning. The number of followers attending might be anywhere between 30 and 300, depending on the day (Saturdays are the most popular) and the prestige of the particular Hunt. A hundred is probably the average. Weather is rarely one of the factors affecting attendance. Fox-hunters seem to ignore it, however foul.

From the Meet, the field moves off, headed by the Whippers-in, Huntsman and Master. Their destination is the first 'covert' (pronounced cover), which may be a mile or more from the Meet. A covert is any place where a fox may lurk — copse, thicket, spinney, hedgerow, outcrop of rock, patch of gorse or field of kale, depending on the nature of the Hunt's terrain. On arrival, the field waits, under the command of the Field-Master, while the Huntsman 'draws' the covert; that is, urges his hounds in to pick up the scent of a fox. Meanwhile the second Whipper-in (often called simply a 'whip') watches for any stray hounds and pushes them back into the pack. The first Whipper-in stations himself on the blind side of the covert, far enough away to see if and where the fox leaves it and what direction it takes.

When hounds 'find' the scent of a fox, they 'speak', or 'give tongue'. The Huntsman urges them on with his voice and short, sharp notes on his horn, which also tell the field what is happening.

When the hunted fox breaks covert and the Huntsman is sure it is well clear and that the hounds are on to its 'line' of scent, he will blow 'Gone Away' — a long throbbing note — and set off after his hounds.

As soon as the Field-Master judges the moment to be right —which is basically when hounds are convinced of the scent, committed to it, and cleanly out of the covert — he takes up the chase and allows the field to go with him. His is not an easy task. He must try to keep up to hounds without overtaking them or getting between them and the fox, and stay ahead of the field. With a big number of eager riders, some able to exercise only nominal control over excited horses in open country, the job might well daunt a Wellington (and the old Duke was a formidable fox-hunter).

Now, the hunt is on. The hard-riding, gutsy horsemen are at the front of the throng, the rest following as opportunity or nerve allows. Hounds travel quickly and can get through and over places that horses cannot — barbed wire fences are a good example —, and it takes courage and ingenuity to stay with them across difficult country. This is the thrill and the challenge. The riders must not hinder hounds and must certainly not try to catch up with the fox independently. It is the hounds' job, directed by the Huntsman, to pursue and kill the fox. The field are spectators, riding as hard as they dare to see as much as they can.

The chase may last ten minutes or two hours. Nobody can tell. The fox is pursued until it either outwits hounds and escapes, it 'goes to ground' (dives down a hole, for example), or is caught and killed 'on top' (above ground). Theoretically a fox should find it difficult to go to ground because, before the hunt, likely holes will have been 'stopped' or 'put to' (the entrances blocked). If the fox does manage to find a hiding place, however — and they often do — three possible fates await it. It may be 'given best' and left alone; it may be 'bolted' by terriers, which scramble into the hole and push it out to be hunted again; or it may be dug out and shot with a humane killer. In that event, if hounds have not been taken to another draw, the fox's corpse may be thrown to them to be 'broken up' (chewed in seconds, bar the unsavoury portions).

That, broadly, is what happens during a hunt, although there are many variations.

Fox-hunters sometimes pursue their quarry until dusk, and they can no longer see hounds and what they're doing. Thus, by tradition, anyone breaking away from a hunt after midday always bids the Master 'goodnight', even if it's only two o'clock on a bright afternoon. 'Cheerio', or 'see you later', will not do.

*

What follows is an account of fox-hunting in Britain today, in the 1980s. It is based on extracts from the hunting diary of a modern Master of Foxhounds. The diaries of most people begin when the year starts, on January 1, although like New Year Resolutions, they often end on January 2. A fox-hunter's year, however, is geared to seasons rather than the normal progression of the Gregorian calendar. This one, therefore, begins when the hunting season begins, with the Opening Meet, on or about November 1.

1 November

Opening Meet at Rushfield Manor, as ever. A distinct success, I think, despite my usual doubts. My ninth Opening Meet as a Master (too many to add up the rest) and I still get a bit fluttery. Enormous crowd. No rain, thankfully, although it threatened all day, and unseasonably warm. Perhaps there'll be no winter this year. Certainly no sign of it yet. One or two people taking snaps but no reporters that I could detect — the antis must have been somewhere else. All splendour, sartorial and equestrian, just about, and the bitch pack really looked the part. I'm sure they knew it was the Opening Meet. I rode Padlock, of course, rock-steady as befits a 12-year-old hunter who's seen it all. Field well up on last year. John [Hunt Secretary] said there were 134 out. Several visitors and lots of silk hats. Hurrah for the diehards. Thank goodness we're not infected with the velvet cap disease that seems to be spreading like foot-and-mouth. Michael Chalmers brought four very smart people, including a gorgeous girl I've never seen before. Don't know where he finds them. All the usual faces, on foot as well as mounted. Nice to see old Mr. Hazlitt out mounted after his fall last season. Ten weeks in hospital. Hope I'm half as fit at 81 — and half as smart. Hospitality not as lavish as last year but good. Alastair [the host] dispensing drinks looking more like a publican than ever. Rumours of antis about. Don't think they'd dare — our people love their hunting too much. Police present and frightfully polite. An inspector I think (peaked officer's cap) actually gave me a salute and called me Master. *Wonder if he'll do the same when he gets his little breathalyser bag out. Drunk in charge of a horse? The hunting less than brilliant. For the record, we accounted for a brace, but with no glory. Against my better judgement we drew first in that scrappy piece of wood Alastair is pleased to call* The Plantation. *Never again. It's far too close to the house, so that half the field were still left strung along the drive all dressed up and nowhere to go. They'd no idea hounds had been put in to draw. Blank*

of course. Master with red coat and red face! Next time
at Rushfield we'll get off the estate, over the road and
into that coppice behind the church where in fact we
killled today.

Lots of mud and splashing about and everybody seemed
to be enjoying themselves. The field halved by about
1 p.m. as usual. I don't know why some of them bother
to come out if they don't want to go hunting. Anyway,
another Opening Meet to cross off the calendar. Tuesday
we're at Whiteways House. Should be good.

The Opening Meet

When the clocks go back in late October, a slight shiver of
regret and apprehension ripples the nation. It gets darker
earlier. Cooler sooner. Cold soon. Double-glazing salesmen
may rejoice, but most of us don't.

Fox-hunters, though, do. They're glad. The end of
British Summertime means the beginning of British Winter-
time. And that's *their* time.

When the Opening Meet happens on one of those
wonderful sun-touched days that are more autumnal than
wintry, it can be a glorious occasion . . .

Leaves are still falling from the big beech trees that line
the mile-long drive to an Elizabethan country manor
house. The drive is generously wide, crisply gravelled; its
grass verges are trim. Smoke sways about neat pyres of
smouldering dead leaves, responding fitfully to an uncertain breeze. Here is residential order, antiquity, continuity,
comfort, inherited wealth sustaining itself in confident,
unostentatious splendour. The land spreading all about
seems as big as a sea. An estate so lordly it should only be
owned by a lord. And it is.

It must occur to many, looking at the sentinel twin
lodges and great wrought iron gates to the drive, that it
was meant for horses, and when hounds are brought here
to open the hunting season, a century of mechanical travel

is momentarily pushed aside.

Horse boxes and trailers have been left well outside the gates, partly because there are so many that they would block the drive, but mostly because experienced riders like to hack the last mile or so to any Meet, to settle their horses and gentle themselves into the saddle. The Meet is at eleven o'clock, and horse boxes have been finding parking places in nearby lanes since ten.

There is quite a lot to do before shining boots are slipped into stirrups. Rug and tail bandage off horse, girth tightened, bridle checked. The rider must be poised and fully ready. Hat, whip, spurs, gloves, flask, snack, hanky. Once you're in that saddle, you could be there for five hours.

The ride up the drive is a delight. It is really the only way to approach such a house. Smartly turned out on a fit, handsomely groomed horse. Nobody would dream of directing you to the tradesmen's entrance. And you're going to the Opening Meet. The distant hum of traffic — cars and lorries droning along boring concrete to workaday destinations — tweaks the pleasure.

Squeeze your horse into a trot. Nice, easily brisk rhythm. Rise and sit to it. And the sky above the trees is pale, clear blue. Even the weather seems to have been ordered from Harrods. Past the home farm . . . the dower house . . . the conservatory . . . the walled rose garden . . .

Cars are coming up the drive now, but all steered considerately by people who understand horses. They need to today. They're being trotted up the drive in ones, twos . . . sixes . . . bunches. It's getting on for eleven o'clock, and the tempo is quickening.

The drive broadens as it sweeps up to the house, becoming a wide gravelled oval with an ornamental rosebed in the centre. There is room to park perhaps 50 cars, but 150 horses may threaten the roses. The thought that they could nevertheless gain coincidental nourishment may console the anxious head gardener. Everything happens for the best, though you may not see it at the time.

Chatter is simmering.

'Good morning, Charles — you're looking remarkably fit.'

''Morning, Douglas — gave up jogging. That's what was killing me.'

'Quite right. Jogging memories is OK . . .'

'What about elbows?'

'Ha ha, jolly good. Yes, nothing wrong with elbows . . .'

'Good morning, Francis.'

'Good morning, John.'

'Is Caroline with you?'

'No, she's not mounted today. Bringing the kids up in the car.'

'That's very noble of her.'

'Well, not really. The au pair's gone barmy, or something. Caroline's furious.'

'Is that the gorgeous one Rodney had to be pulled off at your barbecue?'

'Yes.'

'Perhaps she hasn't got over that.'

'God knows, Hysterics all over the place this morning.'

'Oh dear.'

Conversation on horseback in a confined and crowded space is limited and fragmentary. The subjects are at the superficial evening drinks level anyway, and rendered even more meaninglessly brief by the movement of horses. Much of what would be considered deliberate 'circulating' at an indoor gathering on foot becomes involuntary. Unbidden, a horse shifts and nudges another; that one is moved to accommodate it, which means that another sidles. And so on. Nobody starts any deep discussions because nobody wants his horse kicked.

The main difference between this outdoor equestrian gathering and an indoor pedestrian one is that everyone calls out 'Good morning!' in a clear, confident manner, before passing on to anything more profound. Imagine crying out 'Good evening' to everybody you met at a cocktail party. There's the contrast. Those who are considering taking up fox-hunting and are worried about how they should behave need only bear this in mind. Just keep on saying 'good morning' — loudly to people you definitely know, a little less lustily to those you don't. If you can manage to raise your hat as well, so much the better. No hesitation about the hat if you should encounter the Master — off with it! And say, as deferentially as you feel your social status dictates, 'Good morning, *Master.*' Do not be offended if he only nods acknowledgement. He doesn't have to take off his hat to anybody. Anybody.

The hat will be your greatest difficulty, apart from staying on your horse, but this advice assumes that you are competent in that area. If the hat fits closely, which it should do for safety, it will be difficult to sweep off elegantly with one hand. Best to ease it upwards and loosen it a shade, for relatively easy removal, but remember to jam it down tight again when you set off.

What can inhibit the courtly sweep of the hat is not having a hand to do it with. You have removed your gloves to take the welcome glass of warm punch that has been handed up to you; somewhat rashly, you have also accepted a sausage roll. These would constitute a manageable burden if you were on your feet. But you are sitting in a saddle, trying to hold a drink, a sausage roll, your gloves, your whip — and your reins. Not a good moment to try to salute the Master.

Right. Gloves in pocket for a start — you can put them on later. Whip and reins in one hand. Accept drink *or* morsel of food as delights to be consumed separately. Do not loiter over either — you may not get another.

There are one or two who partially solve this problem by dangling their whips round their necks. This is a bit showily casual and not recommended. There are others who drop their reins, leaving the buckle end to rest on the pommel of their saddles. *Never* do this. The horse is not yet born that can be guaranteed not to be startled by something. Always keep contact with your horse's mouth and have your reins tight enough to deal with any eventuality. You are not pony-trekking.

Once you have drained your glass, it becomes a nuisance to be discarded — or exchanged for a full one — as soon as possible. This is best accomplished by looking helpless and holding the glass out vaguely. Then catch the eye of someone on foot and say 'I wonder if you could possibly . . . ' They will take the hint and the glass, and be glad to. It makes them feel helpful and gives them a sense of belonging to this glittering equestrian scene of which you, as a mounted follower, are clearly a part.

The rumble of chatter gets louder. Healthy laughs sound healthier. It's good, sitting on a horse at the Opening Meet.

'Good morning, Harry — that's a handsome-looking animal you've got there — have I seen it before?'

'No — bought it out of the Belvoir country — hopefully successfully hobdayed.'

'How's it go?'

'Super. Absolutely super; (sternly to the horse) stand *still*!'

'Good for you.'

The hobdaying, a surgical operation to ease a horse's breathing, seems to have worked well enough. The animal is now veering clockwise energetically. Its great thighs and haunches swing with powerful menace to reveal the small red ribbon tied to the top of its tail. Not unlike a Christmas tree decoration, the ribbon looks quite festive and could be thought, by the uninitiated, to be some kind of adornment to celebrate the occasion. It is, in fact, a warning sign that the beast is inclined to kick, and that you stand or ride close behind it at your peril. Harry maintains his seat with admirable calm, appearing hardly to notice the vigorous movement beneath him. Of course, it would be a notably acrobatic horse if it could manage to kick its own rider, so he is in a position of some immunity.

Harry touches his heels to the horse's flanks, converting the sideways movement into forward action for a couple of paces, which distracts the animal from selecting a target for its very capable-looking hind feet. An elderly lady who might well be a frail duchess, with her quilted back towards Harry's horse and suede boots slightly sunk in the gravel, continues to talk obliviously to a mounted friend. She is quite unaware that she was inches away from a sudden, violent and radical alteration to her family tree.

It is one of the conventions of behaviour at a Meet of foxhounds that, whether on foot or in the saddle, one maintains a calm demeanour. Horses, excited by each other's company and impatient to move, tend to fidget, paw the ground, swish their tails (a fairly sure sign of impending disobedience) and even lay their ears back (a definite indication of bad temper). Such actions can easily escalate to bucking or rearing, are potentially unseating and certainly unnerving, yet it is pretty bad form for the rider to look concerned and unthinkable to give the appearance of being at all alarmed. You're English, dammit, and if your hunter is a bit 'fresh', a delightfully bland euphemism for lethal, then all the better. Should give you a jolly good ride.

The most perilous position is that of the pedestrian, yet the unwritten rule applies equally to those on foot. The fact that they are standing amid a herd of a hundred and more horses, any of which could remove even well-fitted dentures with an off-hand blow from their off-hind foot, is ignored.

By and large, despite that coarse aphorism that horses are smelly at one end and dangerous at both, the head is the better part to stand by. Horses have been known to bite people (although the reverse is seldom the case) but a normally vigilant rider should be capable of countering any such urge before it becomes a physical accomplishment, not to say something of a social embarrassment. What can one possibly say to someone who has just had four fingers bitten off by one's horse? 'I say, I'm most fearfully sorry,' could sound a bit limp.

It should not be thought that the horse world is haunted by platoons of fingerless frequenters of Meets of foxhounds, but awareness of such dangers is advisable. To demonstrate such awareness, however, or let it show in any sign of nervousness in the presence of horses, is not done. For example, if one were to leap three feet away from the back end of a horse in totally understandable fear of being kicked, such obvious panic would be deemed unseemly.

Caution is also called for in the matter of where, as a foot-person, one actually places one's feet. If, while talking to a mounted friend, they are situated too close to the feet of his horse, this can result in being trodden on. This is an excruciating experience and presents the victim with a truly terrible dilemma. Horses do not generally wander about looking for people to tread on. What happens is that, being made to stand for any length of time, they occasionally shift their weight for comfort. In a quite small and casual movement, devoid of malice, they lift, say, their near-forefoot and place it somewhere else, two or three inches away.

If one of your feet happens to be occupying that particular piece of ground, the agony will be immediate and tend to make your eyes water. The horse, however, is not likely to feel anything. It will allow most of its weight to sink onto that leg, possibly with a sigh of relief and content. These are not emotions that you will share. Further, apart from the flow of involuntary tears, you may find that your breath has been taken away and that you are unable to squeak, let alone speak.

It is entirely possible that the person on the horse, having a quick word with someone else, is unaware of your predicament. Unable to scream, either through good manners, physical impossibility, or a desire to remain inconspicuous, you will naturally, nevertheless, wish to terminate the scarcely believable pain you are suffering.

Your first instinct may well be to remove your foot. This will not work. You could, perhaps with the assistance of firemen with cutting equipment, remove your leg. But your foot would remain where it was — firmly beneath that of the horse.

Making this discovery will take about a zillionth of a second, and you will doubtless move on to consider what other steps — not literally, of course — you can take. Sheer primitive instinct will provoke you into trying to move the horse, at which point you will learn how heavy these creatures are (half a ton is not unusual) and why they are often described as obdurate. Your situation may be aggravated by your having a sausage roll in one hand and a glass of port in the other. This is a further element of the dilemma.

With your foot trapped, you can exert very little pushing power. You may be reluctant, anyway, to appear to be beating a horse with a sausage roll. Your position is unenviable. Unless gangrene is to set in, you will have to address the rider. Hunting etiquette has no set way of doing this. 'I say, your horse seems to be standing on my foot,' should suffice. 'Gosh,' may be the reply — 'sorry.' The rider will then take a quick pull at one or other of his reins and kick the horse in the ribs. Whereupon it will move its foot. Whether you will ever again be able to move yours will be something that you may doubt, and will depend on the gravity of the injury.

An Opening Meet can be unforgettable.

It is always colourful and very smart. People take great care on the great day. It is no use just yanking your horse out of a muddy field and urging it through the nearest car-wash. If you are as rich as you look — and nearly everybody on horseback at an Opening Meet at least *looks* rich — you will have a groom who will have been at great pains to turn your horse out well. A lot of grooms attend the Meet for no other reason than to appraise the work of other grooms, so they have all been up since very early in the morning.

All the horses should be pretty fit. Anyone who takes hunting seriously will have started 'bringing their horses up' (gradually getting them fit) in August and been cub-hunting for two months. Come the Opening Meet, they should be looking good and feeling keen. On top of that, they will be clipped, brushed until they practically glow, and their manes and tails neatly plaited. Hoof-oil will have been liberally brushed on to impart a water-repelling shine, and leather saddlery soaped to a supple deep sheen. Metal-work — buckles, stirrups, bits and the like — will glitter.

How you look yourself is largely up to you, unless you are grand enough to employ a valet. The general assumption may be that somebody else will have polished your boots; the reality is that you will probably have done it yourself. Likewise your spurs and spur-straps.

Your stock will be bridal white and tied as well as you are able. If you have invested in a new coat, you will be wearing it. Unless you have been guilty of some silly oversight, you should be experiencing a feeling of self-satisfied wellbeing, laced with anticipation or apprehension, depending on how your nerves are standing up to the passage of the years. There are those who say the nervometer starts to drop once you have passed 40, but you may take comfort from the fortifying fact that many men and women have hunted into their 70s and beyond.

So, if your horse is standing patiently, you will have a few minutes to look about you and enjoy soaking up and being part of a very satisfying and picturesque traditional English scene.

'Good morning, Rodney.'

'Good morning, Nigel — haven't seen much of you out cubbing.'

'Some of us have to make a living.'

'Really?'

The crust of the man. Not two pennies of his own to rub together, and surviving solely through acquisitive marital dexterity. That'll be his new rich wife with him, if it's not his mother. Fox-hunting has no more than its fair share of less than worthy participants — and other followers ready to criticise them. There may even be — whisper it — cads in the hunting field.

But the sport can boast one unusual merit. You either do it or you don't. In yacht and golf clubs it is perfectly possible to lean on the bar in appropriate clothing and *look* as though you have just circumnavigated the globe in a Force Nine, or gone round three under par, but in fox-hunting you get on your horse and get on with it, at whatever peril. You cannot tie your horse to a parking meter and guffaw bravely in the clubhouse, because

Hunts do not have premises on which so to perform. Hunting thus tends to sort the men out from the boys.

Gossiping at a Meet or in the hunting field is known as 'coffee-housing', a term that may have originated in the 18th century, when coffee houses were fashionable public venues and gossip-ovens. Dr. Samuel Johnson, perhaps the most famous and fluent of coffee-house clients, was a friend of Hugo Meynell, the renowned Master of the Quorn Hunt, whose influence on hunting and foxhound breeding is still felt today. Perhaps the two distinguished gentlemen discussed hunting over coffee. At any rate, coffee-housing is still common in fox-hunting, and a practice that is acceptable at a Meet, where you can chatter as much as you like, but not tolerable at covertside, when true fox-hunters are trying to listen to what hounds and Huntsman are doing.

The one event that is guaranteed to cause a pause in the coffee-housing at a Meet is the arrival of the hounds, and this is particularly noticeable at an Opening Meet. Hounds, after all, are central to the occasion — its very essence — and their entrance is a key moment that has been carefully prepared by the Huntsman. He and his two Whippers-in will have arrived a good half hour before the advertised time, and parked the hound lorry well away, out of sight of the Meet. The situation is not unlike the theatre. The privileged mounted customers at the Meet could be the audience drinking in the crush-bar and gathering in the foyer; the Hunt staff, the cast getting ready back-stage. It will have taken two or three vehicles to get them, plus horses and hounds, to the pre-selected unloading place.

First of all the Huntsman and Whippers-in will remove the old trousers or overalls they have been wearing over their Hunt livery which, if not new, will certainly be their best. No speck must mar breeches, boots or coat. Hunt servants take good care to see that they look right and are going to *stay* right.

Their stocks have already been carefully and tightly tied. They do not try to achieve the frothily full luxuriant bunch of white that the swells sport at their throats, and which often work loose. The staff anchor their stocks invisibly with a large number of small secret safety pins which barely permit a wrinkle in the stiff white material they favour. This style lacks foppish elegance, but ensures that the stock will never creep up out of their coat collars, and will stay so snugly tight as to provide day-long protection against rain dripping down the back of their necks. Similarly, they tighten their horses' girths so that they stay tight, and pull their forelegs forward to check that the girths are not pinching their skin. Hair neatly trimmed — long hair is unthinkable among Hunt servants — and faces shaved as close as they can, they are ready to get on their horses.

If there is mud about, they will tip-toe delicately like ballet-dancers to avoid puddles, and mount from walls, ramps of horseboxes, bales of hay, or anything else that will make the operation neater and quicker, to reduce the chance of a stray dirty streak on breeches or boots. And, when they are in the saddle, they are *really* in. Hunt horses have to be fit, which often means 'fresh', but Hunt servants seem hardly to notice the sometimes unruly frolics of their mounts. A buck or two is hardly worth an admonitory curse.

Now, white hunting whips firmly in their hands, they are ready for the hounds to be released from their transport. Hounds do not teeter tentatively down a ramp like geriatric spaniels. They pour and tumble down, falling over each other in an eager, energetic and fierce flood. They are never fed on a hunting morning, for obvious reasons, and they are looking to rectify the absence of breakfast. They swirl about the horses' feet, noses characteristically to the ground and sterns waving. The Hunt staff keep an eye on them and quickly reprimand any that look like streaking off on a private hunt, but allow them a few minutes to do what suburban dog owners call their 'business'. In hunting circles this is known more bluntly as 'emptying', and most of it will have taken place during brief morning exercise at the Hunt kennels.

It is understandably not sought on the front lawns of stately homes where Meets are held.

The Huntsman moves off quickly, checking with his Whippers-in that all hounds are 'on' (present). They make a striking sight — around 40 almost identical hounds padding along about and behind the Huntsman's horse, all obviously fit and keen and lively, but none straying far from the horse's legs. The thong of the Huntsman's whip just dangling in front of a hound's nose is enough to remind it of its proper place. Crisp clatter of hooves, bright scarlet coats, gleaming boots, alert and ready riders — the purposeful pageantry can be as uplifting as a marching military band.

Riders at the Meet melt magically to make way for the hounds, which cluster about the place the Huntsman decides his horse should stand. The Whippers-in may have to persuade one or two back into the pack, but most will just sit quietly about the Huntsman's horse, looking up devotedly at their boss and guardian, waiting for his next command. A good Huntsman has more unquestioning control over an entire pack of hounds than most dog owners can manage over a single animal.

Coffee-housing, momentarily hushed by the arrival of hounds, will now resume, and its noise-level increase. More riders will arrive. Joint-Masters will confer. Horses will shuffle about, people on foot will step casually out of their way. Many more hats will be raised and clear 'good mornings' ring out. An Opening Meet is a great reunion at every level. On a big estate old, long-retired employees will wheeze out of their tied cottages and totter somehow to be present up at the big house. They'll get a glass of something to warm them, for sure. It's the beginning of the run-up to Christmas, when they know they will be looked after. It is reassuring for them to see all this evidence of continuing wealth and a grand way of life that they have given their years to sustain.

'Good health, your Lordship.' So late in the 20th century, it seems feudal and therefore reprehensible, but on well-run estates, it still works, putting a bit of jam on the State Social Security bread.

"Morning, Thomas — how's Mrs. Thomas's hip coming along?'

'Mendin' nicely, sir. They took the pins out last week.'

'Jolly good.'

The Meet is an undeniably upper-crust occasion, with the 'them' and 'us' clearly defined and mutually accepted, yet softened and blurred by the unanimous conviction that foxes have to be killed, and by hounds. It would be much simpler if all the people on horses were toffs and all the people on foot peasants, but this is not necessarily the case. The forbidding-looking woman riding side-saddle, with top-hat, hair-bun and veil, may look remarkably like a retired brigadier; the man standing next to you may actually *be* a retired brigadier. The identity of some of the people on horseback could be checked most easily in Who's Who, Burke's or Debrett; with a few, you would be better trying the Yellow Pages.

One of the subtler distinctions is not of class, but of degree of devotion to the sport — real, rural fox-hunters are at its centre, while at the edges are the social fox-hunters, often urban-based. They are not always that popular, because their presence makes fields uncomfortably big, but their subscriptions help keep the sport going.

A quieter conversational exchange between two regular mounted followers:

'Look at them all! Where do they all come from?'

'Opening Meet, old boy. Always brings them out.'

'Christ, it's like August Bank Holiday.'

'Adrian reckons there's 200. Still, I suppose they've all paid.'

'That's not the point. How can you go hunting with all this rabble?'

'We'll probably lose a good few, after a bit.'

'I bloody well hope so.'

For such keen fox-hunters, a field of about 30 riders would be ideal. But their grumbling is conventional and habitual. They know, anyway, that a lot of people will fall out after the first couple of hours. Similar problems of over-subscription and over-crowding exist in other sports — there are waiting-lists for golf clubs just as there are for the fashionable Hunts. But an additional limiting factor in fox-hunting is how many horses landowners will tolerate galloping over their fields.

Once hounds have arrived, they will not tarry more than about 15 minutes. Just time for one or two pieces of select dialogue. A magnificently genial old red-coated gentleman, followed by another, nudges his horse up to the Master's.

'Good morning, Master. May I introduce Sir Richard Ridewell-Fallwell? He's come up from the Chiddingfold Leconfield and Cowdray country.' (Surely he must have rehearsed that?) He pauses as he and his friend remove their top-hats, then completes the introduction. 'Sir Winston Williams-Williams, our Joint-Master.'

The Master nods. 'Good morning. I hope we'll be able to show you good sport.' Such names. And such faces. None are more magnetically beautiful or compellingly ugly than could be found at any similar gathering indoors, but all are much more noticeable through their features being reduced to what can be seen below a black hat and above a white stock. Women's hair is completely hidden, except perhaps for a tightly netted bunch at the back of the neck. It is a severe test. Those that pass it can seem devastating.

The drink-bearers are now collecting more empty glasses than they are distributing full ones. The field will soon move off.

'Have you had a drink?'

'Yes, thanks most awfully, I have.'

'Perhaps you'd like another?'

'I think perhaps I'd better not.'

Wise reply. Inhibitions lifted slightly by alcohol can reduce natural caution and make jumps look smaller.

A slightly worried and ancient-looking butler is glad the party is nearly over. Bits of gravel are getting in his shoes, and he is frightened of horses. It is his least favourite day of the year and he has fortified himself against its discomforts with rather better port than he has been serving to the guests.

'I say, old Jeeves looks a bit wobbly.'

'Pissed, old boy.'

'By jove, I do believe you're right — what a hoot!'

Suddenly, there is a tangible change of mood. The Huntsman squeezes his horse forward and calls out, 'Hounds, please!' He lifts his hat high as riders shift their horses to make way for him. When the Whippers-in, Masters and field follow hounds, there is a great crunching of gravel beneath the horses' feet and, mixed with that sound, the calls of farewell and, more particularly, thank-you to the hosts. For fox-hunters are meticulously courteous at Meets, if not always so in the field.

'Thank you for having us.'

'Have a good day.'

'Don't fall off that great beast, Simon.'

'Thank you for having us.'

'Thank you so much.'

'Have fun, Katherine.'

'Good morning — how are you?'

'Thank you very much indeed.'

'Not at all.'

'Do be careful, Penelope.'

'Thanks awfully.'

Hats are raised. Everyone smiles, those in the saddle, happily; some left behind on foot, wistfully, like guests at a wedding reception when the bridal couple leave. There is a strong feeling that something of significance — an event — is taking place.

And it is.

A tradition is being followed for another year; the rhythm of the countryside is being kept; all is well; it is satisfying.

Moving, even.

The fox-hunting season has started.

There is nothing quite like it anywhere else in the world.

To Kennels to look at the new fencing. Everybody pleased except me, so kept quiet, but can still see no reason for something that keeps nothing in and nothing out. The consensus is it looks better. There'll be roses growing up it next. However, the same people have made a really good job of the wobbly old benches in the bitches' lodge. Really solid. Brian [Huntsman] amusingly indignant. He's found the man at the Hinkley place putting food out for foxes, exactly where we were specially asked to deal with them last month, and did so, handsomely (killed a cub by his runner beans, practically under his nose). Brian says what's the use of us killing them if you're feeding them? Ah, says the man, I like to see foxes about the place. What if they get into your chicken shed again? says Brian — well, I'll have to ring you up again, won't I? Quick look at dear old Lilo [a hound]. Her ear looks terrible to me, and still septic, but Brian says she'll be hunting again in no time. All other hounds fully fit, for a change, and nothing in the hot-house [an isolation area for bitches in season]. The whole time we were talking and looking at the awful fence, Ian [Kennelman] was cutting up a huge dead cow they'd brought in, udders stiff like four candles. Don't know how they stomach it. I had to look away in case I went green. It wouldn't hurt some of our grander members to see what goes on in Kennels and how terribly hard everybody works. All they know about the Hunt staff is how smart they look in their red coats. Ah, well, end of sermon, but they should know why and how our pack is so good.

Hounds, please

A pack of foxhounds moving away from a Meet, tucked tightly round the Huntsman's horse and moving eagerly, tidily, is one of the most rewarding sights the winter countryside can show. It is a scene depicted endlessly on calendars and biscuit tins, and no more stale for that.

Individual Huntsmen's preferences vary, but a pack of 20 couple is usual, and the amazement to the onlooker is how closely they stick together, how disciplined they are, and how similar in size and overall appearance — virtually identical. How can the Huntsman tell them apart? Does he even need to?

He can. And he does. A Huntsman likes his hounds to look level (a uniform 23-24 inches at the shoulder is good) but sees them for what they are — a number of individual animals that he has moulded into a pack. Not the same pack every time out, mind you, but individuals that he has selected for the day's hunting from perhaps 100 or many more.

But whichever hounds he chooses — 'draws' as they call it — will automatically become a pack and work as one. They may be all bitches, all dogs, or a mixture. The factors that determine his draw are many. Among them are which hounds need to be rested, which are sick or lame, which part of his country he is going to hunt, and which bitches are in season.

Dog hounds are reputed to be the more difficult to hunt. They may be slightly more faithful to the Huntsman, but they can be boisterous and inattentive. In a mixed pack, unless chivvied, they will often be happy to let the bitches do most of the work in finding a fox, and then join in the chase that follows — when the real fun starts. Bitches tend to be steadier.

When outsiders ask Huntsmen how they can tell one hound from another, the question baffles, because to them it could not be otherwise. They know each of their hounds instantly by sight and by sound, and could tell you its name and describe its character. Further, each hound knows its name and will respond to it, even though surrounded by 40 of its companions.

To anybody who has had difficulty persuading a single spaniel to do what it's told, even on the end of a lead, the responsive obedience of unfettered hounds just to their

Huntsman's voice is an astonishment. The dazzling discipline, which is never oppressive, is taught in kennels,
where the Huntsman is an all-powerful blend of god and
father.

One of the most impressive demonstrations of a Huntsman's skill and control can be seen at feeding times.
Hounds are not given spoonfuls of tinned dog-food as
they fancy, and tit-bits are unknown. What would happen
to a charitable visitor who slipped a toffee to a fox-hound
is difficult to imagine; perhaps he'd be whipped to death
and fed to hounds himself.

Compared with most overfed domestic pets, hounds
are fed frugally — once a day at most — to keep them in
peak hunting condition, so that when it comes to time to
feed, they are ready for it. Well, more than ready. They
are ravenous. And, because they are usually fed all together, they are in competition. The sight and sound of
50 or more hungry hounds waiting to enter the feeding
yard is unforgettable. Any fox that witnessed it would
resign on the spot, and it would make many human beings
feel a bit nervous.

Some hurl themselves at the feed-yard door in their
eagerness to be first for food, and one might imagine that
anybody foolish enough to enter that door would be in
danger of, at best, being knocked over in the rush, or,
at worst, losing an arm. Yet a Huntsman will stand calmly
in the doorway while he surveys the hounds in order to
choose which ones he wants to feed first. These are those
he knows to be shy feeders, plus one or two his eyes tell
him could do with an extra mouthful. So he will call out
the names, one by one, so that they can enter the feed-
yard and start eating in peace, before he lets the mob
through.

'Diamond,' he will call out, and Diamond, even though
she's on the fringe of the pack and far from the door, will
start to make her way through all the bodies — partly
because she's hungry, partly because she knows she must
respond to the Huntsman, and partly because the others
are *letting her through*. It's amazing. The main body of

hounds will wait for as many minutes as necessary while the Huntsman draws the hounds he wants to feed first, and allows them singly to filter through. When, finally, he opens the door wide to admit the remainder, they surge through like a dam-burst.

Hunt kennels vary in their feeding methods, but the fundamental difference lies in whether they feed raw or cooked meat, always referred to in either case as 'flesh', and always bound to disappear at great speed. Although admirably behaved in other ways, foxhounds are not known for table-manners. Every hound fends for itself and they will climb over each other in their eagerness to get at the food. Fifteen or so hounds, each with a snarling grip on the same piece of carcase and all swaying together as the flesh is pulled this way and that, and then being leapt over and into by another half-dozen trying to reach the same piece of flesh, is a spectacle that makes a desperate rugger scrum look as relaxed as a coffee morning at the vicarage. Hot breath rises like steam above the heaving, struggling bodies. It sometimes appears that in their ravening hunger the hounds might even turn on each other, but apart from an occasional quick squabble — immediately quelled by the Huntsman if it looks like getting out of hand — the feed is finished without real rancour. What's left wouldn't fill, as they say, a hollow tooth.

Opponents of fox-hunting who speak of the cruelty of foxes being 'torn to death' and of their demise being 'lingering' might well stop disseminating such misapprehensions if they saw hounds feeding or, indeed, watched hounds fall upon a hunted fox. It is despatched with an immediacy that rivals electrocution.

Foxhounds, although purpose-bred, do not hunt foxes instinctively. It is not until they are 'entered', as it's said, 'to the cry of hounds', that they learn, from following the example of the old hounds, what foxes smell like, look like and taste like.

The flavour, as it happens, does not appeal to them all that much. If you offered a hound a fox-burger for dinner, you'd earn little gratitude. When hounds break up a dead fox at the kill, they all snarl and bite and tug and struggle over it just as they do over the meat that they're fed in the kennels, and which is gulped down at amazing speed. But they don't find the taste of fox particularly appetising, tearing at it in much the same way as excited terriers worry a rat.

Foxhounds are a hunting breed that is taught to hunt foxes, and could just as well be taught to hunt hare, deer, rabbit, badger, otter, coypu, mink, pussy-cat or postmen. Their ancestors (the hounds' not the postmen's) hunted mainly deer until deer began to be scarce about the middle of the 17th century. Hare were the most favoured quarry until the 18th century, when more and more harrier packs began converting to fox and thus laying the breeding foundations of the modern foxhound. Fox-hunting, in the organised and widespread form that we know it today, is not of great antiquity — scarcely two hundred years.

When hunting or feeding, foxhounds can seem ferocious, yet they are much more docile and friendly than many people's pet dogs. It is common for Hunts to allow parties of schoolchildren to visit their kennels and unthinkable that any harm should befall them. An anxious mother, alarmed that her young son was going on such a visit, once telephoned the kennels to ascertain the degree of danger to which the child might be exposed.

'Well, madam,' replied a straight-faced Huntsman, 'there's always the chance that he might get licked to death.' And it's true. A stranger entering a yard containing 50 foxhounds may well be nuzzled, licked, sniffed and buffeted by great soppy paws on his chest as hounds examine him, but he could be in greater peril in a yard full of labradors.

In all hunt kennels, discipline is strict and the Huntsman's rule absolute. In some, the hounds' devotion to their master is reinforced by his always feeding them and never punishing them, so that he is the kindly father; if they need to be chastised, the task is left to his Whipper-in or Kennelman. In others, the philosophy is that punishment is far more effective if administered by the Huntsman himself, proving that his mighty hand can deliver food, approval or retribution.

Most Huntsmen use the whip sparingly, as a last resort in such emergencies as serious fighting among hounds themselves, 'rioting' (pursuing quarry other than foxes — which could be hare, deer, rabbit or your pussy-cat) or heading pell-mell towards forbidden or dangerous territory — a motorway or electrified railway line, for example. Even in desperate circumstances such as these, there are Huntsmen who can maintain control with their voice alone.

Flesh for the hounds, whether fed cooked, or raw, has more significance to a Hunt simply than the protein it provides. Quite a lot of farm animals die for one reason or another, and cannot be left lying about to putrefy. They have to be disposed of somehow. Having not been slaughtered for the purpose, they are not fit for human consumption, but are acceptable as animal food.

Particularly parsimonious farmers can ring up the nearest abattoir and sell them the carcases of some kinds of animal, but pro-hunting farmers will give them to the local Hunt kennel instead, and kennel staff will collect the bodies for hound food. It would actually be more economical for Hunts to buy meat regularly under contract, but by collecting it from farmers, they provide a useful scavenging service which helps maintain goodwill. The time and wear-and-tear on Hunt vehicles used for this purpose is a major cost that seldom justifies a free but sporadic supply of flesh. In addition, it makes a fairly hefty refrigerating installation a necessity.

Years ago, most Hunt kennels would employ a 'knackersman' to skin and cut up carcases donated by farmers. Today, with increased costs leading to staff reductions, this job is often undertaken by the Kennelman or one of the Whippers-in. It is one of the least pleasant tasks in a Hunt kennels, although selling the resultant bones, hides and fat brings in a quite handy income which is usually the perquisite of the Hunt servants.

Considerable care and knowledge has to go into selecting appropriate flesh for hounds from the variety that comes into kennels. Cows, calves and horses are good grub, but pigs are too fatty and can cause illness, and sheep can make hounds wormy. It used to be feared that feeding hounds dead sheep would give them an embarrassing taste for living lamb, but this has been shown not to be so. If all this seems a bit gory, it should perhaps be remembered that all dogs are carnivorous — even Auntie Janet's little poodle. So are cats. So are foxes. And so, of course, are most human beings. It's just that our meat comes more delicately prepared.

Foxhounds are meticulously bred, their names being registered in the Foxhound Kennel Stud Book, publication of which is supervised by the Masters of Foxhounds Association. Pedigrees can be traced back a hundred years and more, in much the same way as Thoroughbred racehorses' bloodlines can be checked. The breeding of foxhounds is often referred to as a science, and it is almost an obsession with some Masters and Huntsmen, who strive to produce hounds that look good and hunt well. Any that do not conform are put down without hesitation. If the Hunt is fortunate, it will produce hounds that do the job, and win at foxhound shows.

The most famous and prestigious of these is the Peterborough Show, but there are others with foxhound classes and they all offer opportunities for watching the high skills of 'biscuit work'. Hounds are shown by their Huntsmen and Whippers-in, who naturally want their entries to appear at their best, both standing and moving. So, to keep their hounds' attention, they carry a handful of dog biscuit fragments. The theory is that the hound will watch the hand that carries the biscuit, and if the hand is moved cunningly, a bit above nose-level, the hound will maintain a good, alert stance, particularly when the Huntsman feels that he has the judges' attention.

It is a subtle procedure, not unlike conjuring. The Huntsman does not want to appear to be trying too hard, and he must avoid wasting his maximum effort when the judges are clearly examining someone else's entries. Hounds are not going to stand all day watching a hand that never delivers the biscuit, so the Huntsman has to reward them from time to time, in the hope of keeping them mesmerized. Just when he does award them a crumb is quite critical.

Huntsmen put almost as much concentration and effort into all this as they do into pursuing foxes. If they perspire somewhat, it is through a mixture of anxiety and heat — they wear full hunting livery, designed for surviving on horseback in winter, and hound shows are held in mid-summer.

The judges are invariably Masters of Foxhounds, and they wear bowler hats and dark suits, very much in the manner of Guards officers in mufti. Judging foxhounds is a serious and formal matter.

The kind of hounds that win at Peterborough and elsewhere in the 1980s are noticeably different in appearance from the champions of the 1880s, when they were bigger and heavier. Around the turn of the century the belief that strong solid forelegs were necessary for galloping, particularly in uneven, hilly country, led to hounds being so rigorously bred for thick bone that the knees became bowed forward and closer to the ground. The knees tended to knuckle over, throwing the weight forward on to the toes, so that hounds began to look a bit like women in high-heeled shoes, but not so sexy.

The paradox was that ruthless selective breeding for the Peterborough ideal was beginning to produce an almost club-footed animal that was in danger of becoming unsuitable for the job it was actually bred for. Bulldog breeders may well take offence, but there are those who would draw the parallel. Happily, there were Masters of Foxhounds more concerned with their hounds' performance in the field than on the flags at hound shows who rebelled against the vogue and finally stemmed it. Sanity returned to the fox-hunting world and today's hounds are probably better in every way than they were.

A true deformity inflicted on foxhounds right up to

the 1914-18 War and some way beyond was 'rounding' the ears. This meant cutting so that they were less likely to get torn in gorse and brambles. It also gave a pack an appearance of uniformity.

Until fairly recently, experts could tell almost at a glance which Hunt kennels a hound came from because each would breed for its own type of country — thickly wooded, well grassed, mountainous, moorland and so on. While this is still done to some extent, modern farming methods are reducing the differences in the countryside, and this is one of the factors tending to produce a more uniform type of foxhound.

It seems something of a pity that, while judges at hound shows can come to valid conclusions about the conformation of hounds, they are unable to judge what are considered by fox-hunters to be the most important qualities — drive, stamina, nose and voice. If ways of measuring these characteristics were discovered, hound shows might be a great deal more diverting.

The assessment of intelligence in hounds is quite a delicate matter. They are certainly not required to be stupid, but they need to be conformist enough to work unquestioningly as a pack. Really brilliant hounds are not always cherished by Huntsmen because the demarcation line between cleverness and cunning is a thin one.

The loyalty and devotion (dog-like, one might dare say) of hounds to their Huntsman is not cupboard-love. It might be possible to bribe some members of the canine world by consistently plying them with goodies, but not foxhounds. They are working creatures, they enjoy their work, and they adore the man who leads them in it. It actually doesn't matter who feeds them. It's who takes them out hunting that counts.

Foxhound pups — like fox cubs — are born in early Spring, often having been sired by stallion hounds from the more fashionable packs, who exercise considerable influence on breeding overall.

After about a week the pups have their dew-claws removed and are ear-marked — the initials of the Hunt tattooed in one ear, and the pup's litter letter and number in the other. The litter letter is usually the first letter of the sire or dam's name, and becomes the initial letter of the pup's name. This is why so many packs have hounds' names starting with the same letter — Deacon, Decimal, Delicate, Della, Denim, Dettol, Destiny, Dewdrop and so on, although lineal pride might preclude Doubtful. Hounds' names are fascinating, and are often a reflection of national feeling. There have been any number of hounds called Wellington, Waterloo, Churchill, Victory, Montgomery, D-Day, Spitfire and the like. We will probaby never know why the famous Master, Squire Osbaldestone, named one of his hounds Boozer and another, Hernia.

Names usually have at least two syllables to make it easier for hounds to recognise them, similar-sounding names being avoided for the same reason. It is easy to imagine the confusion that would arise in a pack that included hounds called Measure, Pleasant and Leisure.

At about 10 weeks old, the pups are sent off on their great adventure — to live with puppy-walkers. These are the keen and kind people — and every Hunt has them — who are such loyal fox-hunting enthusiasts that they take one or two hound pups into their homes and look after them until they are ready to be returned to the Hunt kennels towards the end of the hunting season in March. This means they may have the pups for up to nine months. Such people are often farmers, who have space enough to care for additional animals and are relatively unsentimental about them. Nevertheless, many of the hounds become household pets and oceans of tears must have been shed over the wrench of them leaving home to return to kennels.

Hunts always instruct these stalwart foster parents to use the hounds' proper names so that they get used to them, but the number of foxhounds properly called Nimrod, Swordsman and Parachute who once answered to Nosey, Sweetie and Puddles must be considerable. Like all pups, foxhounds can be heartbreakingly engaging and, even though it's frowned upon, one or two may develop a taste for spending their evenings on the sofa watching television. Returning to keenels must be like joining the Army and suddenly having to live in barracks.

Few Hunts issue special feeding instructions to the puppy-walkers. They are most concerned that the young hounds should get plenty of freedom and exercise and become used to countryside smells and human beings. Their instinct for the chase is so strong that they will hurtle after almost anything that moves, and are usually capable of catching the odd rabbit to supplement their food. Cats living in the same household as young foxhounds become remarkably agile.

People argue over whether foxhounds, if they were not 'professionals', as it were, would make domestic pets. Those most qualified to say, through looking after them, seem to believe they might, but once they are over six months, they become a shade too big and bouncy. 'A bit of a handful' is a common description. 'Unruly' is another. A wink, as they say, is as good as a nod.

The bond that is forged with their walkers is seldom forgotten. Most Huntsmen have experienced the slight embarrassment of a hound at a Meet suddenly leaving the pack and bounding into the crowd of foot-followers to greet the person who had it at walk.

Once back in kennels, at about a year old, the young hounds are gradually introduced to the discipline of belonging to a foxhound pack. To start with, their exercise is confined to the kennel grounds, and they are taken out coupled to older hounds. A 'couple' is two stout leather collars linked by a non-tangle chain about a foot long, so that everywhere the senior hound goes, the puppy must go too. Not all older hounds appreciate being attached to a mobile anchor, and the puppies, after the freedom of living with their walkers, find it puzzling, frustrating or infuriating, according to their nature. There is a great deal of energetic pulling, and seldom in mutually-agreed directions.

The pack is supervised at exercise by the Huntsman

and his Whipper-ins or Kennelman, who try, not always successfully, to ensure that they're not knocked over. Two lively and uncoordinated linked hounds struggling to pass either side of a human being, at speed and at knee height, can have a scooping effect that affects human dignity and gravity. However, even the most recalcitrant puppies learn quickly enough that there are better ways of covering ground than being dragged along it, and submit, with daily increasing grace, to being attached to another hound.

After several weeks as, one by one, they learn to respond to their names and obey basic commands, the Huntsman lets them off the couple. When they are trustworthy, he takes them out on local exercise with the pack. At first they walk out in lanes close to the kennels, until they get used to traffic and other dangers and distractions. The exercise periods are lengthened; the distances are increased — they're on their way to becoming foxhounds. Soon there is another great event in their lives — the annual puppy show. The occasion might not strike the young hounds as particularly significant, but it is the peak of the puppy walkers' year — the reward for all their months of patience and occasional worries and alarms.

Puppy shows are sometimes held in the grounds of rather grand country houses — the kind at which Meets are given — but many take place at Hunt kennels, and if these are less formal, they are certainly not less important. Preparations begin well before the event. There are rehearsals. The kennels are smartened up. Whitewash is slapped about liberally, grass is trimmed, flowers are planted, and gravel pathways suddenly appear to be more than usually straight and smooth. The atmosphere of urgent activity is very much like that which infects a military camp at the approach of a General's inspection. The analogy is pretty accurate, because puppy shows are judged by visiting Masters of Foxhounds, and within the ranks of puppy walkers a Master is seen as a very senior officer indeed. It isn't simply that he is an MFH. The walkers realise that the kind of Master who accepts invitations to judge hounds has a deep interest in them and will undoubtedly be an expert. They all *know*, of course, that 'their' hounds are far superior to the others in the show and that simple justice and common sense must endorse this. What they cannot foresee are the particular preferences and prejudices of the visiting Master, who will probably be well aware that at the end of the day he will be regarded by some as a genius and by others as an idiot. There's nothing much really in between. There are usually enough rosettes, though, to dissipate true acrimony. With classes for dog hounds, bitch hounds and couples, and first, second and third prizes in each, there aren't really enough disappointed walkers left to start a revolution. Anyway, by the time of the show, they will have already taken new puppies into their care — and there's always next year.

Puppy shows are good country fun, and one of the great summer occasions of the fox-hunting year. They also serve to demonstrate, for those unaware of the fact, that a Hunt kennels doesn't just go to sleep when the hunting season ends. The pace slackens, certainly, but hounds still have to be fed and exercised every day, they are paraded at agricultural shows and the like, and from about June onwards the process of indoctrinating the newcomers — the 'young entry' — is well under way.

Hound exercise in the summer starts very early — five o'clock in the morning is not unusual — before the weather becomes oppressively hot and sunshine begins to soften tarred roads, which are a great hazard to hounds' feet. The outer protective skin layer of their pads can stick in warm tar and be peeled off, leaving them raw, and the hound lame.

In early summer, the Hunt staff conduct exercise on foot, wearing overalls, but adding a touch of traditional hunting formality with bowler hats. Later, as the hounds need to increase pace and distance, the staff ride bicycles. Eventually, when the Hunt horses need to be brought up into condition after their summer rest, hounds and horses are exercised together — with the Hunt staff back in their red coats and in the saddle.

This is the time when a few really enthusiastic hunt followers join the staff and ride with them to start giving their own horses some preparatory work. By now, hounds will be covering ten to twenty miles every morning. The young ones will be getting used to the idea of being with a pack; their pads will be toughening; they'll be getting really fit — hunting fit.

Few dog owners would consider taking their animal for a walk without at least carrying a lead, if only to get it past lamp-posts. Imagine, then, taking out fifty or more loose hounds, armed only with a whip. Huntsmen do this every morning in summer. They use country lanes mostly, but are quite capable of negotiating their charges neatly round a traffic roundabout. The one precaution they take is to have a Whipper-in riding well ahead of the pack to look for likely trouble, possibly in the shape of domestic pets.

If the lookout spots a cat he will signal by holding two spread fingers, like the Churchillian V for Victory sign, by the side of his head, and may reinforce the message by calling out "ware pussy!' Hounds must never be permitted to riot on to cats. It upsets people and doesn't do the cats much good, either.

''Ware' is a warning and command used to stop hounds doing anything or going anywhere that's not wanted. It's short for 'beware', but pronounced 'war', and is taught very early on. ''Ware haunch', somewhat quaintly, is used to keep them away from deer.

Quite when hounds join the kennel choir is really up to them. It isn't a formal, proper choir, of course, and it isn't likely to be heard at Cruft's, let alone the Albert Hall. But hounds in kennel do 'sing' — together and in discernible harmony. One usually starts them off with a spontaneous sustained note about two octaves above middle C, and as the note begins to drop and die away, another hound will come in at the pitch the first began; and then another. Other hounds will take up the song in the same key or an octave removed, like children singing a 'round'. Others will even add something approaching a descant. The melody is somewhat flimsy and there is no rhythm, but there is tangible unison. In musical terms the result could be described as a canine canon; as it develops, with the entire kennel joining in, it can be very pleasing, if a little melancholy. Hounds are more likely to sing like this in summer, and it is taken to mean that they are content.

Sometimes the ringing of church bells will set them off, and the combination of the two sounds rising and falling on a summer evening is an unforgettable country experience. Anyone lucky enough to be able to peep into kennels during choir practice can see how much the hounds enjoy it. As each one comes into the chorus it throws its head up, seeming at the same time to be listening to the total effect with apparent satisfaction. Some Huntsmen can induce their hounds to sing, but this smacks of a party trick. They'll do it by themselves, anyway, when they feel like it.

Not all Huntsmen are brilliant horsemen, but they have a gift for handling hounds. And it truly is a gift. A man either possesses it, or does not. Whatever this quality is, it is obvious at all times, in kennel or out, but particularly when the Huntsman holds morning surgery. Serious injuries are dealt with promptly, lesser ones wait until next day, after exercise and feeding. Hounds are prone to the usual canine ailments, plus the cuts, tears, strains and bruises they gather in the heat of the chase. Barbed wire and thorns are the causes of much of their grief. A hunting day is never stopped through injury to a hound. The Hunt servants carry coiled couple straps in the 'D' loops of their saddles. If a hound is hurt, it can be coupled to another, until it is picked up and taken home.

The sick, lame and sorry hounds are put aside in one compartment at the kennels and wait patiently for their turn to be treated. Anybody who has tried even to give a dog or cat a worm powder will have experienced what a difficult and even perilous task this can be, yet a Huntsman will treat his hounds without fuss. They come to him one by one as he calls their names and submit, through faith, to whatever needs to be done. It would be most unusual for a Huntsman to call in a vet to treat any one of his hounds. Giving injections, lancing sores, extracting thorns, cleaning painful cuts — he tackles all these jobs without expecting struggles and hysterics. If he gets bitten, about once every 100 years, he knows it is only a reflex action to sudden pain. Lameness and stiffness through sleeping after hunting are common and call for the application of 'green oils'. These are an embrocation, rather pungent-smelling but almost miraculously therapeutic.

The life of a foxhound is full and busy and rewarding, but limited to seven or eight seasons. Fox-hunting demands great stamina — they may easily cover 50 miles in a hunting day — and there has to come a time when a hound cannot keep up with the pack, usually because its feet are not longer up to the job.

Such an old hound might be kept on early in the season to help guide the young ones, but as the pack quickens and becomes too fierce for it, its distress is obvious and upsetting. In Hunt kennels it is not the practice to keep animals that are unable to work. They would be desperately unhappy to be left in kennels on hunting days, and would soon pine to finality if they were taken out of the pack and transferred, say, to a private home. So they are put down. In familiar surroundings. Without stress. Calmly, quickly and cleanly. By the man they have come to love and trust — their Huntsman. It is his final kindness. And his greatest sadness.

15 November

Astonishing accident today. About 30 of us waiting at the bottom of the slope at Petts Corner when a girl came flying down and rode right into us at full belt. Horses and bodies everywhere, like a battlefield. God knows how she didn't kill herself and a few others while she was at it. Turned out to be Seymour Lucknell's new groom and apparently a good rider, but the horse just took off. Seymour said it pulled a bit but she'd exercised it in a snaffle and wanted to hunt it ditto. Bet she won't do that again. Never seen anything like it. We heard her coming down the slope and I vaguely wondered why she was coming so fast when there was no need. We were obviously held up and she could have trotted down to us. By the time we realised she was out of control it was too late. We sat there like skittles. Some people tried to get out of the way but there was no room. I didn't move because I reckon its safer to stand still, no horse is going to run into something deliberately. But this one did, or perhaps it could see a gap. Anyway it just missed me and went slap into the rest. Got poor old Oliver midships and knocked him and his horse over. The girl came off and fell on Oliver, and Dr. Hopper's horse went over as well. Incredible. Then the horse sort of scattered the rest and belted off down the ride towards the sewage works — best place for it. Girl a bit groggy and muddy, very apologetic of course. Paul caught the horse and by the time he got back we'd all sorted ourselves out, no bones broken but nobody very happy. Seymour said to lead it back to their box, but she hopped back on as though nothing had happened. Amazing, some of these girls. The horse is too big for her but she obviously knows what she's doing. Didn't see her again but I gather there were no further alarms and Seymour took her home early. Not really my business, but that horse is a puller and that's why he uses a double bridle on it, and he's twice her size and strength. He wouldn't have used a snaffle himself. A bit irresponsible, our Seymour. Not a bad day otherwise. One killed (by the old Army huts) but we never got out of a canter all day. Drizzly and warm. Was tempted to shed waistcoat at second horses but not quite the thing for a Master. Doesn't seem like November.

Out for the Ride

It is axiomatic in the fox-hunting world that there are two kinds of people who follow the sport — those who ride in order to hunt; and those who hunt in order to ride. And the latter are the majority. There is a hard centre of fox-hunters whose pleasure lies in watching hounds work and who simply use horses as the best means of following them across country, but these are easily outnumbered by those who are out, literally, for the ride.

Hunts don't really need anything like the number of riders they attract, except for the money they subscribe. A pack of hounds with a good Huntsman and two Whippers-in could do their work better with a field of half-a-dozen. In fact, this is probably a Huntsman's dream. Certainly the horror of any nightmares he may experience must be in direct ratio to the size of the field behind him. The bigger the field, the greater the noise, and noise is a distraction. A Huntsman needs to hear what his hounds are doing — that's one of the reasons that the 'voice' of hounds is so important.

Then there is the danger of a big field. They'd be reluctant to admit it, but many a Huntsman has 'lifted' his hounds (taken them further ahead) not because of failing scent, but to get him and them out of the way of two or three hundred charging riders.

The field have no vital function. They may be asked to range themselves alongside a road or railway to prevent hounds from being injured, but this is nothing more than assistance that the Huntsman could well do without if they were not present. People who ride to hounds are called followers for the good reason that that's what they do — follow.

One or two might get the opportunity to give a 'view holloa' (a kind of scream emitted when the fox is seen) and that can be of use to the Huntsman if it is done properly. However, anyone about to holloa should be certain that the fox he has seen is the fox actually being hunted; should wait until the fox is out of sight before making the noise, so as not to 'head' it (make it change direction); and should always remember that a holloa is a way of conveying information to the Huntsman, and not of expressing spontaneous joy or enthusiasm.

Some, by the time they've satisfied these quite exacting criteria, deem it more prudent to remain silent, although there are others who would holloa a passing pekingese in Regent Street.

So the people who hunt in order to ride do exactly that, and derive great enjoyment from their sport. If they were not hunting, they would probably be pottering along roads and bridleways, seldom able to get out of a trot or canter and hardly ever getting a chance to jump. Out hunting — provided they behave themselves — they can ride on private land that would normally be closed to them, get a good gallop, fly over all kinds of obstacles and generally give meaning to that old phrase, riding hell for leather.

Just how much hell-for-leathering they can enjoy depends on the Hunt they're out with and, of course, how they shape as riders. In a fast galloping country with big fences, many would be best advised to stay at home. The essence of fox-hunting is to stay close to hounds — to 'keep up', as they call it, and foxhounds move fast and strong, and will get through places that would stop a tank. Ditches, walls, hedges, fences, woods, rivers — they'll plunge over or through the lot. Following them on horseback is exhilarating, demanding and sometimes downright terrifying.

Stories of old-time hunting contain thrilling passages describing horsemen a dozen abreast clearing five-foot hedges with ditches on either side — tally-ho! for'ard on!

the parson's fallen! never mind, he won't be needed till Sunday! Yoicks! — terrific.

But those old hedges could often be crashed through if a horse didn't get up high enough. Nowadays many of them conceal taut strands of barbed wire and should your horse hit that at 30-odd miles an hour you'd probably call out something other than 'yoicks'. A certain amount of caution is advisable in the hunting field, if only to ease the pressure on the National Health Service.

Fences made only of lines of barbed wire strung tightly between upright posts are another hazard, because horses tend to see only the posts, and not the wire. Very good and bold horsemen aim their horses at the posts, but they know what they're doing; and they know their horses.

Wire has troubled and impeded fox-hunters ever since it was invented. Most Hunts have substantial 'Wire Funds' to deal with it. In some areas the money is used to pay farmers to take down wire at the beginning of the season and replace it afterwards.

Where it cannot be taken down, Hunt jumps are constructed in fences. These vary in style, size and nomenclature, but 'tiger trap' is a common term, and most consist of two or three stout logs laid horizontally to a height of about three feet. They make nice, solid, inviting obstacles for horses, but are not usually wide enough across to allow more than one horse to jump safely at a time. This leads to the queueing about which fox-hunters complain so much.

There are parts of Britain — and even more in Ireland — where riders can take a pretty straight line after hounds, but often they have to jink about a great deal to get to Hunt jumps and to avoid trampling on growing crops. Farming is so much more intensive today that far less land is left as stubble or plough. It is swiftly re-seeded and automatically becomes forbidden territory to fox-hunters.

So, while there is quite a lot of galloping over grassland, heath and moor, with horses leaping hedges, ditches and stone walls, much of hunting is trotting and cantering in single-file along bridleways, lanes and round the edges of fields, with just the occasional exciting burst of speed which more often than not ends in a big mob of horses trying to get over a Hunt jump.

This can place a strain on the coolest nerves. It only takes one horse to refuse the jump, or a rider to fall, to create a log-jam of fractious animals. Whether you're in the mêlée, or being borne swiftly and relentlessly towards it, you may find yourself wishing you'd taken up table tennis.

Whether you live through this experience and actually enjoy hunting will depend upon the kind of horse you're on and whether you can actually ride it. Among non-riders there is a popular misconception that riding is a form of transport in which the person in the saddle is a fairly passive passenger. Of the millions who watch show-jumping on television, many suppose that the horses are a species of circus animal and that the rider's task is simply to stay on board and do a bit of steering while the animal performs its tricks.

Anyone who has sat on a horse only once, even for five consecutive minutes, and with the animal taking no more than a few slow paces, knows differently. Riding competently, let alone competitively, is a considerable skill that becomes more difficult to acquire the later in life it is attempted.

Every hunt has its nucleus of good riders — enviably assured-looking men and women who sit well on good horses and are always in front of the field — and they are almost invariably country-bred people who were put on their first ponies, and even taken out hunting, when they were only four or five years old. Surrounding that nucleus there are fairly able riders, mounted on suitable horses, who can be counted on to stay with the field without endangering themselves or others.

And then there are the doubtfuls, in every sense of the word. They may be anything from moderately experienced riders on horses that are a bit beyond their capabilities, right down to complete novices on cobby-looking nags.

The greatest peril among the doubtfuls lies with those whose horses are simply too strong and headstrong for them.

The 'over-horsed' tend to be newcomers to hunting, from urban backgrounds. They've taken riding lessons, become pretty proficient, and are keen to get up and go. They want to go hunting in order to ride, and why not? It's a great sport and their subscriptions help to maintain it. Some, however, would be well-advised to put aside vanity, which demands a best-part Thoroughbred, and settle for a more accommodating beast.

If they looked about them at almost any Meet, they'd see men and women riding well into evident late life. Exceptional people hunt in their eighties, and the reason they have survived is that, throughout their hunting careers, they have matched their mounts to their physical abilities. As veterans, they are content to ride steady, kind, sensible, bomb-proof horses that know the job and won't gallop off with them or drop them on their heads.

That's the sort to end your hunting days on.

And to start them.

At last, after slithering about in mud and rain for three weeks — frost. Just a nice sprinkle of white. Lovely to look at, and there really is going to be a winter. Good for sprouts and good for us. Unfortunately, sun as well, so scent no more than serving, but the pack really got their noses down and Brian hunted them like the wizard he can be on his best days. Amazing start. Hadn't been in Alandale Woods 10 minutes before a fox jumped down out of a tree practically in front of hounds! If he'd stayed upstairs we'd never have seen him. Chopped, of course, almost as he hit the ground. Michael said he must have been asleep. I fell straight in. A fox? cried I — asleep in a tree with hounds thrashing about and Brian blowing? Well, says Michael, maybe he just dropped off. Always the wag. On to draw the gorse on the Gully side and old Mystery opened with his customary accuracy and we were off screaming. Really rattling pace and a straight-necked fox that knew where it wanted to go — the same line as one of its dear departed brethren chose the season before last and left three of the field swimming in the sawmill stream. Great stuff. Same line exactly — right through the sawmill yard like a bullet and right-handed for the stream. No swimming for me, but when hounds jinked right, Brian went for the short-cut like a good 'un — jumped the steel gate (it was open last time) and over the stream, and over the wire beyond and straight up the slope. Got it absolutely right, real Badminton stuff. Too much for me. I followed as hounds ran, lost them in among old tractors and junk and had to go right round the lane way, with most of the field with me. Nobody else tried jumping the gate, and not surprising. On down round Fred Allberry's sugar beet, popped the jump in the corner, then on to the stream where it's a bit less hairy. Padlock slid down to the edge, stopped, then put in the mightiest cat-hop, leaving me half way up his neck. Dignity just saved (a miracle!) and on with one iron lost but back in the plate. Foot back just in time to fairly fly the next stream (Padlock hardly noticed it) and found hounds had checked by a sort of pump-house. Brian cast them forward with a rare flourish and they soon owned the line. Beautiful. There was a holloa from somewhere near the village and a moment later I viewed the fox trotting calmly over the bridge towards *the village. Amazing, and hounds barely a minute behind him.*

When they reached the other side of the bridge, hounds checked. There was a holloa downstream and Brian fairly skidded across the bridge and cast them down by the water virtually in the direction Charlie had just come from. I thought he must be utterly wrong but he was right, and hounds were hunting splendidly almost immediately — a great cry as they worked along beside the water. Along the stream, away from it by Wheelbarrow Lane, left-handed at the old railway coal-yard and away into the scrub and brambles beyond. Thought we'd never get him out of there but he was away on the other side and hounds barely faltered. They coursed him to a hedge, put him to ground and accounted for him near what used to be Tadley Halt. An exciting hunt, with huge splashings through the water, and over all too quickly.

A three-mile point, I reckon, and not much more as hounds ran. Good stuff. Rest of the day slower after second horses and the sun 'unlocked scent', as Father used to say. A fair run over a nice line (yours truly taking a stile in great style) but we gave that one best after another three-mile point. A brace and a good day, with horses lathered and a few empty saddles. The field well satisfied, and winter clearly in the offing. Looks as though we may be getting some real hunting weather soon.

First Frost

Whatever the calendar indicates, or hunting appointments decree, every year there is always a particular day that seems to be the first real day of the hunting season. And most fox-hunters would agree that it is almost invariably the first day that there is frost on the ground. The first morning that the countryside is magically decorated white is the annual reminder that hunting is a winter sport, and that it has now truly begun.

It usually happens in late November, before the trees have surrendered all their leaves. Sometimes there is sunshine as well, and the effect is memorable. Clean and clear. Sharp and challenging. Bright and enlivening. On such a morning, to be on the back of a horse and on the way to the Meet gives even the most cynical old heart an extra tug of anticipation. Dedicated fox-hunters know that the thinly warm sunshine may soon dissipate scent and ruin sport, but it also brightens red coats, brings gleam to boots, sheen to horses, glisten to frost, splendour to the Meet and a halo to the day.

The first frost is a new beginning.

At 10.30 on just such a morning, among thousands making their way to a hundred and more Meets all over the land, there was a young man called Tony. Without doubt, he would remember this as *his* first day of the season — even, perhaps, his first day of hunting.

In several respects Tony, in his thirties, was typical of a great many of today's generation of fox-hunters, who do not all hunt as an automatic birth-given privilege. Although not country-born, he had chosen to live in a rural area and was doing well enough, as junior partner in an estate agency, to keep one horse. He was not one of the county hunting 'set', in so far as such a nebulous body can still be said to exist, but he was known as a regular member of the Saturday field of his local pack. He was in his third season now, and a somewhat better rider than he had been in his first.

By no interpretation of the facts could Tony have been described as a really keen hunter. He had never had the time nor, really, the inclination to go cub-hunting, and he had been known to stay at home in really foul weather. His wife often joked that he only went hunting because he fancied himself in his bowler, and there was a whit of truth in the assessment. He did think he looked rather well in hunting clothes, and he did enjoy the social ambience. His knowledge of and interest in hounds was, like a lot of others', virtually nil. He hunted to ride, and did so prudently, following where others went. He simply enjoyed being on his horse in the fresh air.

His satisfaction, though, as he rode to the Meet on this wonderful morning, was complete. He'd had a good breakfast, his new part-time groom had plaited his horse well (mane *and* tail, at last), he had unboxed in plenty of time, he was perfectly turned out, and had a whisky-and-water in his flask and three pound notes in his pocket ready to pay his field money; he felt right, and ready — a young country gentleman setting off for a day's sport.

What was that old riding adage? Your head and heart high; your hands and heels down; your legs close to your horse's side and your elbows close to your own? Something like that. And that was Tony this morning; man and horse in unison. He'd been very lucky with the animal, a chestnut gelding called Crusader, which he'd bought as a nine-year-old. It was 16 hands, and a made hunter that knew the job and was well up to his 11 stone. Crusader was, in truth, a better mount than he needed or, some might have said, deserved. For Tony had never dared to shoulder his way into the front rank of the local cavalry; never tried to be in the first flight; would never be known as a 'thruster'. The legendary 'quick thing' over old turf and stone walls in a 'flying country' was something that he had only read about, and did not aspire to.

This, anyway, was not that kind of country. It did not require an exceptional horse, and second horses were seldom used except by the Masters and Hunt servants. It was largely a fiddly country, arable, wired up and with a lot of woodland. For the big majority of the field, the only 'quick things' were occasional short bursts over bits of grass, usually snuffed out far too soon by a sudden queue to get over a Hunt jump. There was a lot of single-file creeping round the edge of seed, being nagged by the Field-Master about straying. Nevertheless, the Hunt did have its days.

Tony had left his trailer in a village pub car park, and was enjoying the 10-minute trot to the Meet. Crusader had a high, slightly showy action at the trot, and a more experienced rider would have made him extend a bit to get the ground covered. But the gait looked well, and Tony was accustomed to it. White breeches and well-cleaned saddle met and separated almost imperceptibly at each sit and rise, his weight springily absorbed by his immaculate knees and brightly shining ankles. Nice, swinging rhythm. Natural impulsion contained effortlessly with the weight of the reins.

He glanced down and was pleased to see boot, spur and dangling whip. He glanced sideways and took further pleasure from his and his horse's joint shadow moving along a mellow brick wall. God, he felt like the lord of the manor. Marvellous! How infrequently it was, he reflected, that a man could feel so good — grasp the feeling, experience it, exude it, positively glow with it. He could have laughed out loud with the joy of being on a horse on such a fine morning. Instead, he slightly startled a woman pushing a pram by calling out a ringing 'good morning!' to her. Since she did not know him, nor anyone else who rode horses, she lowered her eyes, muttered something calming to her baby, and continued her journey.

Tony didn't mind being ignored. In truth, if he had been on foot, he wouldn't have presumed to address a female stranger. Riding, particularly in hunting clothes, changed his demeanour. The way he was feeling this morning, he might even have swept off his bowler hat in salute.

The Meet today was being given by one of the Joint-Masters. Tony hadn't been to the house before, but he'd visited the village. In fact, one of his agency's For Sale boards was displayed outside what had once been the village shop. Prices had gone mad, he mused, although not without satisfaction — offers on £55,000? The place was nearly falling down. But this was not a day for business. He was going hunting.

He would have no difficulty finding the Joint-Master's house. He had seen horse-boxes on the village green, and there were four riders well in front of him. He followed them up a lane which opened on to another patch of green, and this was obviously the place.

There were about 20 horseboxes and trailers, some empty because their owners had mounted and gone on, one with a pretty girl trying to persuade her horse down the ramp, and another with a horse tied to it and a hunting whip hanging ready on the arm of the big rear-view mirror.

Tony reined up and looked about to get his bearings. The girl tied her horse to her box and hopped up into the driving cab to make her final preparations. She jiggled her short fair hair into a net, which made her look momentarily like an actress in Coronation Street; then crowned it with her riding cap, which looked more like Bond Street.

The gentleman with the whip hanging from the mirror emerged from the back of his box and lined his horse up ready to mount from the ramp. He was an elderly man, in red coat and top hat, and fortune did not favour his first attempts to get into the saddle. Twice the horse swung away from him, and he had to step down off the ramp and lead it alongside again. The years had eroded his agility somewhat. However, they had given him skill and determination — an essential quality — and, at just the right moment, his ancient right leg went over. Tony shook his head in admiration. The old boy must have been in his 70s but clearly, when he made up his mind to mount a horse, mount it he did.

A group of riders clipped up the lane that Tony had just arrived by, and rode on past the boxes. Tony followed them. He was able to be out today because he'd had to work on the previous Saturday. Going hunting on a week-day was a rare treat that heightened his pleasure. It made him feel almost wealthy, being among fox-hunters who had enough leisure not to have to confine their sport to Saturdays.

Tony followed the riders along a lane, through a wide gateway into a generous drive and, as it happened, generous hospitality. The Meet was perfect — in perfect weather and a perfect setting. As soon as Tony saw the Joint-Master's house he mentally categorised it as the kind of dwelling that would fetch not less than £200,000. Oh, yes, very nice . . . late Georgian . . . well proportioned . . . extensive views . . . paddocks . . . tennis court. He gazed about speculatively. Yes, probably listed, and a pound-to-a-penny there was a swimming pool round the other side. He was almost on the point of framing a tasteful advertisement when his musings were pierced by a female voice. Not addressing him, but the female's female friend. Both ladies were impeccably mounted and clad.

'I always think John's house looks so cosy, don't you?'

'Yes — has he shown you his jacuzzi yet?'

'His *what*?'

'Jacuzzi — I'm sure that's what they call it. It's a sort of bath that swirls round and round.'

'Isn't that rather disturbing?'

'I think it's meant to be erotic.'

'Goodness — naughty old John!'

Two high-pitched, high-class gurgles of laughter followed. Good God, thought Tony, how rich did you have to be to describe a manor house as 'cosy'? That was an estate agent's last desperate euphemism for a terrace cottage almost too small to sell. The chatter — 'coffee-housing' — went on.

There were perhaps 80 at the Meet — quite a big field for a weekday — and they were gathered in a large paddock at the front of the house, below a terraced lawn. It was ideal for the Hunt Secretary, because everybody had to enter through a gate, by which he was able to station himself like a sentry to cap visitors and gather field money.

Hounds were already present, about 20 couple, gathered obediently around the Huntsman in a corner of the paddock. The frost still lay white beneath the long shadows of trees, but was retreating where the sunlight warmed the grass and stretched its way to the front of the house, smoothing its old stones with wintry soft light. With horses, hounds, red coats and black, the scene had an engaging, reassuring flavour of English antiquity. Hounds had met here just like this for over 150 years, and very little had changed, apart, perhaps, from the large number of women in the field. Looking about him, Tony reckoned that the men might well be outnumbered.

A nice middle-aged lady wearing good tweeds and flat-heeled shoes held a tray of drinks up to him. Steam was rising from the glasses. 'Good morning — would you like one of these, do you think? I'm told it's punch.'

'Looks marvellous — thank you.'

'Well, it ought to keep the cold out, at any rate. I think there's some sherry, if you'd rather. Oh! And whisky-mac. Oh, yes, and coffee as well. I'm not awfully good at remembering.'

'No, this is fine. Thank you.'

He took a sip and found it very good. There might have been rum in it, but he couldn't be sure. It was never very clear where these nice ladies came from, but there were always a few wandering with trays at a lawn Meet. Perhaps owners of houses like this always had a little team of O.K.-sounding female relatives on tap. They could hardly hire them from the Women's Institute. By the gate to the paddock were three trestle tables, white cloth-topped, bearing urns, cups, glasses, and what looked like slices of dark cake. When this Joint-Master gave the Meet, he did it properly. Tony had rarely felt so content. It was always nice to be given a drink early on. He never felt he'd really arrived and been accepted until he had a glass in his hand. Furthermore, there'd be time for another.

The field, it seemed to him, were rather smarter than the Saturday lot, although there were a good few Saturday people out, as well. Two of the Members were somewhat conspicuous in the new grey velvet caps, instead of their toppers, but they didn't look as cissy as some had feared. In fact, Tony thought, they were rather smart. But he would stick to his bowler. It had taken a lot of getting used to. The first few times he wore it had left him with a headache and a deep purple line across his forehead, but now it had taken the shape of his skull as though made for him. This was largely due to his having worn it at home — in the beginning, for no more than five minutes at a time — for progressively longer periods until, gradually, it eased. Once, he'd even watched television in it, to the great amusement of his wife.

More people were arriving every few moments. Hearty 'good mornings' were ringing out all over the paddock, with many hat-raisings. How jovial and confident hunting people always were. They didn't look as though they had an overdraft, a mortgage or an erring spouse among the lot of them. Some of them had to have troubles, of course — they couldn't all be as unworried and wealthy as they appeared.

Perhaps knowing that he was going hunting, like knowing that he was going to be hanged, concentrated a man's mind wonderfully. It certainly seemed to cheer men up wonderfully.

'Good morning — don't often see you out on a Monday, do we?' Tony knew the speaker by sight, but had no idea of his name. He was elegantly turned out and mounted on what was clearly a part Thoroughbred.

'Afraid not — usually too busy.'

'Hard at it, eh? Well, you should enjoy yourself today. I expect John'll make us go pounding over his cross-country course.'

'Really?' Tony tried to appear nonchalant, but the word 'cross-country' wrinkled his stomach to the size of a worried walnut. He was not, to put it discreetly, terribly keen on jumping.

'Oh, *rather*. Great fun — John's never got any foxes, but you always get a super ride. You've not been here before, then?'

Tony tried not to squeak. 'No,' he managed to reply fairly coolly.

'Oh, you'll love it — like Badminton without all those people gawking at you.' The elegant horseman nudged his horse away to terrify or cheer someone else, leaving Tony turning slightly pale. Badminton? The three-day event that was always on television, with huge hairy jumps made out of telegraph poles? With drops into lakes? With vast spreads? And obstacles called coffins? Suddenly, the sunshine had gone out of the morning.

A young woman's voice came from below him. 'Is that glass going to be empty soon?' He looked down. She was proffering a tray.

'Er — thanks very much.' He drained his glass, handed it to her and gratefully accepted another.

'Super morning, isn't it?' Tony nodded agreement with a thin smile that didn't convey quite enough enthusiasm.

'Super.' He'd like to have polished off that drink and asked for another, but it might have looked greedy, and the girl was moving off.

His feeling of apprehension grew. Cross-country? Of course! This was where the hunter trials were held. Why hadn't he noticed? There'd be jumps all over the place. He looked about and saw that the gate he had entered the paddock by had a tiger trap next to it, and over on the other side, behind the hounds, there was another. The Joint-Master probably had tiger traps in his bedroom — over a jump and straight into the jacuzzi! Tony began to wonder if he could just quietly fade away, hack round by himself for a bit, box-up and slither off home while he was still alive.

'Hounds, please!' Everybody shifted their horses like the Biblical parting of the waters to make way for the departing Huntsman and his eager pack. Hats were raised in thanks to the hosts in the scrupulously courteous and courtly manner of fox-hunters. The field began moving off in the mood of brave and cheery optimism that always flavours the start of the hunt.

Except for some. Tony, on this bright day, was of their nervous number. It was a bit shameful, he knew, but the fact was that he didn't really know how to jump. He just leaned forward in the saddle and hoped. The few obstacles he had encountered out hunting had been comfortably low and, always being well down the field, he had tackled them when his turn came in the queue. In the portion of the field that he normally straggled in, nobody was in any great hot-blooded hurry to get to hounds because they didn't even know where they were. Bold hunters none of them, they just pottered about following each other, which suited Tony very well.

His great good fortune was that Crusader seemed content to pop patiently and smoothly over little three-foot tiger traps without getting fizzy or fussy. Over he would go, and over Tony would go, and usually they were more or less together. Such accomplishments had sometimes given Tony the illusion that he knew how to jump a horse. He was now acutely aware that the illusion had always been false.

'Shall I take that away from you before you go?' Nice tweed lady again. His empty glass.

'Thank you.' How pleasant and casual the people on the ground were.

'Have a good day. I must say you've chosen frightfully good weather.'

'Yes,' Tony agreed, wishing he'd been more careful about choosing the place. Hounds were funnelling through the gateway now, some squirming over the tiger-trap rather than get left behind. The second Whipper-in saw them through, watched by the Senior Master.

Crusader made an impulsive movement forward to follow hounds, but Tony stifled that intention almost before it was formed. Getting up tight behind hounds was not the idea at all. Besides, it was *very* bad manners to move before the Master, who was looking around now, in confident red-coated command, as though searching for someone. He tilted his chin in Tony's direction: 'Would one or two of you go with Derek and line the lane, when we get there, please?'

Tony's reaction was a mixture of astonishment, pride — and panic. He had never been given a task before. He'd never even been recognised before, except vaguely, as a face to be said 'good morning' to, under a bowler to be raised. And now he was clearly one of the privileged few who were being asked — and by the Master! — to do something positive, helpful and useful, a request that carried

with it the implication that he could be trusted to do
something positive, helpful and useful. He blushed, feeling
like a subaltern suddenly promoted on the battlefield.

The cavalcade moved off, and there was Tony — Tony,
the fox-hunter, flanked by two riders, following *immediately behind* the Master, and at the head of the entire field.
He might have been leading them across Horseguards. It
was amazing. Incredible.

And frightening.

But the fear was mixed with a strong, new, strange
feeling of manly purpose. Of the many Meets he had
attended, this was the very first time he had really felt
that he was participating. Resisting the temptation to
look behind him, he knew what he would have seen — a
long line of riders, heads bobbing at the trot, three and
four abreast, and completely filling the lane for a good
half a mile. He could hear them, anyway, with their
hooves clattering on the tarred surface. Splendid sound.

Normally he would have been trailing at the back of
the procession among a clutter of kids on ponies. It was
unbelievably thrilling to find himself one of the leaders,
and the accompanying fear that corroded the thrill might
have disappeared if he had known more about his chosen
sport. Being selected to line a lane — to act as a kind of
sentry — carried the distinct possibility of being left hopelessly behind and never getting a look at hounds all day.
Real fox-hunters hate it.

Tony trotted on. Or, rather, jogged on. He was beginning to learn that riding a horse behind hounds can be
somewhat uncomfortable, because their pace, when
moving to draw, is faster than a horse's walk but slower
than its trot. Since it is a cardinal sin to allow a horse to
get too close to hounds, and equally unthinkable to slop
about miles behind them, the rider has to compromise
between holding his horse back and keeping it up to
hounds. This calls for a blend of skill and endurance only
achieved after more hours in the saddle than Tony had
yet accumulated. His next few meals, he began to suspect,
might have to be eaten from a mantelpiece, a bookshelf

or perhaps a window-sill. Somewhere, at any rate, high enough to preclude the necessity for sitting down.

Sitting down, as it happened, was what he should have been doing now. And firmly. Crusader was beginning to enjoy himself in the manner that horsemen define as 'not really fresh, but definitely keen'. It may have been that the animal had never been so close to hounds since being ridden by Tony and felt that, at last, it was really going hunting again. What it had been doing with Tony on top for the past two seasons had been Saturday afternoon hacking.

Horses can be infuriatingly stupid, but they have memories that make elephants seem afflicted with amnesia. Whatever the reason, Crusader was now 'right up on his toes', which is another horsey phrase indicating, if not danger, that certainly the rider should be particularly alert and sitting strongly; quietly in command, without communicating any sense of apprehension. It is not easy.

As Tony saw the problem — and he was becoming increasingly aware that that was what he had — Crusader was so eager that he was pulling, seeming intent on hurtling forward to scatter Master and hounds, cannon into the Huntsman, and continue on his way to some unknown destination: Epsom, perhaps. Understandably anxious that this should not happen, Tony was pulling at the reins, and because he was not deep enough into the saddle, he was being hauled out of it. Now he was neither rising nor sitting to the trot, but half standing in his stirrups and attempting to reduce forward progress by sawing the bit. Worse, he was failing. Crusader knew enough to evade the bit's pressure and friction, which Tony was unable to apply convincingly because he wasn't secure, with his bottom raised somewhat untidily. Tiny, almost weightless professional jockets can control thunderous Thoroughbreds from this backside-in-the-air position. But not Tony; nor, in truth, can that many fox-hunters. So Tony's horse broke into a canter. This sudden surge of impulsion jerked him back into the saddle and reduced what little pull he'd been able to exert on the reins. With three clattering strides Crusader plunged forward past the Master to the very sterns of the last hounds and, just as he looked to be about to plough through the entire pack, settled into a lively but satisfied jog. Crusader was a hunter, after all, and knew where he wanted to be.

Tony shortened his reins in the hope of preventing further alarms, but experienced the worrying suspicion that his horse was likely to go off hunting by itself, with or without such influence as he could bring to bear on its behaviour.

The Master now caught up with him. 'Bit fresh, eh?' he called, presumably rhetorically and certainly kindly. Tony, still shaken, would have put it more forcefully, but he knew the conventions and some of the phraseology: 'Just feeling well I think, Master.' The Master chuckled sympathetically. 'Better cut his oats back.' This was fox-hunting patter, which passed for conversation in much the same way as rail commuters impersonally exchange complaints about the train service. It was a comfort, nevertheless, to be addressed. It implied understanding; fox-hunting fellowship; tacit tribal approval. The remark about oats, though, was nearer the mark than the Master could have guessed or Tony known.

Tony understood practically nothing about feeding horses, other than that the bills for fodder always seemed excessive. His groom did the ordering and feeding, except for the evening and Sunday feeds, which she left made up for Tony or his wife to give. The ingredients in the feed buckets were a messy mystery to him, as were the quantities and proportions. As the groom had worked previously in a racing yard, she was a bit too liberal with the high-energy stuff. If Tony had known the inappropriately large quantity of oats Crusader had been getting since the beginning of this season, and their potentially dynamic effect on his performance and behaviour, he would have cut the horse's rations down to a packet of cornflakes a week.

But he didn't know. So, more or less together, he and Crusader trotted on. Or hound-jogged, as the term goes.

Tony remained tense, emotionally and physically, while the Master forbore to make further comment, despite sporadic fears for the safety of his hounds. It was nevertheless with some relief that he saw the Huntsman take the pack away to draw the first covert, while he sent Tony and two other black-coated members of the field off with Derek, the second Whipper-in. Hounds were going to be put into a big patch of kale to the left of a lane in which the field were now halted. Derek's little detachment were to go ahead and line the lane.

Derek apparently assumed that his troops knew what was expected of them, and he seemed to be right because, within five hundred yards, one of them pulled up, calling out, 'About here?'

'That'll do fine, sir.'

The second black coat also fell out and took station a little further on, but Tony stuck with Derek and waited to be given his instructions. The barbed wire edging the kale eventually ended at a corner with a bridleway sign pointing to the left.

'Right, sir,' said Derek, 'this'll do us — if you'll just 'ang on 'ere,' and, squeezing his horse into a canter, plunged up the bridleway. Crusader liked this bit of action, and promptly tried to follow. Checked, he shook his head, lifted his forelegs in a half-rear, and pranced in a way that looks terrific in cowboy films but is fairly alarming for a fox-hunter who hopes he'll never be heading for the last round-up.

To Tony's surprise and considerable relief, when Derek's red coat had vanished up the thickly tree-overhung track, Crusader stood still. Tony patted his neck approvingly. 'Good lad,' he said, in what he hoped was a soothing yet commanding manner. He'd read somewhere that horses were reassured by the human voice, though he couldn't recall the writer saying anything about the trembling human hand. Or the fast human heart-beat that was only just beginning to slow to normal.

He knew enough about hunting to realise what was happening. Kale was a favourite lying-up place for foxes, and if there was one here, the Master didn't want it to cross over the lane. Tony was one of the sentinels.

After a while, four cars came slowly up the lane, passed him, and parked about 100 yards to his right, beyond the bridleway. The drivers, obviously followers, got out of their cars. One of them strolled down towards him and peered up the bridleway. Tony was never certain whether to talk to foot-followers, who often seemed almost secretively silent and self-sufficient. This one, though, shuffled a little closer and asked quietly, 'Anything doing yet, sir?' The 'sir' rather embarrassed him. Tony looked down. 'Nothing so far.'

The man sniffed, hunched his shoulders and drove his hands down into his car-coat pockets with determined pessimism. 'They won't find nothing on a morning like this.' He sniffed again. 'No scent.' The man put a handkerchief to his nose to deal with a dewdrop. So that was why he was sniffing. For a moment Tony had thought he might be competing with hounds, and checking for scent himself.

A neatly sloping hillock of fallen beech leaves lay at the entrance to the bridleway, driven by the wind and then abandoned, like a snowdrift. On the other side of it were the clear prints left by Derek's horse. The going was just about perfect, soft but not soggy. Where frost had crisped the layer of damp fallen leaves, it was the consistency of apple-crumble. Through the gaps in the trees along the track, rays of pale sunshine slanted down, drawing wisps of misty moisture from the now evaporating frost. In the silence and the shafts of sunlight, the tree-tunnel of the bridleway could almost have been a cathedral. For anyone hacking, the track would be an irresistibly inviting canter.

A long way away, there was the sound of shooting. Otherwise, all was quiet. For all Tony knew, hounds might be going away from him, never to be seen again. Would Derek come back and tell him what was going on, or what to do next? Somehow, he doubted it.

After a few minutes, he heard the Huntsman's horn,

but was unable to interpret its message. Just a few rapid short notes, which seemed to be at a good distance. The foot-follower sniffed again and shook his head, as though the sound of the horn finally settled the matter. 'No,' he declared to nobody in particular, 'no scent.' After listening for some moments, he began walking slowly back to the other car followers. Tony felt isolated and conspicuous on his horse, but at least Crusader seemed to have accepted quiet immobility after the flurry upon Derek's departure. Neither did there seem any danger, for the present, of tackling a cross-country course.

Car doors slammed and engines started up. The foot-people drove off, evidently convinced there was a better place to be. What did they know? Where were they going? Tony's feeling of isolation developed darkly downwards into a kind of lonely gloom. He did not feel like a bold, dashing fox-hunter any more.

He looked at his watch, saw that it was nearly a quarter to twelve, and began wondering whether he ought to move. But where to? Up the bridleway? All in all, he thought he'd better hang on. It was as he was coming to this conclusion that he heard a hound speak. Then another. Then the Huntsman's horn, more urgently, it seemed to Tony, than it had sounded a few minutes before. And not quite so far away.

Other hounds took up the cry. Crusader's ears twitched keenly. Tony saw a movement far away in the frost-touched kale. It looked as though a breeze was stirring part of the crop. The horn again. Then, a little closer, a hound leapt upwards out of the kale, and dropped back into it, like a dolphin sporting in the sea. Nearby were the waving sterns of other hounds, just the tips of their tails showing. Some of those, too, made sudden bounds into the air, getting their heads above the kale to see, to seek, to pursue — to hunt.

Isolated excited yelps grew in volume and were joined by a scattering of other hound voices at varying pitches, deep and high. The horn was sounding quicker now and, between the blasts of short notes, there were shouts from the Huntsman, urging his hounds to find. 'Tally-*o*, tally-*o*, tally-*o* — push 'im up, then . . .'

Something was obviously a-foot — and very likely a fox — but Tony could still see no human being, no coat, red or black, to give a clue as to what was really happening and what he might do.

Then, like members of an orchestra tuning up individually and suddenly brought to purpose and performance by the conductor, the random hound voices found unity and conviction. Crusader whinnied and shook his head impatiently. Hounds were truly giving tongue now in a chillingly eager clashing crescendo of different voices that rose and fell and cascaded and crossed each other like cracked church bells rung by the insane; music to hunters, but music of a terrible ferocity. And suddenly cutting through it a long, pulsating series of notes from the Huntsman's horn — the Gone Away.

The fox had broken cover, hounds had hit the line and were hunting in full cry. It is a supreme moment for fox-hunters, especially on what seems a poor scenting day. The Gone Away is as significant and exciting as a cavalry trumpeter's call to charge. When the Field-Master goes, the field goes. And go they do. Or, at least, the goers go. In every Hunt there are those who do, and those who do not.

There had never been much doubt in Tony's mind as to which category he belonged to, but now, having heard the horn, should he leave his post and set off in pursuit of hounds at whatever pace he chose? Crusader was certainly willing. Tony, however, like many other fox-hunters, was a bit shaky on the horn calls and how to respond to them. His normal practice — again, like a lot of others — was simply to move when everybody else did. And stop when everybody else did. All he could discern at the moment was that hounds had been making a lot of noise, and still were.

But the noise was becoming fainter with every second. Hounds were clearly going away from him, and he still had not seen anybody. He was a follower, in fact, with nothing to follow. If he stopped where he was much longer, he might just as well park his horse outside the nearest pub, have a pint and get on home. In fox-hunting terms, he had definitely lost touch.

Wait a minute! No, he hadn't! There was a red coat approaching down the bridleway. Approaching? It was absolutely hurtling. Derek was coming back at a gallop. And calling out urgently, pointing his arm to the left. 'Up the lane, sir — up the lane!' As he got closer he reined back into a canter to round the corner at the end of the bridleway. 'Come on, sir — they're goin' like 'ell!' And he was away, still cantering.

Before Tony could muster any thoughts, Crusader was following Derek's horse, both of them striking a loud clatter from the macadam surface of the lane. Cantering on roads is not recommended — it jars horses' legs and their shoes can easily slip — but a Hunt servant's job is to keep up to his hounds, come what may, and Tony seemed to have been recruited in the same worthy cause. Or, at any rate, Crusader had volunteered.

When the grass verge to the left of the lane became wide enough, Derek put his mount on it, and the noisy road sound gave way to the thud of hooves on turf. Tony pulled at his left rein and was gratified when Crusader responded and got over on to the grass as well. He was less pleased when at the very second the horse's feet touched the verge, it accelerated somewhat alarmingly to catch up with the other horse. But as soon as Crusader had achieved his ambition, he was content to lie comfortably a yard behind.

Derek was standing in his stirrups and scanning the field to the left. It was dark, frosted fresh plough. The Whipper-in seemed not to be in such a great hurry now. It was his nineteenth season in the country, he knew exactly where he was, and he had a pretty shrewd idea where hounds would be running. He gestured to his left with his whip. Tony looked over and saw a line of trees at the far edge of the plough. Dazzled at first by the low wintry sun flickering through the trees, he could not make out what he was meant to be looking at. Then, intermittently, he saw that riders — almost the entire field — were cantering single-file on the other side of the trees, in the same direction and parallel with him.

It was a brave sight on such a morning, and gave him a reassuring sense of belonging. How considerate of Derek, he thought, to draw his attention to it, rather like a foreign tour guide going to the trouble of pointing out a feature of special interest.

The real reason for Derek's gesture was to help Tony re-join the field, to which he properly belonged. A Hunt servant does not want a follower trailing after him all day. Derek maintained a steady canter along the verge until two blasts from the horn made him spur on. It was the signal that the Huntsman needed him. Tony's horse quickened, too, and together they turned left through an open gate into a stubble field. Unhesitatingly, Derek put his horse into a gallop, aiming straight for the far right-hand corner of the field, where there appeared to be a gate or a Hunt jump. Tony, with Crusader immediately tucking himself into Derek's slipstream, was not sure which it was. All he was aware of was that it was some kind of obstacle and that he was being propelled towards it with more rapidity than he cared for. There was a downward slope to the stubble, which increased the pace, and his unease. But, before he had time to panic, the red coat in front of him had risen, so had he, and he was on the other side of the obstacle. It had been a low, easy tiger-trap, and both horses, almost as one, had flown it without having to really get off the ground. Good God! It was like one of those old hunting prints. Now they were pounding across plough. Another jump was coming up and — wheeeee! — dammit if they weren't over that one, as well! Derek's horse veered left, dropped back into a canter over yet more plough and, after a couple of hundred yards, halted. Tony was too busy coping with the unexpected curving movement to see anything but Derek's horse leading the way in front of him, and it was only when Crusader began pulling up, too, that Tony saw before him a most pleasing scene.

A large static group of riders, with quite a few red coats among the black, was assembled in an open space where two bridleways converged. The Senior Master was at the front of the group, as was the Field-Master. They had obviously been held up while hounds checked and had had no diversion in their immobility other than to watch Derek and Tony leaping the last tiger-trap, perhaps even the previous one, as well. A captive audience, as they say.

Tony's pride and satisfaction could not have been greater if he had just won the Derby. He was not certain how elegantly he had cleared the last obstacle, but it had seemed as smooth as it was surprising, and he was still in the saddle, which was good enough for him. What with his breathlessness and barely suppressed feeling of elation, it's a wonder his coat buttons didn't pop off.

What had been happening while he was touring the countryside was that hounds, despite their earlier certainty, had run out of scent. It was that sort of day. The Huntsman had stopped them and gone on to the next draw, which was why he had called Derek in. Now, once again, the field was waiting. Derek set off at once to join the Huntsman, while Tony was left quite close to the two Masters. He could not have moved back timidly to the rear of the crowd, where he normally dwelt, because both tracks were completely jammed with riders. So he stayed where he was and found, oddly enough, that he was quite unafraid. A gallop and two jumps had changed him, for the moment, at any rate, into a bold fox-hunter. Well, bolder than usual.

One of the Masters lit a cigarette and chatted casually to the other Master. Clearly, nothing serious was about to happen, since smoking is frowned upon where scent might be at risk. The mood of the assembly became something like a rather up-market mounted tea-break, and Tony considered taking a swig from his flask. Better, though, he decided, to wait until he was alone. He was not too sure about flask etiquette; whether he should first offer the flask to his nearest neighbour, as he'd seen others do. Or was that only if the neighbour also happened to be a friend? There was niceties of behaviour in the hunting field that he had not yet grasped, on top of which, he reflected prudently, his flask didn't hold all that much. And the day had hardly started.

The dozen or so men and women closest to the Field-Master were evidently regulars, and it seemed it was basically them he was addressing when he said, 'High Wood next, then, good people — anyone fancy the pretty way?' and turned his horse purposefully into a gateway behind him, facing away from the main body of waiting riders.

The regulars followed immediately, as did about 20 of the rest of the field, and since Tony was standing partially in their path, he had little option but to join them. Fox-hunters were not known for their patience nor, in many cases, their manners. When they go, they go, and if there is a non-goer in the way, he may well find that he goes too.

As each horse reached the gateway its quarters dipped as it was squeezed to canter. Some virtually leapt through the space to tear after the others. No horse, it appeared — and certainly no rider — wished to be left behind. As Tony was swept up to the gateway, which was hardly wide enough for three riders abreast, he found he had a horse flanking him on either side, and neither was yielding. Both were ridden by women. Before courtesy could influence the situation, both shot ahead of him and he was squashed out. One called something back over her shoulder. It sounded like 'Sorry!' This meant nothing to Crusader, who, unbidden, broke into a gallop in pursuit of the cantering women, as though intent on revenge. There was still a gap between the pair and inside a few yards Tony shot through it so fast that it made the women look as if they'd stopped for a picnic. 'Sorry!' he shouted into the rushing wind, and tried to induce Crusader to travel at a more sedate pace.

The horse, however, could see no point in travelling slowly when there was plenty of space in front of him, and at least 10 horses still to be overtaken. Crusader could be quite competitive at times. Tony was now experiencing what riders sometimes refer to as brake failure. Earlier, while sitting and waiting, relaxed, he had let his reins slip slowly, and had failed to shorten them sufficiently at the gateway.

Mightily he pulled at the reins, but Crusader was pulling as well, and with a great deal more strength. Tony's arms were nearly at full length and seemed likely to be dragged from their sockets. Every fragment of pressure he was able to exert on the bit was too remote to be effective and only encouraged Crusader to stick his head out further and go faster.

Tony was being run away with.

He desperately needed to shorten rein if he was to have the faintest chance of pulling up. He tried to shift his hands up the reins, closer to the horse's head, but he had to relax his grip in order to claw higher up. As he loosened his fingers, impeded by gloves and whip, Crusader felt the reduced resistance in his mouth, and went straight into overdrive.

Tony won a bit of rein, but lost his last atom of control. He felt the immediate extra, wild, unstoppable animal power surge beneath him; and was frightened. Crusader was now galloping excitedly in the kind of unheeding hysteria that overcomes horses when they bolt, and appeared to be bound relentlessly for the horizon.

Panic gave Tony the brief urge to throw himself out of the saddle, but the speed-blur of the ground passing below him smothered that idea as fast as it occurred to him. He was too scared to topple off, and too stiff with terror to do anything more than hang on to the reins and keep his knees jammed in. In the draught made by his own rapid progress through the chill air, his eyes began watering.

He was racing down the left-hand side of a big stubble field, in the tracks of riders who had gone before. He overtook one pair of black-coated men, then a trio of women. They were all cantering fast, but were no opposition for Crusader, who was now feeling the benefit of all those oats. He flashed past three or four solitary riders and began gaining on two red coats, riding one behind the other. One wore a top hat, and the other a cap — the Field-Master. Top hat heard the urgent thud of Crusader's hooves, turned his head and grasped the situation at once. 'Turn him, turn him!' he shouted.

He might just as well have suggested writing him a postcard, for all the effect the advice had on Tony as he swept past. He was unaware that in an emergency it is sometimes possible to hook one rein over a horse's neck and get enough leverage to pull the other rein so hard that it brings the horse's head round and makes it change direction. If there is room — and here there was — the horse can be brought round in a slowing circle. It's a fairly savage way of stopping a horse, but it beats baling out. And it is certainly preferable to being killed, which has been the fate of quite a few people on bolting horses.

Tony thundered on in terrified ignorance of this useful ploy, and was quickly so tight up behind the Field-Master's horse that Crusader's nose was almost immediately at the Master's offside boot. The Master was now approaching and irrevocably committed to a Hunt jump — three 10-foot logs set sideways in a hedge — and was gathering nicely into it without any expectation of interference. But, as his horse left the ground, so did Crusader, with such superior speed and devastating impetus that he barged the Master in mid-air at the peak of his jump and knocked him out of the saddle. 'Jesus Christ!' cried the Master, just before he hit the ground.

Tony didn't quite catch the remark as he was borne helplessly on, now with the Master's loose horse galloping behind, lit up by the excitement and stimulated by the stirrups flapping free at its sides. It didn't seem possible that Crusader could go even faster but, with the incentive of another horse in the race, he managed to squeeze out a trifle more. They were going downhill now, towards a hedge with an open gate in the left-hand side, directly ahead of them. Far over to the right lay a tiger-trap, which would have been the next inviting obstacle on the Master's 'pretty way', had the Master not been lurching about horseless, recovering his hat, and muttering something about bloody hooligans and getting that lunatic's name.

Horses, like bicycles, go faster downhill than on the level, and Crusader fairly shot through the gateway ahead of him, with the Master's horse in close attendance. Neither had chosen the pretty way, and what lay ahead of Tony looked an ugly one.

He was in plough, which might have slowed down a less impetuous and well-fed horse than Crusader, but failed to have any appreciable effect on his speed. The ugliness of the aspect lay in a thick high hedge at the bottom end of the plough. It was gateless and gapless. Tony was in no position to estimate its height, but if he had been standing by it he would not have been able to see over the top. It was five feet if it was an inch, and he was being carried towards it downhill at something approaching 40 mph.

'Oh, God — no,' Tony whimpered. Even worse, the hedge-top was being trimmed from its far side by a tractor moving slowly right to left. With his vision obscured by the as yet uncut part of the hedge, the likelihood of the driver seeing Tony was remote, and the noise of charging hooves would never get through to him over the throbbing tractor engine and the clattering blades of the trimmer. Given Tony's present course and speed, which he was powerless to amend, he was about to meet the tractor driver without the benefit of a formal introduction.

Tony shouted hysterically 'Look out!' without knowing why and with no hope of his cry being heard. Crusader hammered on as though to jump the hedge just ahead of the tractor. Living in a nightmare, Tony felt a sudden black stab of conviction that he was about to die. Crusader was within ten yards of the hedge . . . five yards . . . then he rammed both forefeet into the ground in a jarring halt, dropping his nose almost to the ground and simultaneously spinning his rear end round anti-clockwise to make off left.

Tony continued his journey alone, in what might be

called free flight.

Launched out of the saddle, he sailed over the hedge in a slow somersault that few Olympic gymnasts would dare to attempt. His landing, however, lacked finesse. His body was bunched in an untidy ball, and made a tangible dent in the soft, seeded field into which, with extreme good fortune, it fell with a muffled thump.

The impact deprived him of consciousness and breath for perhaps half a minute. When he opened his eyes it was to discover that the lids were heavy with fragments of soil, which was also partially blocking one nostril. He had to spit some earth out of his mouth, as well. It was this action that proved to him that he was not, after all, dead.

He next became aware of engine noise and, turning his head in its direction, perceived that the tractor must have passed within a few inches of his knees to be in its present, still hedge-trimming position. The driver had evidently not even noticed the body flying across his path. It was a pity, really. Such an incident might have brought a touch of interest to an otherwise ordinary farming day.

Tony raised himself on one elbow, got to his knees, and finally stood up on his feet. He was trembling somewhat, and had a slight pain in his shoulder and neck, but was otherwise apparently fully fit. He had lost his hat, and the rest of his clothing was no longer as smart as it had been at the Meet, but that hardly mattered. Muddy coats and breeches are quite usual in the hunting field. He took a step, stumbled in the soft earth, and sat down.

The memory of the awful fear he had experienced sped into his mind, and then retreated, pushed out by a strangely pleasurable feeling of relief and peace. He looked up at the wide blue sky, which seemed to him like the Heaven in which, but for the grace of the hunting gods, he might well now be dwelling.

How marvellous that he was no longer on that dreadful crazy horse. His terrible journey was over. He was still alive. He reached for his flask.

'I say — are you all right?' The voice came from a face

peering at him over the hedge, and belonged to the red-coated gentleman who had earlier advised him to turn his horse.

'Yes, I think so, thanks.'

'You dealt old Rodney a mortal blow, you know — plonked him straight on the floor. Never seen a quench like it.'

'Oh, I . . .'

'Oh, don't worry about it. He's all right — miles away by now. Now — let's get you back up again. Your hat's over here.'

Tony had only slight interest in his hat and less, for the moment, in his horse. Get up again? On that mad beast? He was happy to stay on the ground for a while, perhaps even for ever, and began to say as much to the man in the top hat. But *he* was having none of that.

'Nonsense. Must get on again. Walk along to that corner there and I'll catch your horse.' Top hat disappeared on his mission, his brisk, commanding manner leaving Tony with no alternative but to obey. The man was probably a colonel or something, and was not going to allow lead-swinging in the ranks. If a chap could still breathe and move, he belonged in the saddle, not wandering about the fields like an over-dressed tart.

So Tony went hunting again.

Not just that day, but on many more after it.

20 December

Well, we've definitely lost Hubbard's Copse. A nice Christmas present. Rode past on exercise this morning and they've already started — bulldozers, chainsaws screaming, huge bonfires. All settled months ago and we knew it was going to happen, but the reality today, with all the barbarians ripping it up. Stopped and watched for a few minutes and nearly had a little weep. We spent half our lives there when we were kids. A huge machine digging right up the main ride where we had our 'private' jumping course that we kept building and the keeper kept taking down, but he never said anything. And what he didn't know about foxes. Always said their brushes were like rudders and they used them to change direction, and they curled them round their noses when it was cold. Reckoned he'd seen them sleeping like that thousands of times. He could make himself invisible in woods. We often walked right past him and never saw him. Then he'd step out behind us with his 'and where do you think you're going, then?' Made us jump out of our skins. God knows what he'd make of all this wreckage if he were alive today. There's a badger sett in there big enough to bury a bull-dozer in and I'd laugh like a drain if one fell in. God knows how much all that work (destruction) is costing, and all so that they can plough straight through from the lane and save Time and Money. Saw my first fox-cubs in there with old Jack Whitbread, the earth-stopper. We must have drawn Hubbard's hundreds of times since those days, and always foxes in there every season — so they can't mind us all that much! If we'd bought it when old Morrison died, there'd be foxes there yet. Silly to be sentimental, but we've lost a good covert and the foxes have lost a good home, and all in the name of 'progress'. If the antis have their way this will happen all over the country, and when people wake up to the fact, it'll be too late. Everybody knows it but nobody does anything about it.

Charlie Fox

What the majority of fox-hunters actually know about foxes could probably be written comfortably on the back of a hunting appointments card and still leave space to scribble a couple of tips for the Cheltenham Gold Cup. This statement is not as rude as it sounds, because it also applies to most people living in countries where the fox is common — including those who are loudest in their condemnation of fox-hunting.

The truth is that very few people have ever seen a fox. The 'antis' don't know much about them, the conservationists are probably almost as ignorant, and even naturalists have to resort to a great deal of educated guesswork. In short, for all the legends, myths, stories, beliefs and fables, including those so beguilingly devised by Aesop back in the B.C.'s, crafty Reynard eludes our studies and speculations and remains tantalisingly mysterious.

Don't think we haven't tried. Over the centuries, Vulpes vulpes (the proper name for the red fox, although one seldom heard in the hunting field) has been the subject of millions of erudite words written in hundreds of learned books and scientific journals. He's been dissected, sketched, photographed, followed and observed by day and by night. He's been captured and examined; he's been released wearing tags and radio transmitters; his stomach contents, faeces, urine and blood have been microscopically analysed; his (and hers, of course) mating habits have been noted; and yet, despite the mass of facts thus gathered, many are contradictory and confusing and many more will have to be discovered before a totally comprehensive picture emerges.

Physically, foxes are not very big — about two feet from nose to beginning of tail, which is a further two feet long. They measure about 12 to 14 inches at the shoulder and weigh 15 to 17 pounds, with the odd big exception. They can live to be about 12 years old, although not many do, and they spend far less time below ground than is generally supposed. They are sometimes found sunning themselves in the branches of trees.

What does seem fairly clear is that, if foxes are as sagacious as is widely supposed, they don't lose much sleep over being chased by horsemen in red coats. They'll be more concerned about being accidentally poisoned by insecticides and run over by motor cars, or being deliberately shot at, poisoned with strychnine, asphyxiated with cyanide gas, snared or trapped.

Man's inhumanity to man, so famously mourned by Robert Burns, is quite mild compared with his inhumanity to foxes, and will be startling to the many who are unaware of it. In Britain, apart from fox-hunting for sport, foxes are the victims of farmers, who kill them to protect their poultry and lambs; gamekeepers, who kill them to protect their pheasants and partridges; opportunists, who kill them to collect bounties from fox destruction societies; and poachers, who kill them to sell their pelts to furriers.

If British foxes should feel, however, that life is a bit hard for them, they should know that things are a lot tougher on the Continent, where hundreds of thousands of foxes are slaughtered annually because they carry rabies. The carnage is colossal. In France 95,000 foxes have been killed in a single year, while the average in Sweden is 80,000 and in Denmark 50,000. The United States is not a terribly healthy place for foxes, either. In one anti-rabies drive in one state alone, 50,000 were wiped out, and the annual average for America as a whole is in excess of 185,000.

Gassing their earths with cyanide is the most usual method of fox control, although shooting and gin traps (illegal in Britain) are also used. Some of the schemes are conducted with the co-operation of the World Health Organisation, but whether they account for sufficient numbers of foxes to be really effective in controlling rabies is coming into increasing doubt. The dreadful disease is still moving across Europe, with no sign of it being eradicated. Ecologists object to fox control of this kind because it cannot be selective — wholesale gassing of earths for foxes has practically wiped out badgers in some parts of Germany.

There is no point, incidentally, in British foxes emigrating to Australia for safety. About 55,000 a year are killed for bounty in Western Australia because they attack sheep, a possibility not foreseen when they were introduced there for sport over 100 years ago. In Britain, fortunately, foxes do not have to be exterminated to combat rabies, but they are certainly killed as pests and for financial gain, and in large numbers. Actual figures are difficult to estimate, but the annual combined total for England, Scotland and Wales is generally reckoned to be 50,000, of which 20,000 are killed by formal fox-hunting, another 20,000 by fox destruction scoieties and the remaining 10,000 by gamekeepers, farmers and others.

This figure of 50,000, however, is disputed by one of Britain's greatest authorities on foxes, H.G. Lloyd. He believes that, although the tallies recorded by Hunts, destruction societies and the Forestry Commission (which also pays bounties) are reliable, the estimate of 10,000 killed by gamekeepers and others is hopelessly low. These kills are not recorded and are probably swollen by the numbers of foxes pursued for their pelts in response to the increasing prices they are fetching. Lloyd's estimate of the number of foxes killed in Britain annually is therefore 100,000. As any fox would agree, that's an awful lot of Vulpes vulpes. It's believed that some of these extra pelts are claimed by urban amateurs who have taken to hunting foxes that dwell in towns, living largely on what they can find round dustbins and rubbish dumps. This kind of hunting, of course, is relatively cheap. You don't need a red coat or a horse.

What must strike any intelligent person as rather odd is that the vociferous opposition to fox-hunting is aimed only at those who kill some 20,000 foxes cleanly with hounds for sport, and not those who bump off perhaps 80,000 any old how for profit. Killing for gain is OK? Killing for sport is not? It is doubtful if foxes bother to draw such fine ethical distinctions. By coincidence, there are almost exactly the same number of Hunts (200) as there are fox destruction societies, although the majority of these are in Wales, while most Hunts are in England. This may be because much of Wales is unsuitable for hunting on horseback. The societies seldom use horses, but a few of them keep, and sometimes hire, packs of hounds. The manner in which such hounds are employed by some of the societies would send a proper fox-hunter into such an indignant rage that he'd jump on his top hat. They use hounds to drive foxes towards men waiting with guns. The men then shoot at the foxes while trying, presumably, not to shoot the hounds. Or each other. To anyone brought up in a town and not used to guns, this might seem a perfectly reasonable way of despatching foxes. What could be quicker and cleaner than a bullet?

The answer is nothing — if it is fired at reasonable range by a real marksman capable of hitting a small erratically fast-moving target in a vital part of its body. Very few such men exist. Bullets, of course, are single missiles fired from rifles, and require accurate aiming.

Men who shoot at foxes tend — like those who shoot birds — to use shotguns, not rifles. Shotguns make the job easier, because they fire cartridges containing hundreds of little lead pellets which spread out in the air to give a wider area of impact. The further they travel, the more widely they spread, and they rapidly lose velocity and fall spent to the ground. To be sure of killing a fox with a 12-bore shotgun using No. 4 shot, a common combination in the countryside, a marksman would have to be pretty good up to about 30 yards. Beyond that, the fox would simply be wounded, as in fact many are. Given the price of scrap lead today, there may be foxes existing which would be more valuable for their pellets than their perforated pelts.

On a fox drive, nobody minds if pot-shots are taken at foxes that are out of effective lethal range because there is a wide belief that, if a fox is only wounded, it will die eventually, probably from gangrene. This may or may not be true, but it's not a nice way to go, even for vermin.

Many fox destruction societies were formed in World War II, and right up until 1980 the bounties they paid were matched by a Government payment of up to 50p per fox. So a dead fox could be worth £1 to a man, although some societies still pay twice that for a vixen. When one learns, by contrast, that dealers will pay £20 and more for a really top-quality fox pelt, it is easier to understand why many more foxes are killed than is generally supposed. And the dealers — like most dealers — do very nicely, thank you. They sell them on the Continent for twice what they paid for them in Britain. If this trade develops, foxes will have more to worry about than listening out for hunting horns and galloping hooves.

The huge wooded acreages owned by the Forestry Commission are naturally favoured by foxes for the ideal cover they provide when lying up by day, resting from hunting in the neighbourhood by night. The reason that the Commission pays bounties for foxes is not because they damage trees, but because it wishes to avoid being thought guilty of harbouring foxes. That is why the Commission invariably welcomes Hunts on its land.

Human beings seem to have accepted, some regretfully, that foxes are such a nuisance that they must be controlled (a euphemism, of course, for killed) and are left with the dilemma about how best to do this. Nobody really knows how many foxes there are in Britain, or anywhere else, but the effectiveness of control schemes can be judged roughly by the number that are killed every year, and since this does not diminish, it is clear that foxes manage somehow to hold their own, as do seals, deer, rats, moles, mice, squirrels, wood-pigeons, rabbits, bluebottles and one or two other less attractive pests, despite all man's efforts to eliminate them.

Deer offer perhaps the best comparison with foxes in this context. Their crime against man is that they eat shrubs, browse saplings and strip bark from trees. About four hundred are shot in the New Forest every year, but in Scotland, where they have ruined plantations and turn to farm crops when food is scarce in winter, 25,000 and more are shot annually. This is the sport known as stalking. Another word is culling. Unless you spell it killing.

Seal hunting, for obvious reasons, is not classified as a sport — they are shot while helpless on the shore — but thousands are killed because they do so much damage to the fishing industry. They feed naturally on commercially valuable fish at sea, but it is when they get among set nets that they really cause trouble. They rip holes in the nets, eat fish already caught, and let others escape through the holes.

In attempting, not very successfully, it should be said, to reduce this considerable threat to the fishing industry, the Government authorises the killing of seal pups.

The pelts of these have to be inspected to see that the permitted methods of killing were employed, but this can be little consolation to the dead creature or its mother.

People get quite upset over the seal cull, while apparently being unmoved by the fate of rabbits infected — originally deliberately by man — with myxomatosis. Nobody who has seen a rabbit in the process of its blind lingering death from this ghastly disease could condone its use, even on a rabbit that had just polished off a row of prize lettuces.

Neither would anyone be too keen on the use of Warfarin on rats and mice if they stopped to think that it is an anti-coagulant that causes slow death by internal bleeding. Why else is it administered in small doses over several days? Man's — particularly Englishman's — attitude to pests is ambivalent and blurred by a mixture of sentimentality and anthropomorphism. Rabbits are bunnies until they raid the vegetable patch and become a bloody nuisance; moles are velvety little creatures until they get into a smooth green lawn and their hills become mountains. Fox-cubs seem like cuddly puppy-dogs until they grow up and clobber your chickens. Animals only become pests when man decides that they are pests and if killing is the only way to get rid of them then it must seem obvious that death should be imposed as quickly and cleanly as possible.

It would be a specious argument to claim that fox-hunters go galloping across the countryside as part of a fox-control scheme. Most of them do it because they enjoy it as an exhilarating sport in which the the fox does have a chance of escaping and they have a chance of breaking their necks. The result, though, is usually definite and swift. Hounds kill in seconds.

Cyanide gassing is said to be quick, but *how* quick must depend presumably on how much is inhaled and in what degree of concentration. Shooting is chancy. Snares are diabolical, and so are traps. Many regular fox-hunters have encountered three-legged foxes, limping thus because they have bitten off a trapped leg to free themselves. Foxes with broken snares tightly buried in their bodies are also found. The corpses of those poisoned by strychnine are seldom seen because their pelts — commercially unmarked, of course — are fairly swiftly sewn to the expensive collars of ladies' coats.

The use of strychnine to poison foxes, mothers-in-law and creditors is strictly illegal, but it goes on. It is impossible to stroll into a chemist and buy strychnine, but it can be purchased in small quantities by the holder of a permit issued by the Ministry of Agriculture for the purpose of killing moles. Applications for such permits are carefully examined, and once issued, they are not easily renewed, like television or dog licences, but it is impossible to ensure that the strychnine is being used only for mole destruction.

It is against the law to re-sell strychnine but there are no restrictions on its importation and it does change hands. A battalion of gamekeepers swearing on a library of Bibles would not convince a country-dweller that keepers never use this terrible poison. One way is known as open-cast baiting. A dead animal's body is liberally loaded with strychnine and left on a game-trail to be eaten by foxes. Unhappily it isn't only foxes that enjoy a carrion snack. Badgers do. So do quite a number of birds. And so do domestic dogs and cats.

Cats, incidentally, are right at the top of gamekeepers' hate lists — even above foxes — because pheasant chicks are tastier than tinned cat-food, whatever they say on television, and far more fun to play pussy-cat ping-pong with and pounce upon. Most country cats know that, if boredom strikes, there's nothing like a pheasant-rearing pen for an afternoon's diversion. The result is that a fair few rural moggies go to that great cat-basket in the sky because they are illegally poisoned by a vile substance that is supposed only to be used for exterminating moles.

What moles have done to deserve such terrible distinction in death is difficult to understand. It's true that by burrowing just below the surface they kill crops at the root and throw up stones that may damage agricultural machinery. And molehills on racehorse training gallops are a real menace. But they can be kept down by trapping, and used to be when moleskin waistcoats were fashionable and proper plumbers used moleskins to wipe joints. Now that nobody wants moleskins, nobody wants moles, and farmers and gardeners would like to get rid of them. But with *strychnine*? Even a Gestapo Ministry of Agriculture might have hesitated before authorising its use, which induces slow, agonising death.

What the mole murderers do is dip segments of earthworms in the poison and drop them into mole tunnels. The moles munch them up, and that's that. Finding a bit of worm in a tunnel is perfectly natural to the mole, because that's how it gets its grub. Moles don't dig for worms — the worms fall down into the tunnels. A mole that isn't particularly hungry will mangle the worm and leave it for later. So the day that a mole finds a bit of worm in its path is a day, as they say in TV documentary programmes, much like any other. Unless the bit of worm has been flavoured with strychnine, when the day becomes very different, very unpleasant, and the mole's last.

Strychnine acts on the spinal cord, and the first signs of poisoning are muscular twitchings. These become worse until they turn into convulsions which rack the animal's body at intervals. Its muscles stretch until its back is arched inversely, like a bow forced to fire an arrow from the wrong side. The intervals between the convulsions grow shorter until death takes place about 20 minutes later. Not nice.

There are philosophical arguments about whether animals feel pain in the same way and to the same degree as humans, but they are academic. Everyone knows that if you pinch a dog's ear because it pees on the carpet, the dog will yelp. Because you have hurt it. Which was your intention, so that thereafter the dog will associate pee-ing on the carpet with pain, and learn to relieve itself in places where it can do so with comfort and your approval. Empirically, then, as the scientists say, we have demonstrated that animals experience pain. We have also shown that, like fame, it can be the spur. Death from strychnine poisoning is painful. Unspeakably, unjustifiably and undeniably. That it should be legally inflicted upon moles is bad enough; that other animals should suffer, illegally, is disgraceful.

If it is accepted that moles can make an awful mess of arable land — which is true — of what crimes are foxes thought guilty? Why are they so hated and harassed? Aside from spreading rabies, which is not applicable in Britain, foxes are said to be wanton killers of poultry, game birds and lambs. And so they may be, but their predatory activities tend to be exaggerated. While undoubtedly an occasional nuisance to individual farmers, they are hardly a significant threat to the national agricultural economy. Intensive 'factory' farming has produced the battery hen and its impenetrable prison, with the result that free-range chickens and eggs are as difficult for foxes to obtain as they are for human beings.

The risk to game birds is fairly high, but gamekeepers manage to counteract it successfully enough to keep their masters satisfied. Far more birds are bred than necessary and there are always plenty for wealthy gentlemen to shoot at for the £500 per day sometimes charged in shooting syndicates. Interestingly enough, because shooting and hunting interests often overlap, many gamekeepers deliberately limit the number of foxes they kill so that there are some left over for the fox-hunters to pursue. This would seem to indicate that foxes are not such a problem as is frequently stated.

There is no doubt that foxes take lambs, but it is by no means certain that they kill healthy ones. Foxes are not fussy feeders and are quite content to eat carrion, calf and lamb afterbirths and other seemingly unappetising fare.

It is entirely possible that the remains of dead lambs sometimes found near foxes' earths were stillborn or, at any rate, ailing and not likely to survive.

Reports of foxes killing healthy lambs are so rife that some of them must be true, but such kills may be the work of the odd 'rogue' fox or — far more likely — dogs, which kill 5,000 lambs or sheep a year. Heresy though it might seem, it is possible to state that most foxes do not kill lambs, although it is difficult to see why not.

In Britain in springtime there are hundreds of thousands of lambs scattered happily and vulnerably in open unprotected spaces. Foxes are fast, ferocious, strong and cunning; lambs are weak, helpless, timid and innocent.

It must be obvious that if all foxes habitually attacked lambs, there wouldn't be enough left to bother making mint sauce. What is well-known and deprecated is that foxes will kill more than their immediate food needs. Once inside a poultry pen they will seldom be satisfied with taking one bird, but will slaughter the lot and leave the corpses behind. This naturally infuriates and puzzles the owner, and has given foxes the reputation of being malicious, blood-crazed, killers. It is not known why they kill on such a wanton scale, but one theory is that nature has programmed them to kill opportunistically and that, in an enclosed space with victims fluttering everywhere, they cannot switch off the killing instinct. In the wild, surplus prey can often escape.

Although foxes undoubtedly upset country people with raids on chicken houses, duckponds and game preserves, they also command a certain amount of admiration. They are handsome creatures, tenacious and clever, and it is in their favour that they kill lots of rabbits. Actually, rabbits are probably their favourite food, along with beetles, hares, voles, mice, fish, rats and the like, but they owe their survival to being able to adjust their appetites to whatever is available seasonally and geographically.

A scavenging fox would find something to eat in a multi-storey car-park or a farmyard muck-heap. They can often be seen poking their noses into the ground and under fallen trees seeking worms and grubs, although, contrary to general belief, they are not exclusively carnivorous.

They like fruit, for example, a little-known fact that is reflected in the number of pubs called the Fox and Grapes. Quite where a fox would look for bunches of grapes in Britain today is something of a puzzle — unless he prowled hospital wards and sniffed round patients' lockers — but, in Roman times and for centuries after, there were many English vineyards ripe for the raiding. More readily understandable anxieties over foxes' gastronomic preferences are evident in all the pubs called the Fox and Duck, Fox and Goose, Fox and Chickens, Fox and Partridge and so on. Perhaps pubs named the Fox and Hounds were a counter-balancing reassurance that foxes didn't always have things their own way.

Since pubs are places for pleasure, they are rarely named after things and people we hate or fear. There may be one or two Gibbets, Hangman's Nooses and other sinister noms-de-pub, but Kings', Queens' and Dukes' Arms and Heads are far more loyally and happily common. The abundance of pub names featuring the Fox could be taken to signify a sneaking admiration for the villain, and certainly proves how firmly and for how long the fox has fitted into our lives and legends.

As there are Foxes and Grapes, there really ought to be Foxes and Blackberries, because blackberries are far more available than grapes in Britain, and foxes love them. They go blackberrying in autumn with as much enthusiasm as humans, but without plastic bags. It takes enormous patience to see one, but for anyone with enough of this rare virtue and the ability to stay quiet, down wind and absolutely still, a fox blackberrying is an engaging sight. Invariably alone — foxes are solitary hunters — the animal will stretch up on its back legs and, taking great care to avoid the prickles, nibble its way along a hedge for perhaps an hour, fastidiously choosing only the ripest fruit.

If calling a pub the Fox and Blackberry were thought unusual, it would presumably be considered highly fanciful to name one the Fox and Boxing-glove, yet foxes do box, after a fashion. Dog foxes squabbling over a vixen will get up on their hind legs, square up to their rival and slug it out toe-to-toe, as it were. They don't actually punch, but use their forelegs to lean and push against each other, snarling, snapping and screeching, until one is forced backwards and gives up the fight.

Foxes are mostly silent, as befits notoriously furtive and stealthy creatures, but they do call to each other, particularly in the mating season. And the sound they make can be piercingly blood-chilling. Somewhere between a scream, a yelp and a bark, a fox's sudden cry on a black night is enough to put a nervous person in intensive care.

Mating takes place during the winter, largely in January, with cubs being born towards the end of the hunting season in March and April. Under rabies control schemes, this is a prime period for cyanide squads to gas earths, where the cubs remain with their mother for about two months.

Foxhounds, too, could effect a devastating degree of 'fox-control' at this time, but Hunts are on the brink of their close season, and where a Huntsman perceives that the fox his hounds are pursuing is a 'wet' (lactating) vixen out finding food for her young, he will often leave it. This is not a rule, nor even an acknowledged practice. It's just what usually happens. While such reprieves are humane, there is nevertheless a practical side to them. The close season, while vixens have dependent offspring, allows the fox population to recover, ready for the resumption of hunting.

Vixens give birth almost anywhere that is dry and sheltered. They seldom excavate a place for themselves, preferring ready-made accommodation in old rabbit holes, badger setts, the hollows under big tree roots and similar places offering cover. Town vixens sometimes choose cosy holes in graveyards and under garden sheds. They make devoted mothers and will move their litters elsewhere at any sign of danger. They have four to six cubs and suckle them for about six weeks, after which they feed them on regurgitated prey until they are ready to take solid food. Barren vixens in the same family group may help in providing food in this way, as do some dog foxes. Where the vixens have been killed, dog foxes have been known to rear the cubs themselves.

Not much is known about what might be called the family life of foxes, but dogs and vixens usually only stay together during breeding. They are essentially loners — lone outlaws, some would say. Cubs usually begin to explore outside their dens at six weeks, and start living above ground when they are two months old. In play, they ambush, stalk and pounce on each other as kittens do, and by the time they are three months old, are capable of hunting mice and other small creatures. By late summer they are independent, although many maintain loose contact with the family.

Fox-hunters classify foxes as 'local' (the majority) or 'travellers', although quite how static the local populations remain or how far the travellers roam is not known. One of the aims of cub-hunting in late August, September and October is to disturb thickly populated coverts and disperse the litters they contain. The element of chance is one of the attractions of the sport and it would be considerably reduced if foxes were so thick on the ground that hounds were tripping over them. The young foxes soon see the advantages of making themselves scarce when hounds turn up.

The term cub-hunting is slightly misleading, and may give some people the impression that hounds leap on defenceless puppy-like mites. In fact, by the time hunting starts, cubs are well on their way to being fully-grown.

As adults, with their hunting skills developed, they soon find that life is fairly easy. Since the extinction of the wolf, foxes have no natural enemies in the wild, and as they will eat almost anything that walks, crawls, swims, burrows, flies or climbs — dead or alive — they seldom go hungry. The only thing they have to fear is man, and the many means he has devised, mechanical, chemical and diabolical, for extermination. As well as these, foxhounds are a distinct danger, but not such a serious one as opponents of fox-hunting claim, or its supporters may believe.

There are as many types of covert as there are kinds of countryside, and how many foxes they shelter will depend largely on availability of food, but a fairly typical covert might be a 10-acre wood with plenty of undergrowth. Most Hunts have such coverts in their defined areas of operation; some own them and a few even provide artificial earths to encourage foxes to stay in them. Such places are usually 'sure finds' (almost guaranteed to harbour foxes on a hunting day) year after year. Two or three foxes inhabiting an area of this kind, either as a sort of family or, more probably, as individuals would leave it to hunt by night and lie up in it by day, most likely above ground rather than below. They would be content.

Ah, but what about hounds crashing through the trees and thirsty for blood? Well, that would be disturbing, for sure, but it doesn't happen that often. In the average Hunt, covering an area of about 500 square miles, if their hounds can visit the same place six times in an entire season, it's doing very well. Three or four times is more usual, so that there are commonly six-week intervals of perfect tranquillity between raids.

Hounds are a bit of a nuisance turning up cub-hunting at 6.00 a.m. in September and October, but once the proper season starts they are off and gone for the rest of the day. If the hunted fox escapes, as is often the case, he'll return to the covert. Hounds may pick up the scent again, which would lead them back to the covert, but they're far more likely to go off to draw somewhere else.

There really is little reason for foxes to fret themselves over being hunted by hounds, because it is a sporadic, even rare, disruption. If they were constantly being chased about the country every day, they wouldn't be daft enough to remain. Foxes are smart. They'd leg it to somewhere more peaceful!

Whether foxes can perceive danger, and thus experience fear, is not known, but anyone who has seen a fox being hunted would probably agree that they appear unconcerned. It would be stupid, of course, to try to judge by demeanour or facial expression, but assumptions can be made from observation of the fox's pace. Many foxhunters have had the experience of waiting at the side of a covert and seeing the hunted fox emerge, look carefully about it, and then calmly trot away past — or even through — a line of horsemen.

A fox-trot, as well as being a dance, is one of the fox's four gaits. It can walk, trot, canter and gallop, and when it gallops, it can approach 40 miles an hour, as can horses and hounds. A galloping — and therefore presumably alarmed — fox is an unusual sight, except in the last moments before a kill. The emotive concept, sometimes depicted by opponents of the sport, of a harried fox running and urinating in terror as it attempts to elude hounds which are snapping lumps out of it in pitilessly prolonged pursuit before eventually tearing it to pieces alive is false.

Hounds hunt by scent. This they may do quite slowly and uncertainly for some time, while the fox, possibly unaware that it is being hunted, nevertheless moves away, just as it would from any other kind of disturbance. During this period, hounds may well lose the scent and have to give up — all fox-hunters will admit that they hunt far more foxes than they ever catch. Even when hounds get quite close to the fox, it may still proceed at an unhurried trot or easy canter.

It is only when the hounds are near enough actually to see the fox that they lift their noses and start hunting it by sight — 'coursing' it. From that moment the hunt is as good as over. The fox may well now feel fear or some kind of distress, and break into its best speed, but unless it can get into some kind of covert — and very smartly — it has little chance of escaping. The hounds will almost certainly catch it and kill it.

Nobody would pretend that foxes enjoy being hunted, but it may be a far less harrowing and prolonged matter than is generally supposed. And, if the conclusion is the death of the fox, it is at least a quick and certain end.

Scent, and the ways in which it is affected by weather and atmospheric conditions, is a mystery that has irritated and fascinated fox-hunters since the very first one mounted his horse. It will doubtless continue to do so. The men who know most about it are those whose job it is to kill foxes — gamekeepers, terrier-men, Huntsmen and earth-stoppers. They can sometimes actually detect scent with their noses and make pretty shrewd assessments of how fresh it is.

Foxes' scent comes from glands under their tails. They also leave scent from between their pads and to some extent from their fur when they brush through grass. The strength of the scent depends on factors which are not really known — how fresh or tired the fox is, for example. And whether it is engaged in mating endeavour. When very strong, scent is said to be 'screaming'. Foxes also deliberately mark territory with urine, much as dogs do, and will renew these markings regularly.

Sometimes they bury food, and mark the place where it is concealed — or half-concealed, because they often scratch such a shallow hole that the food can still be seen. It is not uncommon for them to half-bury a dead chicken and leave one of its legs sticking out. This must be about the only careless or not very bright habit that foxes have.

For the rest, they are notoriously clever, although some of their abilities have become exaggerated beyond credibility. They are reputed, for example, to raid chicken runs miles away from their home territory and ignore similar targets nearby, so that suspicion will not fall on them. This seems to put them in a rather higher criminal class than is likely.

Feigning death in order to lull prey is another skill that may or may not be true. There are many accounts of them lying motionless until curious or reassured rabbits approach close enough to be caught; they are said to use the same technique for catching carrion crows. Perhaps the most surprising trick that they have been given credit for is catching fish by sitting with their tails dangling in the water. The fish are supposed to get caught in the fur, and are then smartly whipped ashore.

The ruses that they employ to elude pursuit are better authenticated — crossing rivers (they are good swimmers), getting among sheep and cattle and diving into manure to cover their own scent are common examples. Whether they deliberately double back over their own line ('heeling' as it is called) to confuse hounds is not absolutely certain; when a fox retraces its steps it is often because it's been 'headed' (startled out of continuing forward on its chosen line) by a foot follower or other obstacle.

Often, when hunted, one will scramble into a covert and put up another fox. There are people who believe that the fresh fox voluntarily takes over, like a relay runner, to lead hounds away. What is far more probable is that the hunted fox dives for a hiding place it knows, finds it occupied, and that the tenant is frightened or driven out, to be hunted. In hunting circles this is known as 'changing foxes'.

It is something of a paradox that foxes in Britain owe their existence to fox-hunting. At the beginning of the 1880s there was such a shortage of foxes that they were imported wholesale from the Continent. There was an established market in London and some Hunts placed regular orders. They were known as 'bagmen' through the practice of taking them in sacks and releasing them where hounds were to draw.

Occasionally there are still rumours of bagged foxes being hunted, but these are always vigorously denied, and the Masters of Foxhounds Association has long forbidden their use. They are said, anyway, to provide poor sport. Set down in unfamiliar territory, they are confused and soon caught. Hunting has been so well organised for such a long time that Hunts have no need to resort to such unsporting measures. By co-operating with farmers and shooting estates and ensuring that coverts are properly managed, a balance is achieved between keeping the fox population at an acceptable level, and enjoying sport. It is a balance that is accepted in the country and by most country people, despite the claims of opponents of the sport.

What seems not to have occurred to the abolitionists — or perhaps they don't care — is that, if fox-hunting were banned, the fox would probably soon be extinct. At first, foxes would proliferate, but more foxes would need more food and they would be driven to seeking it in places and to an extent that man would not tolerate.

The hedgerows and patches of woodland now preserved as cover for foxes and game birds would be ripped out to make bigger spaces for more economic farming. Deprived of food and shelter in the wild, the fox population would begin to wane, with survivors drawn increasingly to scavenge in towns and cities. Many cities already have resident foxes which are shot or gassed from time to time. If these numbers increased, and they would, and people complained, as they most certainly would, the authorities would have to set about organising big-scale extermination.

Vulpes vulpes wouldn't last long. It is a pessimistic forecast that is nevertheless within probability that if fox-hunting were banned, the day would come when, instead of Britain's countryside being the delightful many-coloured patchwork it is at present, it would be a barley-rich prairie, virtually bereft of cover for wildlife.

The gloomy, almost unthinkable prognosis is that foxes, and many other creatures and birds, might only be seen in zoos. This surely cannot be allowed to happen. Apart from anything else, with no Charlie Fox about, who would we blame for so many rural crimes?

Boxing Day

Jolly as always. Everybody says they hate it, but they all turn out. No real hunting. Hither and thither till we were dizzy and finally one fox marked to ground perilously close to the by-pass, somewhere behind a huge pile of rubble and cement-mixers. Most unpromising. Late by then, and the field looking a bit ragged, so Jack [Joint-Master] gave it best 'for Christmas', which is more than I would have dared. Blimey, said a wag, it must be Christmas. Father used to say Boxing Day was for the gallery and the Hunt servants [traditionally, all 'cap' money and field money goes to the servants' Christmas box on Boxing Day, and followers — and even some spectators — contribute generously] and nothing has really changed except that nowadays they call it public relations — Keep Politics Out of Field Sports stickers all over the place. Maybe we should just parade hounds on the village green, have our pictures taken to show what nice people we are and go home. More cars and people than I've ever seen, and the pub doing a roaring trade. Diana plunged into the throng to get me a whisky-mac, never to be seen again — there ought to be a rule about a Master's wife getting priority! Paul Mannering's new horse gave a marvellous display — bucking and rearing like the Wild West, and scattering people wholesale. Being Paul, he remained icy calm and sat it out, only to have the same performance all over again when we moved off. Bucked all the way to the cross-roads with somebody shouting, 'Ride 'm, cowboy.' Great stuff. Think some of them thought it was a special show for their benefit. Some absolute frights out. Boxing Day always seems to attract a few odds and sods, but these were the absolute end. They seem to think it's some kind of quaint rural ritual that anybody can join in if they've got some dreadful old nag to sit on. I can't stop them watching, but I will not have them following. The worst offender was an incredible woman with the biggest rear I've ever seen squatting on a frightful piebald pony, absolutely filthy and about to collapse under her weight

(15 stone if an ounce). Her clothing was unspeakable, jodhpurs, cap with elastic band — the lot. Diana says I'm a snob over dress and she may be ever so slightly right, but yellow roll-neck pullovers, not in my field, madam. Nice drinks (here) in the evening. Jeremy says I'm an old grump.

Dressed to Kill

Fox-hunters are very fussy about hunting dress. Which is why they look so smart. There may be some who throw their clothes on as though they were just nipping out to fetch the paper, but most dress themselves with as much care as they would for their wedding. Actually, since so many bridegrooms hire their wedding clothes, it may be useful to point out that the most famous London establishment for such connubial hirings is also prepared to rent out hunting attire.

The system is that the customer pays the *new* price for the clothing, as a deposit, and then, when he takes it back, half the deposit money is returned to him, and the other half is retained by the shop as the hiring fee. This would mean that if he hired everything, from boots right up to hat, one day's sartorial splendour in the hunting field would cost him in excess of £200. Fairly astonishingly, there is a steady-ish trickle of such customers, although they are usually foreigners.

Getting them to pay the full price of the clothing in advance is pretty canny, when you come to think about it. The chances are that the kind of person who needs to hire a full hunting rig-out is not a regular man to hounds and possibly not a very experienced horseman. Which could result in the clothes being taken back to the shop in less than pristine condition. Indeed, the customer might be too occupied in hospital, or mortuary, to take them back at all.

But, supposing he survived the rigours of the chase,

how on earth would a foreigner have managed to dress himself properly for his one day's hunting — even though supplied with all the necessary clothing — when English native fox-hunters sometimes get it wrong? Because they certainly do, to judge by the correspondence and editorial columns of *Horse and Hound* and other equestrian publications.

No new hunting season can begin without someone arguing about top hats, bowlers, velvet caps, garter straps, scarlet coats and pink coats, mahogany tops, whips, cutting sticks, rubber boots, spurs, crops, hat-guards, riding macs, chin-straps, and those little silk bows that dangle at the back of riding caps, and shouldn't. Or should.

There are other items, but these are the tried favourites which seldom fail to get the ink flowing and, in extreme cases, the blood simmering. The arguments fall into four main categories: what to wear; when to wear it; how to wear it; and what to call it. The uniting theme is an esoteric obsession with 'correctness', resulting in the words 'etiquette' and 'good manners' cropping up quite frequently.

Nomenclature is perhaps the richest vein of hunting disputation, and it is explored endlessly and voraciously. What colour, for example, should a red hunting coat be called?

'How about red?' the non-hunting clever-clogs with a taste for sarcasm might suggest. Simpleton. In some hunting circles such a slack lower-class solecism could almost get a chap black-balled.

'Oh. Scarlet, perhaps?' Idiot — that's a cissy euphemism for jumped-up parvenus who're afraid to say red.

'Oh, yes! I remember now — don't you hunting people say pink?' Pink! D'you think we're a gang of poofs?

You cannot, as any honest bookmaker would readily admit, win. The use of red, scarlet or pink depends on zones, fashion and generations. Quite a lot of elderly, very experienced and incontrovertibly upper-crust hunting ladies and gentlemen still say pink (especially when referring to Hunt evening dress) and nobody argues with them.

Scarlet is considered a bit of a euthemism by some, but it is still often used. Red is probably best at the moment — blunt, unpretentious and unequivocal, reflecting, perhaps, the spirit of the 18th-century land-owning Tories with whom it was originally associated.

So where did pink come from? Many people believe that it originated with a famous hunting tailor called Mr. Pink, but it has been authoritatively established that there was never any such person. Another explanation is that pink was thrown into an article by a desperate hunting journalist, working against a deadline and feeling that he'd already over-used red and scarlet. He needed a quick synonym and pink was it. It's the same kind of pressure that drives football reporters to write of leather spheres when they mean balls.

To outsiders, who are seldom heard to refer to fire engines and pillar-boxes as being coloured scarlet or pink, these differences in terminology may seem trivial, but in fox-hunting circles, they still matter, although not nearly as much as they used to.

Before the 1914 War, when wealthy families would take a dozen Thoroughbreds up to a rented hunting lodge for an entire season with a crack pack in the Shires, snobbery was extreme, and the cut of breeches, boots or coat could mark a rider as socially suspect. There were even Masters who would send home anyone whose dress did not conform to their views on what was correct.

Strangers at Meets would be quizzed — observed, more or less discreetly — to determine whether they were acceptable, and the first evidence sought was sartorial. So great was the fear of doing or saying the wrong thing that the more timid or insecure would describe a coat as 'not black' rather than take the frightful risk of a blunder over red, scarlet or pink. Even today, careful newcomers to the hunting field may be heard to say that someone has 'got his colours', 'been awarded the Hunt button', or 'put his black coat away' to avoid the possibly dangerous 'has got his red coat'.

There is a saying that 'gin can be pink, but a hunting

coat is either red or black'. But not every fox-hunter would agree. In one or two packs, red is virtually absent, except when worn by visitors. For example, when subscribers to the Duke of Beaufort's illustrious Hunt are invited to wear the Hunt button, they quickly get their tailors to make them dark blue coats with the lapels faced in a buff colour. If you popped up to the Duke's country in your pink coat you'd most certainly be quizzed.

Many Hunts have distinctive livery — like the yellow coats of the Berkeley — although the basic dress is fundamentally the same, and the differences are usually subtle. In the majority of Hunts the Masters, past-Masters, Members and Hunt servants wear red coats with gilt Hunt buttons. Variations can usually only be seen in different coloured lapel and collar facings, which are also worn on the black or dark blue coats of Lady Members. Ladies do not customarily wear red, scarlet or pink, except as lipstick.

Hunt servants' coats generally have five buttons down the front (the hunting horn being tucked between the Huntsman's top two) while gentlemen's coats (whether black or red) have three. In some Hunts the servants wear 'ducal' livery, with coats that have six tail buttons which were once used to catch up the skirt of the coat to keep it clear of mud. The tail buttons were originally a sign that the wearer really was a servant of the owner of the pack, showing that it was not a subscription Hunt.

A few really stylish gentlemen fox-hunters wear 'Johnnie Walker' swallow-tail coats in either red or black, with top hats. If they're not too portly, are really good riders and can fairly fly their jumps, they look anachronistically dashing, rather as though they were hurrying to catch a stagecoach on a Christmas card.

Where fox-hunters are united in terminology is in calling a hunting coat a *coat*, and never a jacket, whether it is black or not-black. Jackets are the flimsy articles worn by show-jumpers, and although they look similar to the garments worn by hunters, they are vastly different. A good hunting coat is warm and heavy, made of thick, tightly-woven woollen cavalry twill or melton cloth, and well-lined. Although not actually waterproof, it is certainly water resistant, taking a long time to become totally soaked. The 'skirt' of it is cut full and long, so that the back drapes over the cantle of the saddle and the front protects the thighs nearly to the knees.

There are several kinds of riding mac long enough to keep the knees dry when it rains, but to wear one of these out hunting is seldom, if ever, done. There are also waterproof aprons that can be worn to protect the thighs, and these are occasionally seen in the field, but not often. People who hunt are very conscious of appearance. And very hardy. In English winters, they have to be.

That's why a waistcoat is vital. There are no special rules about them, but they should be sensibly long and protectively thick. White or yellow are favoured, and some are check. All are worn with the lower button undone, like an ordinary waistcoat, and for the same reason. Whatever that is.

What cannot be seen can hardly be commented upon, and what is worn beneath hunting clothes is a personal matter. Thermal underwear is gaining in popularity, particularly for the comfort of the torso and what are known as, with varying degrees of accuracy, the private parts. But legs are a problem. Woollen longjohns worn under breeches cannot be squeezed into a well-fitting boot and tend, anyway, to bunch at the back of the knees. This makes mounting — often a bit of a huff and a puff for the less agile — virtually impossible.

An undisclosed but considerable number of immaculately turned out and indisputably heterosexual gentlemen fox-hunters have solved the problem by wearing ladies' tights, which fit unobtrusively beneath even the most snugly cut breeches. They do not inhibit insertion of leg into boot and add a layer of gratifyingly warming insulation.

A male patient found to be wearing ladies' tights in the casualty department of a hospital — where fox-hunters do drop in involuntarily from time to time — may be misunderstood, but many think this a risk well worth taking. Being thought a transvestite may be a momentary embarrassment; feeling cold can last for ever.

Frozen feet are another horseback hazard because the almost constantly bent position of knee and ankle while riding affects the circulation. This is not to suggest that fox-hunters are in permanent discomfort. While they're moving, they're fine, and the warm body of the horse between their legs is a kind of central heating.

The chill factor is particularly tangible in rubber riding boots, but these are frowned upon in all Hunts, totally unacceptable in others, and unheard of in some. There may well be affluent fox-hunters who don't even know they exist. Actually, they've improved enormously, are dramatically cheaper than leather boots, and far easier to clean. The better ones now have a leather-look texture, spur-stops, and simulated seams and stitch-marks in the appropriate places. They're pretty convincing but, unfortunately, they look too perfect. They just don't wrinkle and kink as leather boots do — and that's a dead giveaway. Definitely not quizz-proof.

A well-fitting boot is a joy; so snug at the heel and calf that boot-pulls have to be employed to haul the foot into it. These are long hooks, which can be gold-plated (optional, for the man who has everything) with ivory (ditto) handles, and fit into canvas loops stitched, right and left, a few concealed inches down the inside of the top of the boot. The hooks are so shaped that when the foot is rammed firmly home, they can be slipped out of the loops and put back in the safe. The removal of boots is accomplished with a levering device called a bootjack.

To counteract the tendency of the boot leg to work itself down, thus creating those desirable, expensive leather wrinkles, a garter strap is worn. Or should be worn. The niceties concerning these narrow strips of leather are numerous but it can be fairly safely asserted that with 'tips' (black boots with the top quarter made of 'mahogany', 'pink', 'yellow' or other coloured leather) the straps should be white; with plain black boots (known as 'butcher' boots) the straps should be black. To be any more didactic on such a delicate matter would be to risk being lynched.

Garter straps slip through a leather loop at the back of the inside top of the boot and are passed through their own buckle at the front of the leg, with the tongue of the strap pointing outwards and backwards. The correct position of the buckle is between the third and fourth button of the breeches, if the breeches are expensive enough to have buttons.

The strap should be tightly fastened to ensure that it stays in the correct position. There's no point in going to all the trouble of choosing the right colour garter and then finding that the buckle has slipped round to the wrong place. You might just as well not bother. Which is why some don't.

An additional reason is that the boots still tend to slip downwards at the front. Anyone deciding that they are definitely going to wear garter straps should feed them into the loops of the boots *before* donning them. Trying to fiddle a garter into a boot after it's on the leg can easily take long enough to miss the Meet.

One item of hunting haberdashery that absolutely every fox-hunter agrees is necessary is the stock. The hunting world, in this matter, is utterly unanimous.

Whatever the colour of coat or breeches or style of hat, whether the hunter is Master or servant, Member or follower, male or female, child or adult, visitor or even foreigner, he or she *must* wear one. There is no doubt about the colour, either. A stock must be white, if cotton; or pale cream, if silk.

Right.

But it shouldn't be called a stock.

The correct term is hunting tie.

This is a curious and vexatious matter, akin to but slightly more puzzling than the red-scarlet-pink coat uncertainties. Without going to the trouble and expense of conducting a Gallup (or Gallop, perhaps) Poll, it is probably true to say that most hunting folk use the word stock, at any rate in conversation, while admitting that tie is proper.

Stockists who stock stocks call them stocks, in advertisements, on invoices and over the counter, unless the client deliberately manipulates them into saying tie. It is far easier to say stock, because the single word is specific and sufficient. If you say tie, you have to prefix it with bow, neck, hunting, white, old school, mourning, evening, regimental, club, or whatever, to tighten up the definition. But a stock is a stock.

The observant — and this may be of use to those seeking social advancement by way of the hunting field (such aspirations are not unknown) — will notice that the most persistent usage of 'tie', is among the 'U'; those, as it were, who hunt with the Mitford. To these superior beings, *stock* is to *tie* as *toilet* is to *lavatory*, *fag* to *cigarette* and *mirror* to *looking-glass*. A grasp of such subtleties could well smooth the path to the upper echelons of fox-hunting society.

It is assumed that scarf, choker, cravat and muffler can be automatically excluded as inadmissible, but a word of caution about neckcloth. This, in blue with little white dots, was very fashionable among fox-hunters until it gave way to the white stock about 100 years ago, and is still worn by some, and *still called a neckcloth*, when cub-hunting in 'rat-catcher'.

Ah, rat-catcher. This is the term for informal hunting attire consisting of tweed riding coat, buff breeches, butcher boots and bowler hat. Cub-hunting, in September and October, precedes fox-hunting proper. If a neckcloth is not chosen, then it must be shirt and tie. Roll-neck pullovers may be all right when having a fag in the toilet, but not in the hunting field.

For the newcomer to hunting, knowing what to call a stock is less of a problem than working out how to tie it properly. Or how to tie it at all. Assuming that he has reached a terminological truce with his supplier, has bought the right size (the same as his shirt collar) and that he is wearing a suitable shirt (collarless and with stud-holes) he is ready.

First, though, whether or not he habitually washes his

hands after visiting the bathroom, lavatory or loo, he should most certainly do so before tackling his tie or stock. Otherwise, by his ninth attempt to get it right, it will look more like something belonging to a mechanic than a fox-hunter.

On first sight of a new hunting tie, out of its wrapper and laid on the bed, it is its sheer length that tends to astonish. It will be a good five feet long, and shaped somewhat like a double-ended canoe paddle, the twin broad ends about a foot long and three to four inches wide, joined by a slightly curving narrow section about three feet long and two inches wide.

The material will probably be quite stiff white piqué, doubled. Bang in the middle of the tie, at its lower edge, there will be a button-hole, and a few inches to the side of that, a kind of slit across the width of the material. Pretty mystifying, if you've never seen one before, and well worth introducing into aptitude tests. A man encountering his first hunting tie may well react like a chimpanzee on being placed at a grand piano.

Now for the tying of the tie. There are other ways of tackling the job, but the following is recommended: Fasten front of shirt collar band with stud. Pass one end of the tie through its own slit to form a loop large enough to pass over the head like a lasso. Drop the loop over the head with the button hole at the bottom edge of the tie and facing forward. Attach tie to collar stud.

For a moment the white band round your throat will make you look startlingly like a vicar. Don't worry. You'll soon be looking like a fox-hunter. The slit in the tie is now at the back of your neck, with the two broad ends dangling behind you.

Reach both hands backwards behind your ears, catch them up (the ends of the tie, not your ears) and flip them forward. They should now be dangling parallel and vertical down the front of your chest.

Grasp both sides of the narrow part of the tie close to your throat and twist one side over the other, as though tying the first half of a simple knot in a piece of string round a parcel. Pull tight until just before you become purple in the face, and stop. This would be the point at which you would ask someone to put a finger on the knot. You won't need to. You'll find that the knot will stay just as it is.

Make another twist in the tie as though to complete a reef knot (which is actually what you are doing) and gently tighten it up. As you do so, slip a thumb into the forward loop to keep the material flat, and gradually form the reef knot to trap your thumb.

So far, the procedure has been mechanical. Now you move into the realms of manipulative skill, not to say art. While simultaneously tugging at the free ends of the tie, wriggling your thumb and assisting it with the other thumb and forefinger, tighten, squeeze and slightly distort the reef knot so that you end up with the front side of it vertical and as wide and flat as you can manage. The principle is the same as that which governs teasing and shaping a knot in a dress tie.

You now have a neat knot about an inch square, with the two free broad ends of the tie jutting out left and right. They are not likely to be exactly the same length, but that is of no importance — they'll never been seen under your waistcoat. The broad ends will be bunched where they stick out from the knot, so tweak, pull and fiddle them out flat. Next, cross them carefully one over the other and downwards, so that they swell slightly, close to the knot.

Secure the crossed broad ends with a plain gold tie-pin stuck in horizontally and a little below the knot. If the pin is also attached to the shirt, this will preserve the swell in the tie, which should now be both elegant and secure.

Just to make sure the ends don't creep up and flap about, secure them to your shirt with four small safety-pins. One tie-maker packages his product with a little diagram showing how to fasten the tie, but not everyone can quite follow where end 'A' loops through end 'B' without turning the picture upside down, at which point further bewilderment can ensue.

There are purists who anchor the tie with a pin at the back of the neck and a thin piece of white string or concealed safety pin at the front, but this is complicated, unnecessary and asking for trouble.

Hunt servants often use a pin instead of a knot at the front, and then fold up and pin up the broad ends so that they hang down from the collar bones, the material edge-to-edge down the middle of their chests, to make a smooth flat front like a starched shirt. This avoids the gap that is sometimes seen at either side of a gentleman's knot, revealing a tantalising but draughty portion of his yellow or blue hunting shirt. The Hunt servants' method, although supremely snug, is not to be recommended. It requires much practice, assistance, and many safety pins. Further, to help close the possible gap in the edge-to-edge join in the middle of the chest, the tie-pin has to be inserted vertically.

In the event of a fall, this could lead to the Adam's apple being pronged. Hunt servants are safe, of course, because they never fall off. Well, hardly ever. The real secret of getting a hunting tie right is to approach the task in a bold, confident, optimistic, even cavalier manner. Five minutes should be enough time to achieve splendour. It is the timid who fiddle about for half an hour who arrive late at the Meet looking as though they'd just failed a first-aid test.

While a hunting tie undoubtedly looks rather dashing, it is not intended simply for adornment. It is meant to protect the wearer from weather and — if well-tied — injury. By giving support to the top of the spine, it could literally save your neck in a bad fall. It can also be used as a sling for fractures and a bandage or tourniquet for heavily bleeding wounds to people or horses. It's dismal to dwell on accidents in the hunting field, but if someone should hit the floor heavily, it's as well not to rush to tear off their tie. It may be better to leave it in position until someone who knows what they're doing comes along.

Gift tie-pins are a bit of a problem. Those given as Christmas presents often carry ornamental foxes' heads, coiled hunting whips, horseshoes and the equestrian like. This is a great pity and a source of embarrassment, because such embellishments are not approved of in the hunting world.

If the donor compounds the inadvertent blunder by going to the Boxing Day Meet to witness you wearing the pin, then you're really in a spot. Better wear the florid thing just that once and contrive, somehow, to mislay it. Because it just won't do. Members of the Boxing Day field would obviously not comment on an inappropriate tie-pin, unless in sympathetic jest. In truth, they would probably not even notice it, the hangover incidence being fairly high on this annual occasion, and tie-pins being fairly small. What they would undoubtedly not miss, however, is anyone wearing a velvet riding cap with a ribbon dangling from the back.

It is one of the great mysteries of equestrianism in Britain that practically every riding cap sold has a little black silk bow sewn to the back, with the two loose ends hanging down rather fetchingly about three inches. Fluttering, these ribbons can give the rider a becomingly audacious, knightly air, as might a penant. Also, from a practical point of view, the bows absorb rain on the cap and direct it to drip over the collar instead of down the neck. So, the ribbons are rather jaunty-looking and very useful.

But convention dictates that they must not be worn. When hunting people buy riding caps, many of them promptly cut out the safety chin-strap as unbecomingly cissy, and sew the bow-ends up to the inside of the cap where they cannot be seen. Because they must not be seen, in the hunting field, at any rate. The only people allowed to display their ribbons are Masters and Hunt servants. This rule may not be written down anywhere, but it is strictly adhered to in nearly all Hunts.

Thousands of pony-dotty little girls have been bitterly disappointed by this custom. On the first wonderful occasion that they are taken to be excitingly leather-and-new-clothing-smelling riding kit shop to be bought jodhpurs, boots, gloves, stick, tweed hacking jacket and velvet cap, they invariably exclaim with delight when they put on the cap and see the ribbons dangling prettily in the mirror, or looking-glass.

'Oh, mummy — look!'

Mummy, if she is a horse-person, will act quickly, kindly, but firmly.

'No, dear, you must put the ribbons inside — I'll sew them up for you when we get home.'

'But why, mummy?'

'They're only for hunting, darling.'

And then, when the poor child eventually goes to her first Meet and is ready to face the hunting world with ribbons flying, she learns they must remain tucked up out of sight. If she is puzzled, so are most hunting adults. Considering how very few out of the very many people who ride in velvet caps are permitted by custom to display the tabs of their bows, it is surprising that manufacturers continue to bother to attach them. They must account for a lot of extra labour and goodness knows how many miles of ribbon.

It's surprising, perhaps, that women haven't tried to change the convention. The ribbons are certainly decorative and would go to relieve the somewhat stern aspect presented by women in riding caps. Nearly all women — and their children — wear caps, and since females make up about half the people who hunt, they possess a great source of potentially persuasive power. So where are the feminist fox-hunters?

The disappearance of another kind of headgear appendage is also fairly inexplicable. It's the hat-guard, a short length of silken cord attaching the hat to the coat collar. Not so very long ago, hunting top hats and bowlers had little holes — grummets — at the back of the brim, so that the cord could be inserted. The cord ended with a clip that went to the hanging-up loop inside the neck of the coat. It was an inestimably invaluable device. There are dozens of ways of losing your hat while out hunting and, apart from the danger and expense of it getting trodden on by one or more horses, there is the tedium of pulling up and dismounting to recover it, or what's left of it, and then struggling to get back into the saddle. Many a fox-hunter, having gone through this lengthy experience, has found himself utterly alone, with only an approximate idea of where hounds are. How much better, then, to gallop on and leave the hat swinging but safe. Hat-guards were once so common that there were even rules of etiquette about what colour the cord should be — red or black. Now, they have virtually vanished, and modern hats don't have those handy little holes in the brims. Why, it is difficult to ascertain, but three reasons are sometimes advanced. One is that hat-guards are the mark of a cad (!); the second is that the cords are unsightly, hanging as they do somewhat like lavatory chains; the third is that, on viewing a fox, a follower should scream out a 'view holloa', standing in his stirrups and holding out his hat in the fox's direction — a hat being more easily seen than just a hand.

It is just possible that in his excitement, if the rider's hat were attached to his coat and the direction-indicating gesture understandably sudden, he might jerk himself out of the saddle. There is, happily, no authenticated report of this ever having actually happened. Hat-guards would scarcely inhibit the traditional doffing of headgear in salute to the dead fox, since this is seldom an extravagant movement. So their virtual disappearance from the hunting field is something of a mystery.

Top hats are still often called silk hats, although nowadays they're not made of silk. The material is a layered mixture of nylon and cotton stiffened with varnish.

There are no really complex rules about boots and breeches. White breeches, or very nearly white, are worn with red coats and black. Drab breeches are worn by black-coated farmers. Most men stick to plain black boots with black coats and change up to 'top' boots when they are awarded the Hunt button (all Hunts have their own button emblems) and graduate to red coats. In the days of extreme hunting dandyism, gentlemen had their valets polish their boot tops with such exotic mixtures as champagne, egg-white and raspberry jam. Even the most fastidious among today's fox-hunters would not be critical if they learned you were using ordinary boot polish out of a tin.

There is no doubt about spurs. Gentlemen should not hunt without them. They are blunt, and worn with the slight curve pointing downwards. Spurs are said to 'dress' the boot, and cannot really hurt the horse. They do, however, offer a degree of acceleration which indifferent riders would really prefer to be without. They are easy enough to put on, so long as you remember that the longer side of the spur goes on the outside of the boot, as does the buckle on the strap that fastens it.

Whips, too, should always be carried. Or worn, one might say, since few people use them except as a clothing accessory. A hunting whip, refreshingly, is called a *whip* — not a stick, cane or crop. It is in three parts — stock, thong and lash. The stock has a hefty bone handle at the top end and this, for most followers, is the useful bit. It can be used for hooking gates.

The rest of it — thong and lash — is a nuisance, except for people like Hunt servants who know how to use it and have need to. The thong is made of tapering plaited leather and may be as much as four feet long. This can be dangled in front of a hound that's getting dangerously close to your horse's feet, but that's about the limit of its use for the average member of the field. At the end of the thong is the 'dog-cord' lash that makes the stimulating cracking sound if you get it right.

Newcomers who, having acquired a whip, cannot resist the temptation to see how they'd get on in a circus, should practise alone and on the ground, or even sitting up on a ladder to simulate whipping from the saddle. Early attempts should not be made from horseback. Horses that have not previously had the privilege of carrying an amateur Whipper-in will almost certainly become alarmed. They don't like things swishing round their heads and, in the unlikely event that one of the early swishes actually produces the desired pistol-shot crack, may well go barmy.

In matters of dress, ladies who hunt have fewer problems of choice than men. White or fawn breeches, plain black boots, spurs, black or dark blue coat, hunting tie, cap or bowler, and hairnet. Flying hair, except on little girls with plaited pigtails and bows, is not thought right for hunting. Nor are earrings. And scent is considered the prerogative of the fox.

The one glorious choice open to a woman in the hunting field, though, is to ride side-saddle. This elegant echo of the days when a mixture of modesty, vanity and social conformity forbade ladies hunting astride in breeches, is, happily, becoming louder. There are more and more side-saddle classes at horse shows, and the entries increase every year. This re-awakened interest in side-saddle riding is showing itself in the hunting field, to the surprise of many riders, male and female, who have problems enough trying to stay on their horses in ordinary saddles. For those who have never seen a side-saddle — they are, after all, well concealed beneath the habit (not skirt) — it should perhaps be explained that the riders are not just balancing. Slightly to the left of the centre of the saddle there is a curved pommel for the right knee to hook over and give a firm grip.

Even so, it is far from easy, and few men would fancy it. The tricky part comes when putting a horse at a fence. Side-saddle riders can apply the left leg to the side of the horse as well as anyone, but have to use a stick for the right. It takes confidence, nerve, and real riding ability.

Only either bowlers or top hats are worn by such devastating huntresses. Oh, yes — and veils. These are optional and vestigial. Before barbed wire, hedges were thick, often with a ditch alongside — called bullfinches — and were as often crashed through as jumped. Ladies usually had a 'pilot' (sometimes a professional jockey) to ride in front of them and make gaps in such obstacles, but veils were worn because there was always the danger of cuts and scratches from twigs and branches.

Now there's only the danger of breaking hearts.

Off to London tomorrow, so will miss the Children's Meet again. Pity, but unavoidable. Jack [Joint-Master] to take my place as Field-Master, which he relishes not, although can't think why he fusses so. He can't surely be frightened of the little horrors. Good as gold, and a lot easier to handle than some of the adults. I'd like to see certainly one more Meet around Christmas if it could be fitted in with the school holidays. The kids in the top part of the country lost out badly when we were snowed off last year, and their parents can't be expected to drop everything to bring them down this end. Sounds terribly pompous, but they are *the future of the sport. Catch 'em young!*

Children's Meet

The most striking aspect of a Children's Meet is how terribly young some of the participants look — tiny toffs, as it were, still so small that they might not yet be walking all that fluently, let alone riding. But there they are, on miniature ponies, wearing scaled-down riding clothes topped, very sensibly, by velvet riding caps with chin straps where they belong — under their chins. Some of the hats seem a bit too big, but this may well be because smaller ones are simply unobtainable.

These very little ones are not unaccompanied, of course. It's their feet that are in the stirrups and their hands holding the reins, but mummy is at the pony's head with a lead-rein, and daddy is close at hand — so close that, in the event of any sudden loss of balance, he'd probably be able to catch the child before it even reached the ground.

Quite why the children are there so young is not altogether easy to understand, at first. They're hardly likely to be able to grasp what foxes are and why they are hunted, any more than they'd be capable of understanding a cocktail party or a cricket match. And they're clearly not going to be let off the lead-rein to go galloping about the countryside and hurtling over jumps.

'How long are you going to be out?' one mother asks another.

'About a quarter of an hour, I should think.' She glances at her charge. He is about the size of a biggish teddy-bear, perched not very securely — his legs are not long enough to give him any grip — on a pony only slightly bigger than an Irish wolfhound.

A quarter of an hour seems about right.

A newspaper reporter who evidently didn't approve of fox-hunting once asked one such mum if she was trying to indoctrinate her child into blood-sports. 'Good God!' was her loudly astonished reply, and the matter was not pursued. Among fox-hunting parents there may well be a wish to familiarize their young with the atmosphere and etiquette of a Meet as early as possible. But basically, if they consider the child old enough to be placed on a led pony, a Children's Meet is a nice occasion to attend — a kids' equestrian party, and a high point in the Christmas school holidays. This one is in a paddock at the front of a comfortably mature and substantial farmhouse. There are nearly 100 children, all members of the Hunt's Pony Club, and most of them seem to be from eight to fourteen years old.

Girls are in the majority, and they've obviously taken great trouble over their own and their mounts' turn-out. They're dressed correctly but informally, in tweed or dark coats with shirts and ties and velvet riding caps. One or two of the older ones have gone all the way and opted for breeches, boots and white stocks. Most, though, are wearing jodhpurs.

The only red coats out today are worn by the Master, the Field-Master, the Huntsman and his two Whippers-in. There are also two men and one woman wearing formal hunting clothes, making a total of eight mounted adults. So the children are going to be under supervision, but unobtrusively. It really is *their* Meet.

There are stirrup-cups, as is proper, but they're non-alcoholic. And the sausage rolls are supplemented by a tray of miniature chocolate bars. One child is so entranced that she bites into her bar without removing the wrapper. Relatives are present to sip hot punch as the hounds are brought into the paddock. Here, one feels confident, no child, however young, will be heard to utter the word 'doggie'.

One hound bounds towards a nice-looking part-Arab pony with a 10-year-old girl aboard. The pony, having apparently not seen a hound before, takes a few suspicious backward steps. Curious, the hound advances. The pony lowers its head to examine this strange creature and their noses touch. This is altogether too much for the pony, which whirls about, kicks out at the hound and begins to make off for the nearest place of safety.

With admirable aplomb, the rider stops it, executes a very neat turn on the forehand and directs it back to the pack again. Her mother rebukes her. 'Angela — you *must* keep your pony's head towards hounds. You very nearly kicked that hound and you'd have been sent home.'

Oh, the shame! Mum, clearly a fox-hunting person, is quite right. Hounds are definitely not to be kicked and the best way of avoiding such an untoward occurrence is to make sure your horse's front end is pointed at hounds. But the child could hardly be blamed and, of course, she wouldn't really have been sent home.

Anyway, the hound is back with the pack now and Angela's learned one of the golden rules of hunting, which is part of the purpose of a Children's Meet. In furtherance of tuition, the Master moves his horse a short distance from the hounds and gathers the children about him.

'Good morning, everybody. Now, before we move off, there are just one or two things I'd like to tell you. First, you're all looking very smart, which is what we like to see. Now, we're going fox-hunting and we hope we'll all enjoy ourselves, but that doesn't mean we can behave as we like. We'll be on private land, thanks to our generous hosts who've given the Meet here, and we must watch where we're going.

'Don't go racing off by yourselves. Do what the Field-Master tells you. I don't expect there'll be many jumps but if there is one and your pony refuses, circle it out, wait, and join in at the back of the field — you'll soon catch up. If you're the last through a gate, remember it's your job to shut it, unless there's somebody about who can do it for you. Don't get too close to hounds. We don't want them kicked and they can't get on with their job if we're too close.

'When I first came out hunting my father told me the most important rule to follow was never overtake a man in a red coat. If you follow that, you won't go far wrong. Right, let's hope we have good sport.'

The Master beckons to the Huntsman, who calls 'hounds, please!' And the day has started. The proudest members of the field are the five young individuals who have been selected to ride with the Masters and Hunt servants. Each of these key adult figures has one small mounted shadow beside him, to be given an idea of what his duties are in the field.

The girl chosen to accompany the Huntsman is Angela, who has already won a little unwelcome distinction. Now she's tucked in beside the Huntsman, hounds at foot, trotting to the first covert. She looks wonderfully assured and calm, rising nicely to the trot, but must be almost boiling over with a mixture of joy, pride and apprehension. The pony has to extend to keep up with the Huntsman's horse and frequently breaks into an over-excited canter.

Each time it does, Angela sits well down in the saddle to bring the pony back to a trot. She's doing very well. If only mummy could see her now. Of course, mummy can't, and that's one of the frustrating aspects of attending a Meet as a pedestrian. When the field moves off, those who are left on foot have to foot it — but in which direction?

What you have to do is follow other people in the hope that they really are following hounds and not just following their noses back to their cars and home. You also have to hope that they're sufficiently in the know. 'Where are they drawing first?' you'll hear people ask. If the answer is unhesitatingly firm, and you happen actually to know where Plumtree Spinney is, you're all right. Except that, by the time you get there, hounds may have drawn blank, and been taken on to draw somewhere else.

The mothers at the Children's Meet seem fairly well-informed and keep their children in view as much as maternal tenacity can contrive. Nevertheless, they can be seen in anxious clusters peering into the far distance and speculating on whether the movement they can just discern is of hounds or riders.

'There they are!'

'Where?'

'Up by the wood.'

'Oh, so they are, Goodness, they'll have had a long gallop up that field to get there. I do hope they're all right.'

'Mine's frightfully young.'

'Well, they are all together, aren't they? Plenty of people to pick up the pieces.'

'Not too many pieces, I hope.'

'No — ha-ha-ha.'

There's a hint of nervousness in the laugh, and no wonder. If fox-hunting can be dangerous for adults — and nobody should doubt it — how much more perilous might it not be for mites on scatty ponies? The comfort must be that the young enjoy the fearlessness of inexperience. And seem to bounce better. And bouncing past along the lane comes a six-year-old girl on a busily trotting shaggy grey pony at the end of a lead-rein held by a mother riding a cobby-looking grey horse. Only Britain, one feels, could produce such a pair. Both animals are generously coated with mud. The weather is uncomfortably cold. Mother can't risk going across country with the possibility of having to jump — to do so while leading is to risk a multiplicity of disasters — but she's determined to reach hounds.

Poor child, you think, being dragged along like that.

The pace is too hot and she's having difficulty timing her body's rising to the ups and downs of the saddle. Look at her little legs — they're positively flailing. She'll be off in a moment. Oh, she's calling out. She certainly is. 'Hurry, Mummy, hurry! . . .' The legs are flailing not in panic but because she's trying desperately to kick her pony up into a canter even if it means cracking a few of its ribs. If she were out alone she'd probably be about two inches behind the Field-Master — jumps and all. Pony Club children — girls invariably outnumbering boys — can be formidable.

Somebody's seen the fox.

'Look — right in the middle of that field.'

'Where? . . . Gosh, yes.'

'Oh Lord, they're *miles* away.'

It's true. The fox is fox-trotting towards a hedge, seemingly not in any great hurry, and the riders are in the far distance, too far even to distinguish between red coat and black. Hounds cannot be seen at all. A holloa would never be heard. Even the sound of the horn might not carry so far.

'What a pity. Where's he got to now?'

'I think he's in that hedge there.'

'Where?'

'There. That hedge.'

Silence. As the little group of mothers gazes out at a very large expanse of countryside which may or may not contain their children, there seem suddenly to be rather a lot of hedges.

'Perhaps it was a hare,' suggests one lady.

This remark deepens and prolongs the silence. Almost tangibly undeclared is the opinion that anyone unable to tell the difference between a fox and a hare shouldn't be out hunting.

Another group of mothers and female relations is about to have better luck. Wearing regulation green rubber boots, quilted country coats and headscarves knotted firmly if unbecomingly beneath their chins, they've stationed themselves at the corner of a wood within a few yards of a two-foot tiger-trap at the end of a track leading out of the wood. Actually it's a three-foot jump but the top rail has been removed for the occasion.

There seems to be nothing happening, but they either know this part of the country very well or have been given good information. This commodity — information — is about as available in the hunting field as it is on a racecourse. And frequently as reliable. But they're well stationed between two coverts. If a fox isn't found in the first, the field is almost bound to come by here on its way to the second. There may be an easy way round for the less intrepid, but the tiger-trap is the obvious way out of the woods — absolutely on the route the field is most likely to take.

A horn sounds a long note, apparently some way away.

Headscarf: 'What's David blowing — was that gone to ground?'

Similar Headscarf: 'I can't be absolutely sure. Difficult in this wind . . .'

Quietly, they listen, as do the other three in the group. Clearly we're among the cognoscenti here. They know the Huntsman's first name, for a start. And have some idea of the horn-calls.

The silence continues. It is not done to speak when everybody's listening to find out what's going on.

The horn again, sounding several short notes.

Headscarf: 'No. He's calling hounds.'

Similar Headscarf: 'Mmmmmm . . .'

Actually it is very difficult to understand what a Huntsman is signalling, although his Whippers-in know well enough and so do his hounds. As a simple rough rule, short notes mean that the Huntsman is doing something busily with his hounds, and long notes that whatever they were doing has been done. However, there are several subtle variations within these two bare guidelines.

The horn again. This time, closer. Ahhhh!

Within minutes, three or four couple of hounds appear in the track, followed by the Huntsman. He's called hounds to him and they're on their way to try the next covert. This is always an impressive sight — scarlet coat, horn tucked in between top and second gilt button — and hounds eddying closely round the horse's hooves but somehow never getting trodden on. The Huntsman is moving at a purposeful trot and, only a yard behind, rides Angela, his understudy.

It is the most memorable day of her young life. The hounds pour over and through the tiger-trap. The Huntsman calls back over his shoulder. 'Kick on, Angela — tiger-trap!' His horse hops smoothly over the jump with something approaching disdain for such a small obstacle, but Angela's pony has to make a bit of an effort. It sees the jump and throws its head about. She corrects its impetuosity without losing impulsion, puts her heels in, sits down firmly for three perfect strides and flies over with a foot of daylight to spare. Badminton stuff. Perfection.

If only Mummy could have seen.

The rest of the hounds follow, chivvied by the Whipper-in, his whiplash ready to check any that stray away from the main body of the pack. He sees the last hound over the tiger-trap, puts his horse neatly over it and trots on. Very orderly and as it should be. But now comes the rest of the field, practically throbbing with excitement. The first four riders are girls in their teens, well-mounted and able. They are evenly spaced out in single-file, their ponies going calmly and not getting on top of each other. They take the jump creditably.

Headscarf approves but is not demonstrative. This is not a football match, after all. Quietly but briskly and to nobody in particular, she says, 'Well done.' The riders certainly can't hear her.

Well, now, after the Lord Mayor's Show, as they say. The next girl, aged about nine, approaches the jump sideways in a manner seldom described, and never recommended, in riding manuals. Her pony is getting fractionally but nervously nearer to the jump with every excited step, but using most of its energy in a sort of bunched-up cantering action that looks as though it might escalate into a rear or swift departure.

Neither pony nor girl is particularly happy with these circumstances and before they can arrive at mutual intent they are overtaken by four other assorted ponies that are enjoying hunting and going to catch up with the Huntsman whatever the wishes of their riders. They fly over the jump, with their jockeys miraculously still on board.

This activity induces the sideways-travelling pony to execute an interesting spinning movement in which it whips about completely in a tight circle and follows the others over the jump with a leap that would do it credit at the huge puissance wall at the Horse of the Year Show. And — yes! — the girl is still in the saddle, although neither she nor anyone else can understand how.

Headscarf: 'Well done.'

More young riders are coming down the track towards the jump, in varying degrees of control and at rather greater speed than the first half-dozen. Their mud-dotted faces reflect a mixture of elation and anxiety. They're only moving on to the next covert and the Huntsman is only moving at an easy trot, but they're getting slightly behind, so are cantering. This is partially because they want to catch up, but mostly because their mounts want to catch up. All members of the horse family tend to be gregarious and are not fond of being left out of things. The hooves splatter in the mud.

As each pony sees the jump and agrees to take it, it accelerates, and the sound of its feet cuts to a moment of silence while it's in the air, then there's a thump as it lands on the other side and scurries on.

Headscarf: 'Well done.'

The entire field has got over one way or another now, and even the tail-enders are almost out of sight. The little group of spectators gaze in the direction the riders have gone and shift their cold feet a little, thinking where to go next.

Headscarf: 'I didn't see your daughter, did you?'

Similar Headscarf: 'No.'

Headscarf: 'Will she have fallen orf, do you think?'

Similar Headscarf (to whom this possibility had not

occurred until now): 'I hope not.'

Headscarf: 'Oh, look — here comes someone else. Is it your daughter?'

Similar Headscarf (peering anxiously through the trees): 'No. I don't know who that is. Little dot of a thing.'

Approaching, the little dot becomes a slightly larger dot, but it is not big enough to be called a blob. It is a girl of perhaps seven, certainly not more, trotting along on the kind of small shaggy pony normally only seen in humorous cartoons. Her riding cap is somewhat too big for her and tilted forward so far down towards her nose that she has to peer upwards to determine where she and her pony are going. She is quite unaware that anyone is watching. Both she and the pony perceive the tiger-trap simultaneously and react in different ways. She puts both her jodhpur boots vigorously into the pony's sides as an encouragement to continue forward movement.

The pony stops dead, as though it had walked into the side of the House of Commons. The sudden loss of impetus tilts the girl's cap even further forward, impairing what little vision she has left.

'Get on, Timmy!'

Timmy evidently cannot hear too well.

'Get on!' Three more swift applications of boot.

'Get *on*!'

Timmy remains motionless, conveying the impression that he hadn't been too keen on coming out hunting in the first place, and has now abandoned the idea altogether.

The girl has been well taught. She has applied the appropriate 'natural aid' (an 'aid' is an equestrian euphemism for an instruction or signal given by rider to horse — the rider's legs, hands and seat are 'natural'). She must now resort to an 'artificial aid' (spur or whip). She is not wearing spurs, but she has a stick. Raising her right hand, she swishes the stick downwards with as much force as she can muster. There is a convincingly loud slap.

Headscarf: 'Well done.'

Not quite so well, actually. This aid is supposed to be applied to the pony's side, just behind the girth. Unfor-

tunately the little girl has only succeeded in hitting her
own boot. 'Ouch!'

Timmy is indifferent. If riders wish to punish themselves in this fashion, it is no affair of his.

The little girl improves her aim. Three great thwacks
follow each other — right on the mark and heavy enough
to knock dust out of a brand-new carpet.

Headscarf: 'Well done.'

Timmy ignores even this assault.

Now it's well known in the horse world that if you
have an argument with your mount, you *must* win. Or, at
any rate, you should. The little girl must have heard about
this, and raises her arm again. Timmy is going to go forward and take that jump, or be thrashed into dog-food.
But the arm doesn't come down. The girl sighs loudly.

'Oh, come on then, Timmy.' She climbs down to the
ground, takes the reins over Timmy's head and uses them
to lead him to the jump. Timmy doesn't mind this at all.
He's quite willing to go to the jump. Even look over it
and admire the view. But jump it? Together, girl and
pony arrive at the jump and gaze at the now quite empty
field beyond. After a moment, the girl remounts and
turns the pony's head in the direction they've just come.
The pony turns round. She gives it a natural aid, a gentle
squeeze with the legs.

Timmy moves into a pleasantly steady, willing trot.

He is taking her home.

Headscarf says nothing.

Children's fox-hunting is exactly the same as normal
fox-hunting except for the almost total absence of adults
among the field, and the deliberate choice of easier
terrain. The one or two grown-ups are specially asked by
the Master and are in attendance to keep an eye on things,
catch riderless ponies, restore their riders to their saddles
and encourage the hesitant.

They may carry a few extra tissues in case called upon
to dry a tear, but this is a fairly unlikely eventuality.
Young fox-hunters, male or female, are pretty resilient,
not to say tough. The very young ones on led ponies just

potter about gently until their parents decide they've been out long enough. Those old enough to ride solo will stay till the end — not forgetting, of course, to say 'good-night' to the Master.

1 February

Daphne Reynolds, of all people, rang up this morning to ask if she and her daughter can wear the new safety hats with chin-straps, and should she write and ask the other Joint-Master. Apparently she even hesitated about approaching me direct on the phone in case it was a breach of etiquette. Didn't know quite what to say but I've given permission and said I'd tell the others that I've done so. Not certain that people need permission any more — the Association has really said use your own discretion. Can't have the poor woman writing to three people she knows socially anyway, but I do appreciate the gesture. Good manners cost nothing, as Father said so often. I think chin-straps look frightful and as good as said people might stare rather, to which she said, 'I'd rather look daft than dead, Master.' (Think she may have read that somewhere.) Also think her example might well be followed. They're both good horsewomen and go well to hounds, and well-known for it. Makes me feel old-fashioned and rather sad. I'm sure if I read this when I'm an old man I'll see it as the beginning of the rot setting in. There's no question that I was right to give permission — how could I deny two very nice people the right to hunt safely? Although I do just wonder what Daphne would have done if I'd refused — given up hunting? Well, there it is — perhaps we'll all end up looking like motor cyclists. I quite like the grey caps idea, despite my reservations. No use droning on about it. I shall wear a black cap till my very last day and I wouldn't wear a chin-strap even if the Duke of Beaufort ordered me to. So there!

Danger Ahead

Fox-hunting is dangerous — dangerous, as in dead. There are no specific National Health Service statistics for fatalities in the hunting field — they probably come under 'general' or some such heading — but every season probably a dozen people are killed or seriously injured while out hunting.

The fact is that riding horses is a pursuit that carries risk, and riding them on roads and a full-tilt across country and over jumps is even more perilous. Horse and rider can easily part company; the rider hits the ground; that ground is hard tarmac; and that, very often, is that. Irreversible brain damage is frequently the chilling medical evidence at the subsequent inquest, and death by misadventure the melancholy verdict.

Really, though, it's death through vanity. Or pride. Or etiquette. Or tradition. Or conformity. Or, less kindly, stupidity. Head injuries are the cause of most riding deaths. Protective headgear is available, yet it is spurned by the huge majority of fox-hunters because it doesn't look right. They wouldn't, they declare, be seen dead in it. And, unintentionally, they're absolutely right — they wouldn't. Jockeys and Event riders aren't seen dead in it. Because they wear it.

There are several other sports that could be said to involve as much as, or even more physical danger than fox-hunting — motor-cycle and car racing, hang-gliding, pot-holing, canoeing, mountaineering, parachuting, polo and so on. But the one important element that makes them safer is that the participants protect their heads, either because commonsense urges them to or rules tell them to. Even Cabinet Ministers, visiting industrial sites in circumstances that must surely be conspicuously free of peril, don safety helmets — because regulations so dictate.

But commonsense and rules are replaced in fox-hunting by a mixture of tradition and etiquette. And tradition and etiquette ordain that the proper thing for a gentleman to wear on his head while hunting is — a top hat. For those who have not worn, examined or handled a top hat, be assured that it would provide scant protection against a flying blancmange, let alone collision with a tree trunk.

If a gentleman wears not a red coat, but a black coat,

he may choose to wear a bowler hat instead of a topper. Both, if designed for hunting rather than attending Ascot or an office in the City, are specially reinforced, but even their manufacturers would hardly dare claim that they are anything more than nominally impact-resistant. You can easily dent them with simple thumb-pressure, so that the kind of thump they are capable of diminishing may not have done you all that much harm if you'd been hatless.

The only other kind of headgear acceptable in the hunting field is — or was, until the 1983-4 hunting season — a black, velvet-covered hard riding cap, which is considered to be a bit safer because the good ones carry British Standards Institute seals of approval — the so-called 'kitemark'.

Until 1983, the tradition in most Hunts was that black caps were worn with red coats only by Masters, Field-Masters and Hunt Servants. This was to distinguish them, as officials in the field, from red-coated gentlemen followers. The caps could also be worn by farmers hunting in black coats, and by their wives. Neither safety nor snobbery influenced this distinction. Without farmers, there would be little land to hunt on, so farmers have always enjoyed sartorial and financial concessions.

Children could also wear caps, and so could women, but usually only after applying to the Master for permission to discard bowlers. Women who rode side-saddle, however, were expected to wear bowlers or toppers.

For many years these subtle and complicated-seeming distinctions were not merely tolerated by the hunting fraternity. They were enjoyed and understood as part of the mystique of the sport.

Then from the 1960s, as more people took up riding and some aspired to hunting, proportionately greater numbers began falling off horses, and an awareness of the perils of equitation began to grow. In the less stringently ordered Hunts, black caps were seen occasionally on the heads of gentlemen who wore black coats but were evidently not farmers. This was seen not only as a breach of etiquette and an abuse of the farmers' privilege, but as causing confusion in the field.

In the heat of the chase, a red coat and top hat identified a gentleman follower, while a red coat and black cap meant someone in authority. That was easy. Similarly, if a Field-Master saw a man in a black coat and cap, as opposed to a top hat or bowler, he would know at once that he was a farmer and could be trusted not to leap into someone's — quite possibly his own — winter barley. Such certainty was eroded when newcomers to hunting (who wear black coats) began bobbing about in black caps because they felt safer in them, because they were cheaper, or because they would have felt a bit ridiculous in bowlers or toppers.

Some, it must be reported, were sent home.

As the '60s slipped into the '70s, and fields grew larger, one or two Masters turned a Nelsonic eye on these black caps, but they were seldom welcomed and often banned. And why not? All clubs and similar bodies have rules, and those who wish to enter must abide by them. If a restaurant won't let you in without a tie, then you either borrow one from the doorman, or eat somewhere else.

However, very few people have starved to death through being turned away from a restaurant, and even fewer have strangled themselves with a borrowed tie. In the hunting field, though, there were fatalities that might have been avoided had the victims been wearing safer hats. Correspondents wrote to newspapers and magazines (particularly *Horse and Hound*) and a talking point grew into a cauldron of controversy that bubbled anew every time someone had a hunting accident.

At the very beginning of the 1982-3 season, a most distinguished horseman and experienced fox-hunter was killed when his horse slipped and fell on a road, while out hunting. He was wearing a top hat. The fox-hunting world was fairly stunned, but nobody stopped hunting. However, the controversy over safer headgear came to the boil, with top hats being described as dangerous, anachronistic fancy-dress, and the like.

Eventually the Masters of Foxhounds Association felt obliged to relax the rules. They announced that individual Masters could exercise their own discretion in matters of dress.

Fine. A Master could allow people to hunt more safely. But the Association also advised Masters that if followers wished to wear riding caps or bowlers, they should only do so with black coats. On the face of it, this didn't seem unreasonable. It preserved the identity of those in authority in the field. If a man in a red coat decided he might live longer by jettisoning his top hat, all he had to do was get a black coat, which he probably possessed anyway.

But. Say it again.

But — gentlemen fox-hunters don't wear red coats at whim, just because they think the colour suits them better than black. They *earn* the right to wear a red coat. It may take several seasons with a Hunt before they are awarded the Hunt button and formally *invited* to wear red. It is an honour, a kind of promotion, a distinction, a privilege, a mark of status; a matter of great pride. To the particularly sensitive, going back to wearing a black coat is like being reduced to the ranks.

So that piece of advice didn't go down too well. Further, a proliferation of black caps and black coats eroded the distinction enjoyed by farmers.

Fox-hunters, however, are resourceful folk, and one Hunt devised a compromise which was quickly adopted by others. This was that any follower, red-coated or black, could wear a riding cap — so long as it was *grey*.

Phew! The controversy was resolved. Visible authority was preserved, confusion avoided, traditional red coats retained, and everybody could not only breathe again — they could hunt honourably and safely.

But not very safely.

The sad fact is that most riding caps worn today, whatever the colour of their velvet covering, are not terribly safe; and certainly not safe enough to satisfy the neurosurgeons who have to deal with riding head injuries, and their often terrible consequences. The caps are not tough enough, and they do not give enough protection to the sides and the back of the head.

In order to qualify for the British Standards Institute 'kitemark' the caps have to be capable of withstanding 'impact energy', which could be translated as the force of a good clout, and is scientifically measured in units called 'joules'. Jockeys' skull helmets have to withstand rather more joules, and motor-cyclists' helmets even more. It is easy to understand that motorbikes travel faster than horses and that anyone catapulted from such a machine and striking his head on a lamp-post might build up a formidable number of joules.

But what about the horseman? Well, the unfortunate ones are quite good at generating impact energy. What kind of a rider ever just fell out of a stationary saddle and hit the floor? Accidents happen when horses bolt, shy, slip, buck or rear. Or they happen at jumps when horses stop suddenly, veer sharply to avoid the jump, 'peck' (stumble forward on to their noses) on the landing side of a jump, jump too high or jump too low. There may be even other ways of dislodging riders, but what is certain is that anybody who leaves a horse involuntarily does so with considerable velocity which must give him a (literally) flying start when it comes to collecting joules. Further, a rider so unseated may well get kicked by the horse, as a kind of bonus. And a horse's kick is Crown Joules.

It should not be supposed from this that cap manufacturers are callous or the British Standards Institute careless. There are now riding caps on sale that cover more of the head and are even tougher than the jockey skull helmet. But they are not favoured by the hunting fraternity because their extra strength makes them a bit bulkier. Less becoming. Not traditional-looking. And, even worse, they have single chinstraps, or double safety harnesses with chin-cups — just as are worn compulsorily by jockeys and Event riders.

Any kind of chinstrap, in the hunting field, is a very rare sight indeed. Fox-hunters hate them. For years they've been cutting them out of velvet riding caps to save the bother of tucking them up inside, out of sight. Two quick snips soon get rid of what is contemptuously referred to as 'knicker elastic'.

And yet it is axiomatic in riding circles that if a person gets thrown from a horse, his body will land in one place, and his hat in another. Hats of every kind almost invariably fly off in riding accidents. Unless, of course, they are firmly attached to the head.

It must be said that fox-hunters are not alone in not favouring hats with chinstraps. Most horse riders dislike them because they feel cumbersome and because they interfere with the wonderful sense of freedom that goes with riding. Fox-hunters have additional and, to them, entirely valid reasons — chinstraps are an impediment to hunting etiquette, which calls for quite a lot of hat-raising.

At the Meet, it is customary for a gentleman to bid others good morning and, in doing so, to raise his hat — most especially to the Master. On setting off from the Meet to start hunting it is good manners to thank one's hosts — and raise one's hat. And these are not sloppy little nominal gestures — no mere touchings of the hat brim or peak. The headwear is doffed — removed, and the head bared — and by some, in a positively elegant sweep.

Many Huntsmen and Whippers-in, when they take hounds from a Meet, hold their caps up at arm's length in an extravagantly old-fashioned kind of salute that borders on the theatrical. It is courteous, traditional, and very nice to see. On viewing the hunted fox a follower is expected to stand up in his stirrups, holloa, and indicate the direction the fox has taken by holding out his hat. It is also customary to doff the hat in salute to a fox upon its death. Finally, the hat is removed again when saying 'goodnight' at the end of the hunting day.

How could such traditional gestures be made gracefully with chinstraps flapping about?

Those who do not hunt may think all this pretty insignificant. What, they might argue, does it really matter if a minority of anachronistic nutters want to gallop about in fancy dress, killing themselves in between taking their hats off to each other?

Quite so.

But interest in riding as a leisure pursuit is growing rapidly. There are at least three million riders in Britain, and even if few of them aspire to hunt, they are influenced to some extent by hunting, and the eminent riders who enjoy the sport. Show jumping is another influence. And in both these equestrian spheres the disregard for safety is hardly believable. Of the show-jumping stars who appear regularly on television and are watched by millions, only one is ever seen wearing a proper chin-harness. And it is well-known that he has only done so since returning to the sport after a fall so serious that he was clinically dead at one point. He cannot afford another accident.

As show jumpers enter the ring to tumultuous applause, they raise their caps, proving to the millions of children who idolise them that there is no cissy chinstrap to impede them in the jump-off against the clock. What mother, after such a dazzling example, can persuade her nine-year-old son to wear his hat and chinstrap properly when he goes hacking round the common with his friends? Pony Clubs and good riding schools are very strict about safety, but far more riding is done outside their supervision than within, and much of it on roads, where most of the really dreadful accidents happen.

Traffic upsets the horse. It slips on the smooth surface. The rider is thrown. Hat off head. Head on road.

It happens to fox-hunters, as well.

No sign of the snow disappearing, which makes three days' hunting lost. We go on Saturday, though, whatever happens. *On foot, almost certainly. Might be quite fun. Early start, 9.30 at Kennels, and see what happens. Whips and wellies — spurs will not be worn. I'll phone round a few of the old faithfuls on Friday. Not like the old days. They used to hunt so long as the snow hadn't reached the top of the kennel door. How did they do it? Snow balls up under the horses' feet, so you can't ride. May be a touch of romance about those old stories, or did they mean hunt on foot? Horses presently being lunged on a straw circle in the field. God knows what they'll be like when we can get them out again, but don't want to cut their feed. If we go on foot we'll hunt just the Common and round Desmond's plantation. The main road is clear so we can use the lorry —* the new *lorry! The ever-amazing Supporters' Club have bought us a new one (or new secondhand). Brian told me this morning. Apparently this was all decided at their AGM but they said nothing about it in case they couldn't raise the loot. None of us knew. The great unveiling is to be at the Kennels, where the S.C. is giving the Meet on the 27th (by* kind permission of the Joint-Masters — *I didn't even know!). Shudder to think what the lorry cost, or what it's like. The Supporters are absolutely astonishing. A new saddle at the Terrier Show, and now this. What would the antis say? — we must have corrupted the peasants, or some old claptrap. They love their hunting, and that's it and all about it.*

The Supporters Club

If Hunts charged farmers and other landowners for getting rid of foxes, an invoice might read: 'To killing one fox — £500.' Of course, such a bill would never be sent — and it certainly wouldn't be paid! — because permission to hunt over the land has long been the quid pro quo. But £500? To kill a fox?

Well, it doesn't cost that much to account for every single fox despatched by hounds, but it is not such an outrageously unrealistic figure as it might seem. It undoubtedly costs £50,000 a year to run some Hunts, and a Hunt that had a season's tally of only 50 brace would not consider it shamefully low. So — £50,000 divided by 100 foxes equals £500 per fox. Even a schoolboy without a pocket calculator (if there is such an underprivileged creature) could do the sum in a twinkling. And supposing the tally were doubled, it would still be £250 per fox, which sounds a bit steep.

There are Hunts that kill more foxes for less money, but the fact remains that hunting with hounds is expensive. So, as it happens, is game bird shooting. By an interesting coincidence, when a man has paid £500 for a day's shooting, he often takes away only a brace of pheasants — which comes to £250 per bird. Still, at least he can eat them when he gets home, which is more than can be said for the catches of coarse fishermen.

The high costs of killing foxes with hounds may well surprise a great many people, including quite a few foxhunters who have never bothered to work it out. More surprising still is the fact that a high proportion of these expenses are met by people who never ride to hounds because they don't want to, or couldn't afford to even if they knew how to ride a horse. They are members of the Hunt Supporters' Clubs.

The Clubs began to emerge as an integral part of the hunting world in the 1960s and '70s, when the social base was broadening among those riding to hounds, and when car ownership began to be common. There had always been people following hounds on foot, but they were mostly local rustics, many of whom went out in the hope of getting tips for opening gates and helping to catch riderless horses.

When people started to follow hounds in motor cars, they were barely tolerated. Cars in the hunting field are a noisy smelly nuisance. But their numbers increased so greatly that they gradually became an accepted part of the hunting scene. Some Hunts even cap them (take small subscriptions from the drivers) as though they were visitors on horseback.

It should be made clear, perhaps, to those who don't know, that the cars don't actually join in with the horses and go belting through wood and meadow tooting their hooters in concert with the Huntsman's horn. The cars are driven to the Meet, so that their owners can attend, and then follow roads as close to the direction of hounds as they can. When they reach a good viewing place, their owners get out on their feet. So they use the cars to stay in touch with hounds as best they are able. But it is out of this fairly new pursuit that the Hunt Supporters' Clubs came to be formed, and they are now in such strength as to be a tangible force that has lowered some of the sport's social barriers and is a formidable defence against its critics.

Some of the Clubs are particularly strong, with 3,000-4,000 members, lapel badges, car stickers and regular magazines. Even Masters are not above serving as Chairmen. An old-time fox-hunter would be amazed at this development, and many contemporary ones are not fully aware of how much their supporters contribute. Britain's most distinguished and respected fox-hunter, the late Duke of Beaufort, described the Supporters' Club as 'the financial life-line of many Hunts'.

What has happened is that Hunts, in the face of rising costs, have had to increase subscriptions, but dare not go too far in that direction for fear of squeezing followers out. Thus, subscriptions may only cover about half the costs of running a Hunt, leaving half to be found elsewhere through such fund-raising events as Point-to-Points (always a good one), horse trials, sponsored rides, the Hunt Ball, terrier shows, barbecues, skittle matches, darts tournaments and so on. This is where the supporters come in, organising, providing helpers, selling tickets and collecting cash with indefatigable zeal.

Even Hunts that are ticking over very nicely, thank you, can be embarrassed by a sudden need for capital expenditure — major repairs to the kennels or stables, for example, or a new horse-box. Time and again, the supporters find the money. Changes in hound-feeding have come about through the purchase of big deep-freezers. At one time the carcases of donated dead farm animals were kept as fresh as possible for as long as possible by putting them in water, or turned away if there was a surplus. Nowadays, into the freezer they go. And who found the funds for the freezer? Almost certainly it was the supporters.

One of the side-effects of their many activities is that they make people more aware of hunting, thereby improving what the media call the sport's 'image'. To the outsider, it must seem surprising that so many supporters work for and subscribe to a sport in which they do not participate — at any rate, on horseback. It is rather like the NCOs and Other Ranks of an infantry battalion having a whip-round to send the Officers' Mess on a ski-ing holiday.

If you ask why they do it, most supporters will say that, basically, they like to watch hounds working for their Huntsman. They don't care in the slightest about the expensively clad wealthy members of the mounted field, except in so far as they add to the colour of the spectacle. But this they could do without. Their loyalty and pleasure lie with the hounds, and they will do everything in their power to ensure that they do not vanish.

By no means all of the supporters are true country dwellers. The patterns of modern life are such that probably most have to work and live in or near towns. Fox-hunting gives them a link with the countryside, and an opportunity and reason to enter it and be part of it.

16 February

I was 'the governor' today, as my clever sons insist on calling it. Paul [the Senior Master and a JP] busy locking up burglars. Met at the Farmer's Boy, Woldrington. Very cold, but lovely atmosphere and a gratifying absence of cars because they can all park round the back of the pub, even the boxes and trailers. Only about 60 out and nearly everybody looking right. Old Mr. Thrush hadn't bothered to plait up, and there were even bits of straw in his horse's tail (unbelievable) but I suspect he can no longer afford a groom. I'm getting more like an Orderly Officer than a Governor! Brian not to be drawn on his assessment of scenting conditions, but looking quite genial. Mixed pack and his favourite number, 19½ couple — he reckons it's the extra odd one that catches the fox! Trays of drinks floating about but no sign of money changing hands that I could see. Take it somebody settled up but 'the pace was too good to enquire'. Off on the dot and a nice easy jog to the Lowdown piggeries. Slight breeze and great white clouds scudding across blue sky. Really beautiful day, so nothing for the field to moan about. A text-book draw in the gorse above Stratton, hounds in almost constant view and a fox soon unkennelled. With high chicken wire in front of us, everybody was wondering whether we'd have to go left or right and a fair few were edging surreptitiously to the left in anticipation. They'd seen Brian take hounds through the gate to the left and assumed that was the only way through the wire. O ye of little faith! When we took off the field split into two halves, with hounds going like stink — a proper cry. The ones who went with me to the right were miles better off. If the others had taken the trouble to keep their eyes open they'd have seen the new Hunt rails to the right. An easy pop and half a mile saved, while they were all struggling with the gate and ended up going in the wrong direction. They were probably following fat Percy, a know-all who knows bugger-all if ever there was one. Set off in fine style and it really looked as though we'd got a straight-necked fox that would take us out of the county. A good holloa (car follower) by Widgetts and I had half a dozen of the best with me as we took the in-and-out over the lane (bar Wally, the first victim) down the ride on the other side and then over the tiger-trap at the end. Marvellous sight. Fields stretching away miles to the downs, half a dozen jumps virtually in a line. As we took the first, hounds were at the third and moving as though under the classic tablecloth. Now, we thought, this is hunting. First run of the season. Brian well up and a fox that's set its mask for somewhere distant, Macklesworth, as like as not. And then damn me if hounds didn't throw up — totally at fault. Foil of some kind, freshly scattered fertiliser, I think. Brian cast them left, beyond a hedge, they quickly owned the line but I don't believe it was the hunted fox. Anyway in minutes they'd marked to earth near a tree with a ladder up it. The ladder has elbow rests at the top and has been there for years — Prescott's game-keeper shoots foxes from it. It's within yards of the biggest earth in the kingdom and it most certainly should have been stopped. Classic Master's dilemma — to dig or not to dig. A very *frustrated* field, horses and people steamed up, and all wondering what you're going to do. Brian blew for the terrier-man and he took for ever. When he eventually got there he scratched his head and said the earth should have been stopped, which was a great contribution. I looked at the people, and they looked at me. We could have been there a fortnight, so I told Brian to get on down to Glover's kale. For'ard on! Very, very disappointing and the rest of the day an anti-climax. I was right as it happened. They were digging out for an hour and killed a vixen. We found and killed on the Linkley side of Smiley's, but a most unenterprising dog fox. So, a brace at the end of a day that was pleasant but looked as though it was going to be a classic. Brian to have a word with the guilty earth-stopper because that earth's been there about 500 years, but perhaps he wasn't sent a card, and he's a volunteer. Can't really rate the man if you're not paying him.

Marked to Ground

The purpose of fox-hunting, it may seem superfluous to say, is to kill foxes. But this unpleasant fact is ignored by many who go hunting. They enjoy wearing distinctive clothing, the social occasion, the fresh air, the excitement of riding across country . . . but the kill, which is the point of the whole endeavour, is an event that very few witness, or indeed, even care about.

Ask the average fox-hunter if he's had a good day and he'll very likely reply 'super!' — a much-used adjective in his social sphere — and go on to describe how he and his horse behaved, with the emphasis on galloping and jumping.

He'll be telling you about the thrill of the chase. Ask 'Did you kill?' and he may not know, except by hearsay.

Foxes are often killed above ground out of sight of the Huntsman, let alone the field. And, if he's up with hounds at the kill, it would be unusual for there to be more than a handful of the field up with him. Most foxes die unseen by the majority of the riders because they are much too far behind to view anything but the backsides of the horses in front of them. By the time they actually catch up, there is nothing much left to see. Hounds have done their work.

For all the foxes that are killed 'on top', there are just as many that are 'marked to ground'. That is, they've managed to escape and hide in a badger sett, rabbit burrow, field drain or other refuge too small or inaccessible for hounds to follow. Hounds will scrabble and scrape at the place and make a dreadful din of frustration, while the Huntsman blows 'gone to ground' — a long mournful note on his horn. By now the field may be arriving, horses and riders sweating and puffing and barging into each other as they pull up. But even those who get closest will only see the 'sterns' of the hounds (tails is not an acceptable word where foxhounds are concerned) 'flagging' (not wagging) vigorously in a frenzy of balked zeal.

When it becomes obvious that the hounds cannot reach the fox the Huntsman, on the instructions of the Master, will either leave the fox where it is, 'give it best', or blow three notes on his horn to call in the terrier-man. Hounds may then wait to see if the fox can be 'bolted' (pushed out to be hunted again), or be taken on to draw again somewhere else.

Whatever happens, very few members of the field actually witness that which they have set out to accomplish — the death of the fox. When they move off and leave it to the terrier-man, they turn their well-clad backs on an aspect of fox-hunting that, perhaps, they would prefer not to think about.

Terrier-men are the unseen — or seldom seen — side of hunting. They do not ride horses or wear smart red coats. They dress in practical country working clothes and usually trail the Hunt in muddy Landrovers. They seem humble and scruffy alongside the splendour of the Huntsman and Whippers-in but they are a vital part of the Hunt staff. Terrier-men often double as earth-stoppers and in any event are closely associated with them.

Successful hunting depends very largely on thorough earth-stopping, which means blocking foxes' dens while they're out doing their own hunting, so that they cannot duck back into them when they themselves become quarry for hounds.

Earth-stopping is murky work that used always to be carried out at night by men whose social status was only a notch above poachers, or the unfortunates who removed what was euphemistically called night-soil. Hunts would often fine them if a fox managed to get into a hole that should have been stopped. Nowadays it isn't too easy to find men willing to creep about on cold nights filling holes for a few bob, so the work is often done the day before, sometimes with the help of the Hunt staff and terrier-men.

Earth-stoppers are no longer social outcasts; in some Hunts they are sent cards telling them where to operate, and the late Duke of Beaufort treated his to an annual feast at which he might be heard joining in the chorus of some fairly earthy songs.

Some Hunts block breeding earths for the entire season, and reopen them afterwards; others stop them before a hunt, and open them again at the end of the day.

The best way of stopping earths is probably to have permanently-tied bundles of sticks which can be rammed into the entrance, hooked out afterwards, and used again when required. Mostly, though, almost anything that's handy is used. Unhappily and untidily, there are not many pieces of countryside today that fail to yield discarded fertiliser bags and plastic insecticide containers. Most earth-stoppers carry newspaper which they soak in diesel and stuff into the hole before they block it. Foxes have a highly developed sense of smell, and will go nowhere near it. Another technique is for the earth-stopper to ram a rolled-up newspaper into his wellies. This becomes warmly foot-rich as he walks about, and a whiff of one sheet is usually enough to deter the fastidious fox.

For all this ingenious sophistication, it is difficult to block every hole and well-nigh impossible to guess which way a fox will run. So, inevitably, holes are left un-stopped, and hunted foxes get to ground in them. When they do, it is the terrier-men who 'dig out'. This is a procedure that disconcerts many people, both among those who hunt and those who do not. At best, it is considered unfair and distasteful; at worst, cruel and disgraceful. Terrier-men would not agree. They regard foxes as destructive vermin — on a par with rats — and have no qualms whatever about killing them.

When summoned to the place where the fox is hiding, they first establish the way it got in. This is fairly easy, because this is where the hounds will have been trying to get in, too. They then look for possible exits — there could be several, for example, in a rabbit burrow — and seal them, sometimes with nets, or by plunging a garden fork firmly into the ground, so that the prongs become like the bars of a cage. Just shovelling in some soil will not do — foxes are very good diggers if the need arises.

With the exits firmly blocked, the terrier is put into the entrance, with its collar removed in case it catches on anything. Trembling with eagerness, it needs no persuasion to enter the hole, although experience must tell it that it's likely to be half suffocated, mauled and bitten. They are fiercely tenacious little dogs.

Now the terrier man, perhaps with one or two friends to help him, starts to listen. Someone will probably put an ear to the ground. The noise they are waiting for is the 'baying' of the terrier when it reaches the fox, although the sound coming from below will be more like a muffled yapping.

They will also sometimes poke sticks into the ground to trace 'pipes' (tunnels), always being careful, of course, not to impale the terrier. Only one terrier is put in at a time, for fear of two encountering in the darkness and fighting to the death.

Terriers' tails, if left to grow naturally, curl round to 12 inches or longer. Those bred for hunting have their tails docked so that when the animal is fully grown, the stub is four to five inches — just enough to be handily grabbed to pull the dog out of a hole. The docking, in early puppyhood, can be carried out by a vet. In Hunt kennels, more often than not, the job is done by the Huntsman, who feels up the tiny tail for the right vertebra, and uses a penknife.

Once underground, the dog will either drive the fox to one of the blocked exits, or to a point at which it can move no further. No fox, they claim, will ever get back through a tunnel past a terrier, but they often block the original entrance, behind the dog, in case there is a loop tunnel leading back. Viewed from above ground, it's impossible to tell.

If the fox is not driven quickly to an exit, the subterranean conflict may last an hour or more. Many a fox has been dug out by torchlight. The burrow may be deep and the tunnels long. Badger setts can be particularly complex. The terrier will never give up; the fox has no option but to try to defend itself. Squeezing its body forward in the blackness, it will be snapped at from the rear. If it can turn round to face its ferocious little enemy, it will do so.

Terrible and bloody battles take place thus in the deep, dark earth, while the men above wait and listen. Sometimes they will have other terriers with them, and the canine tension, or extra-sensory awareness of what is taking place, sends them into a kind of trembling frenzy. Although tied up, they will strain against their collars almost to strangulation, and hurl themselves against the restraint. Their angry frustration will even make them attack each other, if they get the chance. Their owners will swear, thump and separate them while they try to tear each other's ears off; then re-secure them, and carry on listening.

*

This is such a scene . . .

A fox has been marked to ground in a rabbit hole in an old gravel pit in the middle of a big grass field. The Hunt has moved on. The terrier-man and two companions are gathered about the entrance to the burrow. They have blocked the only two exits they can find, and put the terrier in. Its urgent, scurrying little white rump disappeared into the hole some minutes ago. All the men can do for the moment is watch, wait and listen. It is a very quiet, still day. In the distance, from time to time, the hunting horn can be heard. Two terriers belonging to the terrier-man's friends are tied to the bumper of the Hunt Landrover. The dogs are tense, but silent.

'There he is!'

Somebody has heard something. It is a faint, muffled, desperate sound from deep in the ground. It is not likely to have been made by the fox. Whatever the stress of the circumstances, foxes tend to remain resolutely silent.

The men listen further, and decide to dig down towards a point just ahead of the source of the noise.

Ten minutes later, jackets are taken off.

The terriers on the surface strain at their leashes, best part hysterical. The men dig on, widening the hole so that they can stand in it, to dig deeper. The pile of excavated earth is growing higher and beginning to slip back into the hole. They shovel the pile further away to make more room to dig. It's going to be a longer job than they thought.

They have dug like this many times over the years. One man makes a joke of it.

'If we was to get all the 'oles we've dug and put 'em together, I reckon we'd 'ave a bloomin' swimming' pool.'

'Whatya want a swimmin' pool for?'

'Bloody swim in, 'course.'

'You can't bloody swim.'

'That don't make no difference — still 'ave a pool, can't I?'

'Tell you what — you want a swimmin' pool that much you can dive in 'ere with that bloody spade.' The man down in the hole clambers out to make room. They all chuckle a bit.

The hole is looking like a small grave.

Eventually their spades break through into a rabbit tunnel. The terrier man lowers his head to listen.

'Yeah, he's there, all right.'

'Which way?'

They are all very quiet as the terrier-man listens carefully, and then crooks his arm to feel into the tunnel with his hand.

In the distance, the hunting horn is sounding again.

'Can't feel nothin'. Give us that stick down.'

He slides the stick into the tunnel about four feet. There is an indistinct sound of animal anger or pain. It is impossible to tell. A mixture of growl, snap and snarl.

''e's a bloody long way in.'

''as 'e turned, d'you reckon?'

'Dunno. Give us the net.'

They bundle the net into the hole they've dug, so barring the tunnel that the fox can't get back that way. Unless there are side tunnels running off the one that they've exposed, the fox is now trapped somewhere between two blocked exits, trying to fight off the terrier. Whether it has turned round or not is now immaterial. Almost inevitably, it will be forced to the exit, where a fork, like a portcullis, will stop it; its way to the other exit, where the net is, is almost certainly guarded by the terrier.

Guessing again, they start digging another hole in the ground between the two barriers.

A few minutes later, there's a sudden cry from three yards away.

'The fox!'

And it is. Behind the prongs of the fork barring the exit from the tunnel, dark, ginger-coloured fur can be seen. It moves. Vanishes. Reappears, and vanishes again. Strangely, there is no noise from inside the tunnel.

The men wait, not knowing quite what to make of the situation. Why isn't the terrier growling behind the fox? Perhaps the dog is stuck somewhere, but even if it is, the fox won't be able to get back past it. They know now that their job is almost over.

Intently, they gaze at their portcullis, their cage. Their trap.

Then, the waiting is over.

The fox is back again. Its 'mask' (they don't speak of head or face— appears behind the prongs.

Sharp snout.

Bright eyes.

At bay.

But silent.

The hunting horn sounds again, louder than it was. The hunt is coming back this way. 'Go and get David' (the Huntsman).

One of the men runs off in the direction of the sound.

The fox, from darkness, looks out at the light it cannot reach.

The terrier man takes out a pistol and loads it. He moves the handle of the fork slightly so that he can press the barrel of the pistol behind the fox's ear.

The fox does not move, or make any sound.

The terrier man fires. It is only a .22 pistol and the sound it makes is puny, like a gunshot in amateur theatricals. Unconvincing.

It is, however, sufficient. The fox's head tilts and rests on one ear.

It is dead.

The terrier man pulls out the fork, takes the fox by the neck and tugs at it. For a moment, the body is stuck in the narrow tunnel. Then, almost like a cork from a bottle, the body is pulled free and cast, floppy, on the ground.

There is no sign of the terrier.

The terrier man pushes his arm into the hole. 'Sam! Come on, you little bugger.'

Nothing. Perhaps Sam has exchanged his life for the fox's, but the two men do not seem concerned. No fox, in truth, is any match for a terrier.

'Where's 'e got to, then?'

''ave a look down the other 'ole.'

They examine the big hole they dug earlier and remove the net.

Still nothing.

They finally find Sam at the original entrance to the tunnel, where he entered it in the first place. He is peering through the prongs of the fork that blocks it. Black wet snout. Bright eyes. Trapped, just like the fox. Sam whimpers slightly and, as the fork is pulled out, leaps into the arms of his master and licks his face.

'Give over!' complains the terrier man with simulated irritation at this display of affection. 'Let's 'ave a look at yer.'

He takes the dog by the scruff and holds it away from him to inspect it.

''e ain't got much blood on 'im, look.'

There is the approaching thudding sound of a horse cantering on grass, and the Huntsman arrives with his hounds. Half a mile away the field — about 100 riders — have been told to wait.

They have not seen the fox dug out and shot and they will not see what now takes place.

The Hungsman approves the furry body. 'Well done.'

Even as he dismounts and hands the reins of his horse to the terrier man, the leading hound falls upon the limp body of the fox, and the rest of the pack crowd and struggle and push to find space for their jaws. The Huntsman blows a few short blasts on his horn and urges the hounds on, crying repeatedly 'Tally-O-tally-O-tally-O-tally-O' in a loud high voice. He's exciting and inciting them, reinforcing their instinct, breeding and training.

They don't need the encouragement. Within three minutes there is nothing left of the body but fur, skin and entrails. Were it not for the mask and 'brush' (tail) the remains might easily be taken for an old dishcloth. There has been no sign of blood-lust or unhealthy passion in the Huntsman's action. He's been doing his job. Some men show rather more emotion when they throw a stick for a spaniel and call out, 'Fetch it.' Particularly if the spaniel won't.

The Huntsman remounts and rides off with his hounds to draw the next covert. The terrier man throws what's left of the fox into the back of the Landrover.

It adds to the tally.

The field is still waiting.

The ever-growing problem of car-followers came up at the meeting last night — my least favourite subject, as they well know. Apparently some idiot parked his car slap in the entrance at Benson's farm, and old Benson wanted to move some sheep. Car firmly locked, of course, and the occupants God knows where. Benson said his men had to bounce! the car out of the way, which must have done it no end of good. Serves them right, of course. Nobody knows who the culprit was but evidently 'one of ours'. The upshot is that we're going to draw up a set of rules, or rather, ask the Supporters' Club to draw up a set of rules for car followers. Apparently they have such traffic jams up in the Beaufort country that they go round putting cards on people's windscreens, so now Muggins has got to write to the Duke and ask for one of the cards, as an example. I suggested we should have two rules — Rule One: Park your car at least 50 miles from the Meet; Rule Two: Stay in it. Just a joke, of course, ha-ha.

Foot Followers

At every Meet of foxhounds, there are people present on foot — perhaps half as many as there are on horseback. A lot of these pedestrians are unmistakably OK, and some of them frightfully OK, as one can observe from their demeanour, accent and dress. They're at the Meet because they belong to the upper echelons of the local fox-hunting fraternity. They probably know the owner of the large house where the Meet is being given, as well as several of the more elegantly-clad riders. They are at ease with horses and each other and convey the impression that they themselves hunt, or used to. One of their distinguishing characteristics is the ability to talk upwards to someone on horseback without looking as though they're being talked down to by the person in the saddle. This is possibly an inherited social skill.

Their clothes are about the same colour as army lorries, and have an almost military uniformity. Waterproof green boots are pretty standard, with either quilted green jerkins or sloppy-looking wax-proofed jackets, topped by cloth flat caps for the men and headscarves for their women. Viewed from the front, the caps are worn horizontally level, the peaks half an inch above the eyebrows and inclined downwards over the eyes in a rural version of the Guards manner that only partially impairs vision. The headscarves, of expensive silk, are folded in half to make a triangle, and tied beneath the chin in the fashion that may have first been introduced in Windsor Great Park and makes all the women look faintly Royal. Conversation is confidently clear, not to say ringing, and reveals more about the Public School system than the Comprehensive. It concerns, in the main, horses. For some reason the word 'yes' is often rendered 'yop' or 'yar'.

For most of these people, the Meet is a brief social occasion that ends when the field moves off.

There are, however, other pedestrians at the Meet for whom the gathering is not a social event. They are there to go fox-hunting — on foot. Every Hunt has its regular foot and car followers, most of whom are members of the Supporters' Club and known and respected by the Master and Hunt staff. They are a bit of a mystery to the majority of mounted fox-hunters, who would find it difficult to imagine following hounds on anything but horses. Oddly enough, the successful pursuit of foxes is frequently aided by the efforts of these people on foot, some of whom know more about hounds and hunting them than the horse riders.

Foot-followers are usually not so well-off. They're mostly working (or retired) ordinary country folk, although ex-officers and nice middle-class ladies are not unknown. Class distinction is not evident among them. They are friendly and helpful to each other. But, by and large, they go hunting alone.

At the Meet they often pay a small 'cap', but whether

they're given a drink and a bit of cake, like those on horses, depends on the judgement of the people carrying the trays. These stirrup snacks are a vestigial reminder of the old days, when hunting started early in the morning after a big breakfast. They are intended principally for the mounted, although those apparently attached to the mounted are often treated as guests. But people on foot at the fringes of the gathering, where the foot-followers tend to cluster, are likely to be taken for casual bystanders who may have nothing to do with the Hunt. So they sometimes miss out on the punch, but it is doubtful if they care. They've got hot flasks in their cars. And sandwiches. And a little drop of something stimulating. And shooting sticks. And rugs. And spare boots. And extra coats. And goodness knows what else.

They're all right, thank you.

Quite a few of them are also equipped with dogs. These are almost invariably small, of the terrier type, and are seldom let off their leads. This precaution is to avoid the dogs taking off and confusing the Hunt, or to prevent them being eaten by myopic hounds.

Sartorially, the foot-followers are somewhat less conformist than the upper-crust earthbound, and a shade more practical. Their dress is based on the assumption that the weather will be dreadful and the certainty that they'll be out in it all day. Stout wellingtons are favourite footwear, although thick, clumpy hiking boots have their adherents. Coats tend to be thicker, more waterproof and longer than the bum-freezing and often sleeveless quilted jerkins of their apparent social betters who've only gone to the Meet to see someone orf. Foot-followers have no wish to be mistaken for wealthy racehorse owners and know that their photographs and starkly un-hyphenated names will never appear in Jennifer's Diary. They just want to be warm and dry and are content to be anonymous. Anoraks with draw-string hoods are seen, as are Harold Wilson macs and après-supermarket-cum-car-rally coats, sometimes adorned with badges advertising petrol companies.

Headgear is varied. Where men choose cloth or man-made fibre caps, these may be worn at a slightly jaunty angle. Deerstalkers with earflaps lowered are seen, as are nylon versions of the fur hats so popular round the Kremlin. Knitted woolly hats, the odd balaclava and even the pork-pie trilby, with or without small pheasant feathers in the band, provide occasional sightings.

That's just the men, of course.

Women foot-followers are fewer, but just as tenacious and possibly even more hardy. They are often bare-headed but resort to sensible woolly hats when the temperature drops below zero. A small proportion of the women seen during hunting do not qualify as foot-followers because although they accompany their husbands, they never leave their cars. Except, presumably, for reasons totally unconnected with fox-hunting. These are amazingly patient ladies, often contentedly post-menopausal, who knit and read and take no interest at all in their husbands' obsession. They are abandoned in their cars at remote rural cross-roads and near gateways to fields, and probably wouldn't notice if a horse jumped over the bonnet.

It is difficult to estimate how many people regularly follow foxhounds on foot. At a weekday Meet attracting, say 100 people on horses, there might be 30 on foot. At a Saturday Meet, the numbers swell proportionately, so that 50 and more on foot would not be surprising, with very many more on special occasions such as Opening and Boxing Day Meets. There's no doubt, anyway, that the national total must be expressed not in thousands, but in tens of thousands. Which is rather an interesting fact to lay before opponents of the sport who assert that it is followed exclusively by equestrian snobs.

But how do they do it? How do they follow hounds on foot when riders frequently fail to keep up with them on horseback? Do those energetic welly-clad feet fly across ploughed fields, over jumps and ever onwards?

Well, obviously not. They'd soon be left far behind.

No. What the foot people do is employ a mixture of experience, strategy and guesswork to anticipate where hounds will appear next. Some of them are so good at it that often they're in a good viewing position before the field gets to it. Everybody who has regularly followed hounds on horseback has had the experience of cantering confidently to some point, knowing he's well up in the field and in close touch with hounds, only to find a foot-follower already there, sitting on a gate in close touch with his sandwiches.

They do have their blank days, of course. A good fox may lead hounds and field far away and leave the foot people in the wrong county. It is this uncertainty, and the need to be constantly working out what's going on, that the foot-sloggers enjoy. Some of them have been following hounds in this way since they were children, seem to know almost instinctively the direction a hunted fox will take, and can be of great help to the Huntsman. They act like scouts, in a way. They understand hunting, move about quietly, and know how and when to 'holloa'. They don't crash through undergrowth, pop up over boulders and scream out if they see a squirrel.

About the 'holloa'. It's pronounced 'holler' and means a loud drawn-out mixture of scream and shout. Every exponent has his individual style, but the resultant sound is usually something like 'whoooooeee', ending on an upward or downward inflexion. There is a wailing, carrying quality to the noise that makes it seem quite eerie in a thick wood. It is uttered once and is a signal that the fox has been sighted. Or, rather, that it was sighted a few moments before.

The good foot-follower only holloas *after* the fox has passed him, so that it isn't startled into changing direction or, worse, going back over its own line. The holloa is meant for the Huntsman, although hounds will sometimes respond to it. If a foot-follower is in open country and thinks the Huntsman can see him, he may supplement his holloa by pointing in the direction the fox has gone, or waving a handkerchief. It can be very exciting to hear hounds 'speaking' loudly to a strong scent with short blasts of the horn urging them on, and holloas confirming the line of the fox and tracing its progress.

It's more than exciting for the fox, of course. But a lot get away even when their end seems inevitable.

Foot-followers are often referred to as car-followers, for the good reason that they use cars a great deal — a great deal too much in the view of most Masters. Motor vehicle engines make a noise, and they smell, both factors that are not conducive to good hunting. But followers are supporters, and supporters are an important element in hunting. They raise a great deal of money for the sport and are a bastion against its opponents. These are facts that are often overlooked by the people on horses, for whom part of the appeal of hunting is that, in the saddle, they can escape from motor cars — including their own.

When they're trying to squeeze their horses down a narrow lane past a line of followers' cars, the word 'cars' is frequently prefixed by 'bloody'. But the riders smile and call out 'thank you'. Roughly translated this means, 'Damn you for getting your car in my way but thank you for slowing down/stopping/not actually running my horse over.' The hunting field is a sphere of great courtesy, much of it implicit.

Occasionally, horses and cars have hunting accidents, giving rise to insurance claims. The following are actual statements made on insurance report forms:

'My horse collided with a stationary car coming the other way.'

'The guy's horse was all over the road. I had to swerve a number of times before I hit him.'

'In an attempt to view the fox I drove into a telegraph pole.'

'I pulled away from the side of the road, glanced at my mother-in-law, and headed straight through the pack.'

'Hounds had been running hard and as I galloped into the lane a hedge sprang up, obscuring my vision, and I did not see the supporter's car.'

'I had followed hounds by car for over 40 years when I fell asleep at the wheel and had an accident.'

'To avoid hitting the two riders in front, I struck

a pedestrian.'

'An invisible horse came out of nowhere, struck my car and vanished.'

'The hound had no idea which way to run, so I ran over him.'

'The indirect cause of the accident was a fellow on a small grey horse with a big mouth.'

'In avoiding a supporter's car, I was thrown from my horse as he left the road. I was later found in a ditch by some stray cows.'

'The lady's horse backed into my window into my wife's face.'

'An "anti" hit me and went under my car.'

All true. Really.

But now, come to a Meet and get the feel of a day's hunting by car and foot.

The first thing is to find out the projected shape and order of the day. Meets are not spontaneous gatherings. They are known about well in advance and are usually held at old-established venues that are used perhaps two or three times every season. Be the Meet at a village green, cross-roads, pub, farmhouse or stately home, the place will be known to all the regulars, who will also know where the nearest coverts are and what order they are likely to be visited in.

If you ask someone where hounds are going, the reply will be, 'Well, they usually draw so-and-so woods first, and then go on to Wobbly Down,' or wherever. There is often an established pattern, although this can easily be altered through circumstances on the day — a change of wind direction, for example. The Huntsman will almost certainly have visited the area the day before and made an outline plan, which will be ratified by the Master at the Meet. It's not done to ask the Master or Huntsman where they're going to go, but it's easy enough for someone to overhear them telling the people who have to know — the terrier-men and the like — and the information soon spreads.

So, we commence. Hounds move off with the Huntsman

and Whippers-in, followed by the Master and the field. And, as the last few horses fall in at the rear of the column, the supporters climb into their cars and drive along behind them, except for the diehards who keep to their feet and will try not to use their cars at all.

It is always an impressive sight along a country lane, with hounds, horses and riders in a long line. One could almost believe that the 20th century hadn't happened yet, if it weren't for the bloody (sorry!) cars. Well, it cannot be argued that they enhance the pageantry. In any sense you like to take it, they spoil the atmosphere. But they are part of hunting today, and likely to remain so.

After probably not much more than a mile, the field will turn off the road and into the country, perhaps entering a field or going down a track.

It's from this point that you start to devise your strategy. If you get out of your car and pound after the horses, you may well catch them up, perhaps mustered at the side of a wood, waiting while hounds draw it. But you may then find that, before your breathing has returned to normal, the horses move off, leaving you as a diminishing dot in your wellies. You can plod after them, of course, but you'll see more hunting country than actual hunting. A ploughed field that had once contained 100 horses can look very empty very quickly.

Now, if you watch other people on foot, you'll see that they seldom rush anywhere. They stand. At a distance. And wait. And watch. And listen. They know roughly where the Huntsman has put hounds into the covert and they know that they'll hear his voice and horn, which will tell them the direction he is drawing in.

If hounds begin to 'speak', the followers will keep on listening until they're fairly sure which way the fox is going. Then they may start to move a bit, although always ready to stop and listen again.

If they hear the horn blow 'gone away', meaning that the fox has broken cover and is running, combined with the stirring sound of hounds in full cry, then they're happy, and hunting. They won't necessarily see anything, but they'll enjoy *trying* to see. It's more than likely that the fox will have broken on the blind side of the covert — the side they cannot see — and that the wood in front of them totally obscures their vision.

The more energetic ones may try to get round the wood; most will probably get back to their cars and drive to where they hope the fox is making for. It is fortunate that fox-hunting does not take place in cities, because fox-hunters tend, when hounds are running, to be somewhat cavalier about traffic regulations. It should never surprise you to see a car approaching you up a lane in reverse. As soon as the driver finds a gateway or a bit of space, he'll turn his car round and proceed frontwards. In the meantime, he is going in the direction his passion dictates — the direction of the fox.

Followers with farming connections can sometimes stay closer to hounds by bumping across the fields and up muddy lanes using vehicles with four-wheel drive. But most of the foot people only have ordinary saloon cars, and drive circuitous miles by road to make quite small territorial progress. It is a sure sign that there's hunting going on somewhere if you come across a dozen such, parked and empty, on the verges of a country lane. Their owners may be up to a mile away. Waiting. Watching. And listening. But probably not in a group. Not acting in concert. Foot followers are essentially loners, making what they can of the day. The mounted field may be a cohesive force — a kind of cavalry troop commanded by the Field-Master — but the foot people follow their individual lines and inclinations. The flow of the chase may influence them to drive almost in convoy on occasion, but it is not uncommon to see one suddenly take a unilateral side-turning, and by no means certain that the rest will follow.

Again, if four or five of them happen to be standing together, one may stride off on his own, without it being likely that the remainder will follow. Each has his own concept and respects the others.

They are endlessly patient and oblivious to bad weather.

They stand for hours staring out towards apparently empty pieces of landscape, while cold, rain and wind chastise them for their curiosity. Hunting is a winter sport, and they spend far more uncomfortable time waiting, watching and listening than they do walking, driving or simply sitting in their cars. Some of the clues to what is happening in the hunting field are visual — the movement of animals and birds, for example — but more are aural. The Huntsman talks, shouts, whistles and blows his horn. Followers holloa. Hounds speak. So foot supporters listen. And since listening properly precludes talking, they certainly don't go hunting for the conversation. They do talk, however, during lulls, and much of their talk concerns 'Charlie'.

A fragment of sample dialogue might go like this:

First foot-follower: 'I seen Charlie, right enough.'

Second foot-follower: 'Where was that, then?'

First foot-follower: 'Down the bottom of the common, by the cottage on the corner.'

Second foot-follower: 'Oh, ah. What, after they come down by the chicken farm?'

First foot-follower: 'That's right. But they wasn't speakin' to 'im.'

Second foot-follower: 'No, they wasn't speakin' to 'im. I was down there, 'n all, and then I come up 'ere.'

Charlie is not, as one might suppose, a foot-follower who is not being spoken to because he's been placed in some kind of rustic Coventry. Neither is he HRH the Prince of Wales, although *that* Charlie does hunt, with various packs, in a splendid coat he devised himself — dark blue with scarlet collar and cuffs.

The 'speaking' being spoken of is the speaking of hounds, and the Charlie they failed to address is Charlie the Fox. How the fox earned this soubriquet is not certain, but one theory is that it was named after Charles James Fox, the great 18th-century British statesman. Whether this was meant as a compliment to either must be left to your view of history and your opinion of foxes.

Anyway, 'Charlie' is an acceptable word for a fox and

is commonly used in the field. Something that perhaps should be made clear is that foot-followers do not imagine that they will ever catch a fox. That is not their purpose and is, anyway, the job of the hounds. What could a person on foot do, after all — bring the fox down with a rugger tackle and pop it into a plastic bag? Nor do they entertain very high hopes of being in at the kill.

So why do they do it, once, twice or even more times a week for six months of the year?

First of all, because they enjoy it, but that is self-evident and hardly an answer. Second . . . well, if you could speak to enough of them to reach a consensus, it would probably go something like this:

They love the countryside and enjoy being in it. Hunting gives them a reason for doing so — a purpose — and allows them to go pretty well where they like.

They enjoy watching hounds work as a pack, which to them is far more fascinating than, say, watching sheepdog trials. They like working out what the Huntsman is up to and matching their strategy to his. And they enjoy the occasional glimpses of something that can be spectacularly exciting — a fox stretched in full flight, hounds hard after it; galloping horses, flying clods, splashes of mud, falling bodies, cries of alarm, shouts of joy, the shrill pierce of the hunting horn, flashes of scarlet coat . . .

It can be like a brief vision of our historic past. A touch of colour, of dash. Even, at moments, of splendour.

And that's rare enough to stand about in the rain for.

14 March

It is now agreed that Gone to Ground is to be blown by Brian at old Tom Leigh's funeral tomorrow, by special permission of the Vicar. He'd been worried that it was 'pagan'. Jack said no, sir, it was a bit like the Last Post! There was talk of throwing a fox's brush on the coffin, but that would have given the Vicar a fit. Can't think Tom would have minded either way, but he was certainly a stalwart old hunting man. Told me once that he'd been to over 50 Opening Meets and then stopped counting. First went hunting with his father, who always hacked to Meets. Fantastic, 15 miles to a Meet, a day's hunting, 15 miles back, and do farm chores before and after. Chavingly Park today and we had silence for Tom before hounds moved off. Looked down and saw that daffodils were already showing, a sure sign that the season's almost over. Closing Meet on the 20th. Hope there's a good turn-out tomorrow, we ought to show the flag.

Pagan Rites

Fox-hunting is a blood-sport, although the preferred and softer term today is 'field-sport'. Blood, however, is certainly shed when a fox is killed, and children out hunting for the first time are sometimes 'blooded'. This sounds more gory than it is and amounts to no more than a Huntsman daubing a blood mark on the child's forehead or perhaps cheeks. At one time no child could escape this ritual initiation into the hunting tribe, but nowadays a Huntsman will only daub if requested by the parents. It would be an unusual child of a hunting family that objected to being so marked. Kids used to be so proud of the initiation that if they were blooded on a Saturday they wouldn't wipe off the stain until church on Sunday. Today the number of children so initiated must be even smaller than the number who attend church.

Trophies are sometimes awarded in the field, but with nothing like the hysteria that marks similar awards in Spanish bull rings. If someone — particularly a child — has ridden hard and well and kept up to hounds, a Master may well award the fox's brush. And the kind of child that is gutsy enough to take jumps on level terms with adults will be dizzy with pride and delight.

Fox-hunters are no more sentimental about death than anyone else, but they will often seek to honour someone who has served the sport with devotion over a long period. A Huntsman who has put in 30 and more years' service with a particular Hunt — and this is not uncommon — is likely to be buried to the sound of the hunting horn. And a lone hound may follow the coffin. It is a deserved and appropriate tribute.

Where sentiment and emotion are missing is at the Closing Meets. While most Hunts open the season with a glad flourish, the closing of the season is more of a fizzle-out than anything spectacular.

There is no official closing date but, as winter fades and spring approaches, the end is nigh. Traditionalists say that there's 'no real hunting' after February; the majority of Hunts probably pack up in March, but some go on into April and at least one never stops until it has killed 'a May fox'.

On hunting appointments cards the last date bears the phrase 'to finish the season', and that's that. What can be guaranteed is that there won't be even half as many people present as attend the Opening Meet.

A definite anti-climax.

The Hunt stables and people who keep horses only to hunt, then begin to 'rough off' horses. An animal that's had six months of high-energy feeding and lots of work cannot simply be thrown out into a field and left till the next season. Its food and exercise are gradually reduced and, when the weather is warm enough, it's put out to grass by day and brought into stables at night. Eventually it is let out permanently, or 'turned away', with its shoes removed.

Once that has been done, it is said to be 'summering'.

The horses that keep their shoes on and are very much on their toes are the 'qualifiers', those racing in the Point-to-Points that proliferate from February into the beginning of June. Such horses have to have certificates, signed by an MFH, that they have been 'fairly hunted'. As steeple chases were originally cross-country races from church steeple to church steeple, so Point-to-Points were from one prominent point or landmark to another — and very hairy, competitive, fierce and dangerous they were.

Point-to-Points were once rather relaxed and jolly, informal occasions at which the best horses in a Hunt raced against each other and against those of adjacent counties, largely as entertainment for the farmers whose land they had ridden over during the season. They are still more casual than Cheltenham, Ascot, Goodwood and Aintree, but are very much more professional than they used to be, with better horses, specialist jockeys, bookies and the Tote. And dope-tests.

For the spectators, they're a good day out in the country, with the chance of a flutter, and busy (if draughty) beer tents. For the Hunts, they're major fundraising events. Few Hunts could survive without the annual financial boost of the Point-to-Point. They're almost as important as the 'points' that hounds make — the distance between find and kill, measured as the crow flies, is called a point.

9 August

Very very hot still. All family tanned after Italy but actually just as hot here by all accounts. Where did all the time go? We'll be cubbing soon, and don't I know it. Went on hound exercise this morning to 'cast an eye' as Brian puts it. Early-ish at the Kennels turned out to be 6 a.m. Very good for the soul and very different from Italy. Rode Orbit, who's supposed to have been in for a fortnight but still grass-fat and idle. Very hard work, kicking and squeezing till I had no more squeeze left, which the cunning old devil soon worked out. O.K. for the first hour but then I was an ambulance job. Wonderful to be out, though. No traffic till we were getting back to the village, then one really snotty lorry driver who thought we were holding up commercial enterprise and started trying to nudge us down the road. Brian waited until he'd got room to put the pack into Fairbrothers' entrance and then took his hat off to the driver with a loud 'thank you very much'. Puppies looking quite good, except for Trumpeter (walked by the Thornes) who may have to go. Over shy, but we'll see. Early days yet. Stubble everywhere and not much more corn to come in. Brian (check) says hounds need till the end of next week before cubbing. Might try for 22nd. Must get out again at least once before then — ancient muscles stiffening already. Sweating when we got back and had to slide gently on to the mounting block in case I just fell off. Cubbing already. Only seems a couple of months since the closing Meet. Old age creeping up.

Smoke Signals

There is a widespread belief that the ability to read smoke signals is a dying skill possessed today only by a few frail and elderly Red Indians. This is not strictly true. Mohicans in the United States may be getting a bit rusty, but fox-hunters in Britain can read smoke signals as easily as they can read their electricity bills.

When great smudges of smoke rise high to obscure the sunshine in pale blue July skies, fox-hunters get the message — another hunting season is about to begin. The grey-black clouds sail up from burning fields of crop stubble, and although this smoke is not intended as a deliberate message, it is certainly read — and welcomed — as a signal that the harvest is coming in. And when the harvest is in, horses and hounds can get on to the land again. There may even be one of those old rhyming rustic maxims — 'harvest in: hunting begin'. And there may not, but that's the truth of it.

Horses and hounds cannot go crashing through standing crops, but once the combine harvesters — massive machines half as big as council-houses and nearly twice as expensive — have rattled, rumbled, reaped and threshed through the fields, the way is clear. The waste they leave is set alight as the easiest and cheapest way of clearing the field ready for ploughing again.

The dry stubble burns fiercely, roaring, scorching and crackling across the smooth acres to mark the great peak and pivot of the rural year — the harvest.

As any old countryman will tell you, harvest time isn't what it used to be. Not so very long ago, to burn stubble would have been thought heresy. It was ploughed in and harrowed and the earth then often left fallow for a year. Wheat was stacked in sheaves, to be carted away by patient horses. There was beer and bread and cheese in the shade of hedgerows, where rabbits scurried and apple-cheeked maids might be wooed by gaitered lads. There were harvest homes — festive farmhouse suppers with good food, more beer, and any number of verses of earthy songs like 'The Threshing Machine', and 'A Farmer's Boy' . . .

'Oh, I'll plough and sow and reap and mow, to be a farmer's boy . . .'

Today, hardly anybody knows the choruses, let alone the verses. And, what with intensive syndicate farming, mechanisation, winter barley, plastic fertiliser bags, cereal subsidies and VAT, a good crop is as likely to be recorded at a board meeting as celebrated at a harvest festival service.

Yet, for all the changes (and all the complaints from environmentalists about the nuisance of stubble smoke) the significance of harvest time remains. The crops still depend on the weather, and gathering them still involves a lot of anxious hard work — and will go on doing so even when combines take in wheat at one end and spill out ready-wrapped sliced bread at the other.

A good harvest safely brought in still brings a tangible feeling of relief and satisfaction to the countryside. That's something that has never changed and is never likely to.

Equally unchanging is the tremor of anticipation that harvesting brings to fox-hunters. They've read the smoke signals. Soon, as August advances, they'll be out — cub-hunting.

Since the whole of agricultural Britain is not one vast cornfield (yet, some pessimists might add), the start of cub-hunting is not governed everywhere solely by harvesting. There are many accessible crop-free areas harbouring foxes a-plenty, but fox-hunters observe a voluntary close season until at least into August.

This is not to say that all foxes enjoy carefree, undisturbed summer holidays in which to rear their families. Because they are regarded as vermin, foxes are always in danger from man and, with their well-known taste for birds, 'man' usually means gamekeepers. Game birds are protected outside the shooting season, which lasts from autumn to early winter, but are always liable to figure on a fox's menu.

To ensure that satisfactory bags are available for expensive guns, gamekeepers keep a very sharp eye out all the year round. Any day they can kill a dog fox is a good day; any day they can kill a vixen is better; and, if they should be lucky enough to destroy a vixen together with her litter of cubs, that's worth an extra pint down at the local that night.

It sounds brutal, and it often is, but the keeper has to protect his master's interests, and his own. That birds so protected are reared and preserved simply to be blasted out of the sky is a paradox that may well puzzle many (the birds themselves, perhaps, as well as the non-shooting public).

The word 'cub' is emotive, just like 'kitten' or 'puppy'. The young of any species are vulnerable, often appealingly pretty, and tend to arouse our protective instincts. Fox cubs, when very young, can be delightfully engaging. They look like puppies and play like kittens. By August or September, though, they are usually so well developed as to be virtually indistinguishable from adult foxes. They are independent and out hunting for themselves.

Nevertheless, cub-hunting means killing young foxes, and that makes it a particularly repellent and propaganda-worthy aspect of the sport to its opponents, and distasteful even to some of its followers. For the many, however, who believe hunting with hounds to be the best method of controlling the fox population, 'cubbing', as it is often called, is vital. Primarily, it teaches young hounds their job, destroys a lot of foxes, and breaks up what might otherwise develop into fox colonies, which would irritate those farmers who permit hunting on their land on the understanding that foxes are kept down. That's the basic country bargain that sustains the sport — 'You can gallop over my land *so long as you kill my foxes*.' There is a variant, carrying a second proviso — 'You can gallop over my land so long as you kill my foxes and *don't disturb my pheasants*.'

In some places the bargain is never struck, either because the land-owner is exclusively dedicated to shooting, or is quite simply opposed to hunting. There are those, of course, who won't tolerate strangers on their land for any reason, and although this obdurate attitude may bewilder many enthusiastic fox-hunters, they are careful to respect it. Some of their hunting forebears were notoriously arrogant and rode where they pleased. Nowadays they watch their step, very conscious of upsetting anyone or provoking bad publicity.

It must not be supposed, though, that all is disagreement and doubt in the fox-hunting world. Shooting and hunting dwell in harmony for the most part. The horses tiptoe round the bits where they're not wanted and, as sure as the seasons change, cub-hunting begins when the harvest is in. It is part of the rhythm of the countryside.

As the smoke signals spread, so do rumours about when cub-hunting is to begin. The rumours, inspired as they are by hope rather than by actual information, are invariably wrong. Nobody really knows until the last minute, not even the Master — and he's the one who finally decides. The decision depends on progress with the harvest, which is dictated by the weather, and even Masters of Fox-hounds, as close as they are to heaven, have little control in that area.

When the date is arrived at, it is after consultation with farmers, and sometimes gives those concerned as little as 48 hours' warning. Actually, very few are directly concerned. All the rumours flying about are naturally of interest to the fox-hunting fraternity, but certainly don't affect all of them because those who are to go cub-hunting do so only at the Master's invitation.

Almost invariably, these are the dedicated, privileged inner circle of a Hunt, people who have hunted for years and are known and trusted followers. Some of them will have walked puppies, ridden out on hound exercise and will even be able to 'name' hounds, or a fair few of them, at any rate. To name hounds means the ability to recognise individual animals and, obviously, know their names. There are few greater crimes than to address a hound by another's name. It confuses the animals and is likely to induce cardiac arrest among the Hunt servants.

The first morning of cub-hunting is a joy to the real enthusiasts, who practically live for hunting. Their interest is in the hounds and how well they work together, and what really gives them a thrill of apprehension is how quickly the new entry will learn their job and settle to it.

The new entry are young hounds that, after being

'walked' by individual supporters and then having spent perhaps six months in the Hunt kennels, learning the discipline of belonging to a pack, are now to be taken hunting for the first time. They are usually about 18 months old by now, but all future references to them — in Hunt hound lists, at shows and in the Foxhound Kennel Stud Book, for example — will bear not their year of birth, but their year of entry. Hounds are referred to as Blackberry '74, Fearless '73, Playfair '83 and so on, to indicate the year in which they began their working lives. So, for several reasons, the first day's cub-hunting is an important one. The youngsters will have been taught to stay up with the pack during weeks of roadwork, but quite how they will behave when they start earning their keep is another matter altogether.

The new recruits may number anywhere between two couple and 20 couple, depending on each Hunt's requirements. An average might be 10 couple, and with that number most Huntsmen would probably choose to enter them in two or three lots, filtering them into the pack as it were, rather than risk putting them all in on the first day.

Whatever his decision, it is certain that the older hounds will sense what's going on. They are taken out on exercise every day throughout the summer, but when they are going hunting again, they know, and let the neighbours know, as well. There is such a noise from the kennels on the first morning of cub-hunting that nobody living nearby would need to be told of the occasion. It may be that the hounds pick up the Hunt servants' feelings of anticipation and anxiety, the extra urgency and briskness about them.

Whatever the explanation, the hounds are noticeably more boisterous and vocal as they are loaded into the hound lorry. The sound they make gives great pleasure to keen followers — it's akin to church bells ringing-in the New Year — but perhaps rather less to non-hunters still a-bed. With an early harvest, the departure from the kennels may well be at four o'clock in the morning, a shade before most alarm-clocks are set to jangle.

The aim is not, as some might suppose, to surprise the foxes before they're properly awake, in the manner of police making dawn raids on criminals' lairs, but to get hounds out before the sun climbs high and hot enough to reduce scent. For this reason, there are packs that go cub-hunting in the cool of evenings.

The fundamental difference between cubbing and formal fox-hunting is that, in cubbing, foxes are 'held up' (prevented from leaving) and killed in covert, while in hunting proper the aim is to push a single fox out into open rideable country and pursue it. So the first might be described as work (training hounds and culling foxes) and the second as play (hunting for sport), although the two often overlap and blur such simple distinctions. In moorland areas 'holding up' is rare because of the lack of coverts, and in thickly wooded territory foxes frequently break out of well-guarded coverts and make a run for it.

Cub-hunting, particularly on the first morning, is a private affair, quite unlike the colourful and crowded Meets of the season proper. There might be only two or three dozen people present — the Master, the Huntsman and Whippers-in, with perhaps 15 people on horseback and another 15 on foot.

The foot-followers wear whatever clothes they think suitable for the weather, but those on horseback are smartly and correctly clad. The two or three Hunt servants are in red coats, the Master and the remainder in rat-catcher tweed or cavalry twill coats with bowler hats or riding caps. And stocks or shirts and ties. It may well be summertime, but fox-hunters are not expected to slop about in open-neck shirts.

Hunting has started. They know it. They're glad of it. And they're properly dressed for it.

Mr. and Mrs. Palmer down this morning from Sheffield to take their daughter home after her fall, thus concluding a career as a Hunt groom that lasted exactly two weeks. I felt really dreadful. Her leg will mend all right, but she's such a tiny little thing and hasn't got the hang of using crutches. I was praying that she didn't fall over in the yard and break the other leg as well. She kept saying, 'Sorry, sir,' which made me feel even worse. The parents very pleasant and quiet, but obviously very concerned, and no suggestion of a complaint. In their place I'd be talking to my solicitor by now. We employed her and she was injured while carrying out her duties — cut-and-dried. Perhaps they'll get round to it when they've got over the shock. Our insurance is OK, but the sad truth is that she hadn't had enough riding experience and a big Hunt horse was too much for her. She'd have been all right in a couple of weeks. I'm getting on Diana's nerves talking about it, but I feel to blame. Working pupil at a riding school up north but never been in a hunting yard before. Brian interviewed her and said she'd improve and I thought no more about it. OK on hound exercise and then, bang. What a way to start a job. She wants to come back when she's better! I said we'd have to see. No. 1 task now — find somebody else. We'll be cubbing three days a week before we can turn round. Poor child, never even saw a Meet.

Learning to Ride

In fox-hunting circles, the ability to ride a horse is acquired early and pretty well taken for granted. The offspring of well-off country parents are popped atop their first ponies when frighteningly young. It's nappies off and jodhpurs on, almost before they've been put down for Eton.

Then follows a natural progression: riding in the hols; Pony Club gymkhanas; first children's Meet. Meanwhile, as ponies, boots and riding clothes are outgrown, they are replaced. In no time at all comes the great day, almost as significant to a fox-hunting family as the adult initiation ritual in a primitive tribe, when the youngster moves 'out of ponies' and 'into horses'. Equestrian graduation has taken place. The fledgling is off. Or on, rather.

Of course, not all such lucky children take to riding and hunting, but many do, and theirs is a common route to the hunting field. Others, lacking this financially and geographically ideal background, may go to riding schools, or just mess about with friends' ponies. But, one way or another, it is a fair assumption that the majority of adults out hunting will have learned to ride as children, and forgotten that they ever needed to learn.

What, then, of the newcomers to hunting — the many who never bestrode a pony when they were young, and have absolutely no knowledge of horses, yet whose circumstances and inclinations lead them to contemplate riding to hounds? It is unlikely that anybody, especially any urban body, ever woke up suddenly one morning and decided that he would like to go fox-hunting. It is, after all, a remote and mysterious sport to those who have no connections with it. Curiosity about it may come through meeting fox-hunting friends, possibly after moving into the country. However the urge to hunt is induced, the certain fact is that there are a lot of men and women to be seen in the hunting field today who were not brought up with horses and had to face the problem — as *adults* — of learning to ride.

The obvious way of setting about this is to go to a riding school. There are plenty of these available nowadays — a new one seems to open every week — but it cannot be said that they are all of a good standard. With increased leisure and higher wages, many more people are taking up riding, and some of the establishments formed hastily to meet this growing demand, lack the desirable quality of horses and of instruction. The difficulty here is that the complete beginner has no way of knowing whether a place is properly run, or is just a scruffy kind of circus with a few under-fed, over-worked, nappy old nags, inadequately supervised by three teenage hooligans whose only qualification is that they possess a pair of rubber riding boots (possibly between them).

By and large, if the place looks well-kept, has an indoor school, is run by a rather severe-looking lady, is approved by the British Horse Society and seems expensive, it will be adequate. They are all expensive, anyway, as is practically everything to do with riding. An ordinary bucket will cost twice as much if it's called a horse bucket. Much the same applies to clothing. Put the word 'riding' in front of such simple pieces of attire as hats, coats, breeches, boots, gloves, macs, scarves, shirts, socks or underpants, and up goes the price. This, the beginner will soon learn.

Some of the expense can be avoided at first. It's as well, though, to get a decent pair of jodhpurs, to avoid the insides of knees becoming chafed to the consistency of cheap steak. And a hard hat is essential — good riding schools will insist on it. Jodhpurs rather than breeches, because with breeches you will need high boots, which are much more costly than jodhpur boots. The latter can always be worn as ordinary shoes, should the flame of equestrian endeavour flicker out. Give the discarded jodhpurs to Oxfam or a passing jockey, and grow geraniums in the hat. With a few holes drilled in it, it will serve very nicely as a hanging basket.

The most depressing aspect of an adult's first riding lesson is that it may make him unexpectedly aware of the approach of senility. However brilliantly adroit in other spheres, he will discover that in this one he is clumsy, inept and possibly ineducable. His sense of inferiority will deepen as he sees that, apart from his instructress, he is the only person in the school over twelve years old. Feeling conspicuously foolish in a ridiculous, uncomfortable hat and strangely shaped trousers, he may well wonder if he mightn't have been better advised to join a geriatric unit rather than an equestrian centre.

This is just unfamiliarity, of course. Similar emotions grip British grown-ups the first time they try to ski. The discovery that they cannot even stand up on those awful foreign planks, while five-year-old Austro-German-Italian kids shoot past them down the mountain at 60 miles an hour — perhaps even yodelling — is not nice.

Assuming that the establishment is well-run and the instructress firm but understanding, the client will find that he has quite enough space in the indoor school — he may even have it to himself — and anyway is in no danger of being trampled to death by the group of Mothercare jockeys carrying out advanced movements at the other end.

He will then meet his horse. This can be a nasty moment for the nervous. The animal will be quiet, obedient, and not too big for him. Nevertheless, it will be a horse. It really has to be. He may now discover something that had never occurred to him — that he is frightened of horses. He was unaware of this previously, because he has never been so close to one before. Its very proximity seems to hold menace. So does its eye.

'Right, Mr. Rider,' (of all the names to be born with — aren't there people called Learner?), 'let's see if these leathers are OK. Slip the stirrup under your armpit and hold your arm out straight like this.' (Is she mad?) Puzzled, he nevertheless does as he is told. The stirrup feels strangely cold, and heavier than it looks. He reaches out to touch the saddle, as instructed, doing so gently for fear of upsetting the horse. The instructress explains that this rule of thumb method is pretty reliable; for some reason, the distance from armpit to fingertips equals the appropriate length of the stirrup leathers.

'Now, let's get you into the saddle.' He is surprised to observe, watching her demonstration, that she starts off by facing the rear end of the horse, not at all like the cowboys he has seen in TV Westerns, who approach stirrups like bicycle pedals. She says this is because, if the horse should suddenly take off, its forward movement would tend to push the foot further into the stirrup and might assist the mounting process, while if she were facing forward, the movement would tend to dislodge the foot or, worse, drag the rider. (If the horse should suddenly take off? Drag the rider?) The pupil's nerves are not improving.

'Right, now, let's mount shall we? . . . reins in the left hand, so . . . that's it . . . left hand on the neck here . . . yes, grab hold of a bit of his mane if you like . . . foot in . . . that's the idea . . . face the back of the horse . . . try not to kick him in the ribs . . . good . . . good . . . now, clasp the cantle — yes, the back of the saddle — get a good grip . . . that's it . . . now, *push* up with the right foot . . . oh! Never mind. Keep hold and push again . . . no . . . that's it . . . straighten the left leg . . . good . . . now, swing the right leg over . . . that's the idea . . . now, move your right hand forward to make room for your leg and eeeeease down into the saddle. Good!'

It is far from good. He believes he has wrenched his right shoulder, and possibly his left as well. In his confused and awkward scramble, he has landed in the saddle with a heavy thud from which neither he nor the horse may recover. His thighs are spread farther apart than he would have thought humanly possible. He feels apprehensive about being so high up in the air. His legs are trembling, either through physical effort, or nerves. He is fairly sure it's nerves. He feels unhappy, uncomfortable, awkward, self-conscious and frightened, and wishes to God he'd never seen a cowboy film, let alone been stupid enough actually to get on a horse.

'How does that feel, then?'

'Fine.'

What else could he say, poor man? Anyway, he has learned one vital lesson. Horsemen don't cry.

The instructress says that in future lessons, they'll practice mounting and dismounting. But, first, she wants to get him used to being in the saddle. He can ignore the reins — the horse won't go anywhere — and concentrate on his seat. He now begins to learn that he is possibly the most clumsy and thick man in the school — the world, even. He also finds that he has a failing he had thought unique to his wife when he tried to teach her to drive — he has difficulty telling left from right. Until getting on this horse, he had always been confident of making that fundamental distinction.

The simple instructions come to him at bewildering pace — heels down, lower leg slightly back, knees in, toes forward, head up, don't hollow your back, sit up straight, elbows in, don't-look-down-at-the-floor-or-that's-where-you'll-end-up, hands resting lightly on the thighs for now . . .

She is a good, patient teacher. It is not her fault that the wheel of equestrian fortune has dealt her a congenital idiot.

'Don't worry — it won't all come at once. We'll soon split you up.' (We'll soon what?!) It could have been more happily put. She means regard the human body as having three sections, all capable of independent movement in the interests of creating and controlling impulsion. (Wow!) She is not sure those leathers are quite right for him.

'I think we'll come up a hole.' He has to push his thigh away from the saddle so that she can reach in to haul on the strap and put the tongue of the buckle in the next hole up, thus making the leather shorter. He feels a bit embarrassed and helpless, as though he were receiving slightly intimate attention from a hospital nurse. He tries to make the adjustment easier for her.

'No — never take your foot out of the stirrup.' It is not a reprimand. Simply good advice. But it increases his feeling of pathetic dependence. She takes hold of his knee and heel, to push them snug against the horse's side. The action is impersonal, but it aggravates his unease. Finally, she is satisfied that he is sitting as well as he is able at this stage.

'Now, we'll try walking on. Forget the reins for the moment. You can take hold of the pommel, if you like.' He hesitates, not being sure what the pommel is, so she takes his hands and places them on the front of the saddle. This makes him feel like a retarded child at his first lesson with a knife and fork. She presses the hands firmly. 'If you feel at all insecure, just pull yourself down into the saddle. Try pulling now.' He does so. 'There, see how safe that feels?' He does not, but he nods.

'Right — off we go. Just relax and sit comfortably. Don't try to do anything but sit.' Don't worry, miss, he won't. Gently she takes the horse's head and leads it forward, very slowly. Although the movement of the horse is very slight, it feels volcanic. Each slow step seems like a lurch which is likely to dislodge the useless, over-weight, sloppily-filled sack that for years he'd been convinced was an able body.

He grips the pommel with fear-given strength. He tries to hang on with his heels. His toes, were they the hands of a clock, would be showing about a quarter to three. His knees spread outwards. He is infected with a kind of terrified paralysis. Each time the horse moves a leg, Mr. Rider's equilibrium is placed in further doubt. He is convinced that soon he will topple from this terribly high position that he has so rashly allowed himself to occupy. He is not far wrong.

'Whoa, boy.' She stops the horse and contemplates the man.

'Now, we're not relaxing, are we?' No, we are not.

She rearranges his body.

'Right, now let's try again.' They set off on another mini-journey.

'Nice and relaxed . . . that's it . . . don't look down . . . press those heels down . . . that's the idea . . . squeeze with the knees . . . no, you're pointing your toes down . . . good . . . heels down . . . sit up straight . . . straighter . . . chin up . . . that's the style . . . relax . . . go floppy . . . try to go with the horse . . . relax . . . you're slouching . . . head up . . . that's better . . . toes forward . . .'

After fully four minutes, during which, miraculously, he has not slid slowly into the sand, he realises that the horse has completed a very small circle. They stop.

'There we are. You'll soon get the hang of it.'

He has just the glimmerings of the beginnings of the faintest feeling that he might just be going to start to experience a very slight sense of achievement. He wouldn't put it any stronger than that. But he's still in the saddle, dammit.

After a few more sedate circles, during which the horse has behaved with reassuring docility, Mr. Rider is feeling more like a rider and less like a stricken coward. He then learns that he is moving on to the next dimension.

'Now, we're going to take up the reins and I'll put you on the lunge.' (The lunge? Doesn't that sound a bit wild?) She shows him how to hold the reins. It is very simple, but because his incompetence has now reasserted itself his fumblings have all the frustrating flavour of a first attempt at learning to knit. Eventually, he manages to hold the reins more or less in the approved manner, and hopes that his doing so will not be taken by the horse as a signal to move.

He is not to know that he is sitting on the oldest animal in the establishment and that movement of any kind, except back to its loose-box for something to eat, is the last thing it has in mind. The horse may be bored, having to stand in the ring with its bit being rattled against its teeth, constant shifts of weight on its back and the occasional jab in the ribs by inexperienced feet, but it has become accustomed and indifferent to such proceedings. Riding schools do not place complete novices on Grand National hopes.

'Elbows hanging loosely to your sides . . . that's it . . . thumbs uppermost . . . pretend you're squeezing a sponge . . .' He is sufficently confused now to want to throw in the sponge, never mind squeeze it. But steel is beginning to enter his soul. A hint of determination. This, unhappily, evaporates as soon as the instructress clips on the lunge rein and pays it out as she steps further away from the horse. And further. He has seldom felt so alone. So high up in the air. So vulnerable.

And she has a long thin whip in her other hand.

(Blimey!) Perhaps the excellent British Horse Society should advise its examinees to explain to new students that the whip is seldom used for beating inattentive pupils and, indeed, only usually trailed behind the circling horse's legs to keep it up to its paces and out at the length of the lunge. Mr. Rider fears that the horse may be about to receive a crack across its backside that will send it galloping off into the next county. Before this night-mare vision sets him a-tremble again, there are instructions that distract.

'Now, don't worry about the horse. He won't do any-thing. Just feel the weight of the reins. Don't try to pull them or do any steering — I'll be doing that — and if you feel a bit insecure, get hold of the pommel. I don't mind if you let the reins go altogether. We just want to get you sitting right, for now. OK?'

He nods.

She makes a clucking noise with her tongue. 'Walk on, Satan.' (Satan?!)

'Satan! Walk on!'

Satan is gazing at the far wall, his poor old equine mind miles away.

'Squeeze him on, Mr. Rider.' (Eh?)

'Close both legs firmly.' He tries to obey, but finds he has very little strength. The enormous bulk of horse be-tween his knees makes squeezing exceedingly difficult.

'And again . . . that's the idea . . . give him a kick . . . WALK ON!'

The sudden loud, positively commanding voice, coupled with the faint taps in his ribs, remind Satan what he is supposed to be doing. He begins to walk. And Mr. Rider is on his back. By himself. Holding the reins. He is not particularly comfortable, nor confident, yet he is un-doubtedly sitting on the back of a moving horse. Which means, in a sense, that he could be said to be riding.

The instructress is encouraging. Says he's doing well.

'Now we'll change the rein.'

They go round in the opposite direction. Plod, plod, plod. Creak of saddle-leather. Muffled sound of horse's hooves in the sand. An occasional blowing of Satan's breath, which the pupil suspects may be a sign of rebellion but is, in reality, a kind of world-weary sigh. It may be a great and daring adventure to Mr. Rider, but Satan has done it once or twice before. The instructress wonders, after a while, if her student is up to trying to trot. She believes, personally, that this is more valuable at the start than trying to convey elementary aids. She also believes that pupils should be taught to sit to the trot from the outset, and learn rising to it later. In this belief, she is at odds with the principal of the school. So Mr. Rider will rise.

Exactly when to start a pupil trotting is a bit of a knife-edge decision. Leave it too late and the pupil may become bored, or feel that he is making no progress. Start too soon, and you may put him on his head and frighten him out of further lessons. As she ponders this, watching Mr. Rider the while, she glances at Satan. He has no opinion in the matter. Given the option of trotting, walking, or standing still, he would unhesitatingly plump for the latter. She makes up her mind.

'Right, Mr. Rider, I think you're ready for the trot now.'

With Satan contentedly immobile, she persuades her pupil to press down with his feet and raise his bottom slightly from the saddle. This strikes him as a highly precarious procedure which, in truth, it is for him.

Gradually, though, he absorbs the knowledge that detaching his rear in this fashion does not necessarily involve being precipitated into the sand. Up and down, up and down. He feels and looks ungainly but, as she explains, it will be much easier when the horse begins to move. It will also be much more uncomfortable, but there is no point in telling him something that he will rapidly find out for himself.

Experienced riders, who can get on any horse and immediately adjust to its gait, rise to the trot effortlessly and automatically. Some even do so gracefully. They forget that it is a skill that has to be acquired, and that the acquisition can be both painful and frightening.

Anybody is liable to be a little scared the first time they experience the power of a horse moving beneath them, and discover how easily they can be propelled forward and backward and jolted helplessly in the saddle. That the sensations thus induced can include pain is more readily understood by male pupils, whose anatomical arrangements are ill-suited to being bounced up and down with their legs apart. How will Mr. Rider fare when it comes, as they say, to the crunch? Not too badly, as it happens. When Satan actually starts to trot, the pupil finds the action so violent that he feels as though he has been rocketed, by mistake, into a Wild West rodeo. In fact Satan's version of the trot is only a slow, reluctant, lumbering movement that wouldn't topple even a bag of potatoes if it were reasonably well tied on.

Mr. Rider clings to the pommel like a shipwrecked mariner in a heavy sea. His body rises and falls. The saddle goes up and down. Body and saddle do not coincide. For some unaccountable and singularly uncomfortable reason, the saddle always seems to be going up just as he's coming down; these collisions send him upwards, only for him to come down again for the painful thud to be repeated. He leans on the pommel to cushion the blows.

It won't do. The instructress halts the torture before he ends up round the horse's neck, and patiently explains what Mr. Rider is doing wrong. Everything, actually. But gradually his body and his mind soak up the beginnings of the basics.

They try again and, miraculously, he finds that there is the odd occasion when body and saddle are both going in the same direction at the same time. His teeth are rattled less frequently.

'Sit, rise; sit, rise; sit, rise . . . don't push with your feet . . . let the saddle throw you up . . . sit, sit, sit, sit . . . that's it . . . well done . . . sit, sit, sit . . . good!' Mr. Rider's pleasure at hearing that he has actually done something right astonishes him. He glows. Having been put into unfamiliar circumstances that have made him feel childishly inept, this fragment of praise has almost restored him to adulthood.

They go round on the other rein. He certainly doesn't manage to synchronize his and Satan's every movement, but he is starting to grasp the principle of rising to the trot. He is pleased. Much less frightened. Gaining a tiny bit of confidence. It is a good first lesson. He is actually sorry when it's over.

'Free your feet from the stirrups. That's it. Now let your legs hang loosely at the horse's sides. We'll do some dismounting in the next lesson, but you might as well do it properly. Place your hands on the pommel and swing your right leg back over the back of the horse.' It is a simple enough instruction, but it requires more gymnastic ability than he would have thought or, as it turns out, he now possesses. His efforts to stay on the horse, squeezing at the huge, wide, unyielding bulk between his knees, have so strained his calf and inner thigh muscles that he cannot swing his right leg back. In a less than smooth manner, he manages to descend to the sand.

'You've done very well, Mr. Rider. Don't worry if you feel a bit stiff. We'll soon have you in shape.'

After the lesson, he drives to a pub. He had intended to change into ordinary clothes, feeling a bit daft in jodhpurs. But now he is a slightly different person.

As he enters the bar, his walk is very close to a swagger. He is proud to be in riding kit. It no longer seems like inappropriate fancy dress, but the costume of bravery. Nobody is to know that he's just had his first riding lesson. For all they can tell, he might just be having a drink after spending the morning exercising racehorses.

The slightly stiff feeling as he sits on the bar stool enhances his sense of well-being, of achievement. Of having ventured and overcome.

'Pint of lager, please.'

He takes his first, deep sip, puts down the glass, wipes his mouth with the back of his hand, and sighs happily.

'Yes,' he mutters to himself, 'I might try hunting one of these days.'

Must record something about cub-hunting, although there's precious little to report. Best thing is that the groom problem is over. Jean is back with us. It's all off with her boyfriend in Canada and she just walked into the yard for a chat! Just moved back into her old room and that's that. A thousand times better than the little Sheffield girl. Came out with us this morning. She could easily whip in to Brian. Last couple entered this morning, Rupert and Rumbelow. Only fair, Brian says, but far too early to say. Likewise Trumpeter. A babbler, I fear but, again, it's early days. So that's 8½ couple, and we'll see how they're beginning to shape come October 1. Endlessly dry for nearly a fortnight and scenting worse than poor. Lucky to have managed 2½ brace so far, but there's rain about. Fawcetts on Tuesday, starting in that great dip where Brian had his famous fall. Must hold foxes. Ronnie says they've got the corn in on the railway side so it should be easy to hold up, so long as we have a few bodies. There are rumbles about reviving the Hunt Ball, after two seasons. About time, too, but not in the Guildhall. There's also talk of a 'Hunt Dance' at the Royal, as something to attract the younger element. Neither Diana nor I interested. 'Ball or nothing at all.'! Might even go mad and try the big Horse and Hound *do in London.*

Aye-Aye-Aye

It is half-past six on a morning in early September. It is going to be another hot day. Farmers have been lucky. Not a drop of rain during harvest. Now they'd like to see some. And fox-hunters are practically praying for it.

A dozen of them are sitting on their horses beside a high open-sided shed that shelters a combine harvester and three tractors. This is the unusually well-kept farmyard of a man who both shoots and hunts and can practically guarantee that there'll be foxes on his land. Standing about quietly are about a dozen foot-followers. Nobody, in fact, has very much to say so early in the morning.

They are gathered to participate in the least-publicised and most controversial side of their sport — cub-hunting. This is only the third time they've been out so far this season, and they have not been conspicuously fortunate. A total blank the first time; one old fox killed the second. This isn't the idea at all. The old hounds need to be in blood again; the new must be blooded. It's the same in many parts of Britain. No rain. Dry land. No scent.

Maybe things will pick up this morning.

Horses, riders and foot people wait a few moments while the Huntsman and his Whippers-in get their horses out of the lorry and mount up. Then, a nod from the Master, and hounds are released. If the Hunt servants did not know their job, chaos would be immediate. The old hounds are excited, and the young ones have little idea what's going on; they pour down the ramp of the lorry like an invading army charging out of an assault craft without any clear idea of what they're supposed to assault. They've hit the beach, but now what?

The red coats cope; new names are firmly spoken as whips dangle over eager young noses. 'Dumbbell! Dumbbell!!' Rebuked, the hound scampers back to the group safety of the pack. 'Lifebelt!' Once is enough for Lifebelt, and order is quickly imposed.

There are 21½ couple in the pack, two couple of which have never been hunting before. As it happens, there are other neophyte youngsters present, in the shape of what might be called 2½ couple of young girls. They are privileged children, in several senses; nieces of one of the Joint-Masters, and daughters of the host farmer. They each possess ponies and are still on summer holiday from their expensive boarding schools. Born into the hunting set, they will never have to aspire to enter it. They are aged between 11 and 13.

Coming from horsey families, they are all capable riders

and are neatly and correctly dressed. Three of them have
never been allowed to go cub-hunting before and, aware
of the significance of the occasion, are naturally excited,
but managing to conceal the fact. They have been told
exactly what to do and how to behave, but already the
instructions are being reinforced.

'Sarah, you must say good morning to the Master —
have you said good morning to the Master?'

'Yes, daddy.' She has, too, although somewhat uncertainly, because suddenly to be saying 'Good morning,
Master' to someone you've been calling 'Uncle Peter' for
years seems a little strange. But Sarah will soon get used
to the conventions of the hunting field and, in time, pass
them on to her own children. There is a strong sense of
tradition among fox-hunters.

In cubbing, there is no ritual of assembly, stirrup-cup
and chatter, as at Meets in the season proper. Dispositions
are quickly made and the hounds move out of the yard,
over a lane and begin crossing a field of stubble.

The horses' hooves raise puffs of dust as they strike
hard dry ground. They and the foot-followers' shoes
make a crisp swishing sound as they pass through the
stubble. There is very little else to break the silence of
the bright early morning . . . a distant wood-pigeon
mutters; a foot-follower clears his throat; a snaffle bit
chinks against a horse's teeth . . .

The advance across the stubble seems fairly casual.
Hounds and Hunt staff are some way ahead; the horses
follow in three separate groups, mostly walking, with one
or two trying impatiently to trot; the foot-followers are
scattered. There is little appearance of organisation or
intent, except that they are all moving in the same direction. There has not been, as yet, a single sound from the
Huntsman's horn. A stranger might get the impression
that this was some kind of very early morning ramble.

If he were close to the Huntsman, though, he would
sense the urgency of the proceedings. A Huntsman has
always to be positive and decisive, and, with 43 keen
animals in his charge on an early day of cubbing, these

qualities are imperative. A bit of luck wouldn't hurt, either. The older hounds' noses are already close to the ground, questing eagerly, but with the earth so dry, scent is not likely, and the Huntsman is doubtful if they'll get the quick find he'd pray for if he were a religious man.

The young hounds are just bounding about, enjoying themselves and sniffing out of instinctive curiosity, but with no real purpose.

Where the stubble ends, at the far edge of the field, there is a fence — upright posts linked by three taut strands of barbed wire. Beyond the fence is a wood that harbours foxes. The Huntsman knows this because this is a covert that has contained foxes pretty consistently for something like 60 years — since before his time. There are old breeding earths in it that have been used so regularly that it's a wonder they haven't got electric light.

A Landrover has already been driven round to the far side of the wood, half a mile away. In the vehicle are the terrier-man, the terrier-man's wife, and the Huntsman's married daughter. They can be trusted to spread out to guard the corner of the wood, where it narrows and peters out on a hillside. The covert is shaped like a triangle, with the base to the Huntsman's front as he approaches a gate in the fence. The gate is old, broken and open, leaving enough of a gap for a horse to get through to a broad but overgrown track that divides the copse into equal halves.

The Huntsman intends to draw the right-hand half first, moving right-handed. With each side of the triangle about half a mile long, it should be possible to ensure that no fox gets out. That's what the followers — foot and mounted — are there to do.

As the Huntsman takes his hounds through the gate, the first Whipper-in rides forward up the track; the second trots round towards the far right-hand side of the wood. Some of the foot-followers have already moved in that direction, and the riders split up into two parties to line the sides of the triangle as best they can. There aren't enough to really seal off the area.

'Don't bunch up, please, people,' says the Master, and

soon the field is set. Very few words have been spoken. Now, there is a great silence. This part of the countryside is so remote and it is still so early in the morning that even the normally inescapable hum of distant traffic is absent. For fox-hunters, perfection, except for the poor scenting conditions.

Every member of the field is in his own little patch of isolation now, in the saddle or on foot. Waiting. Listening. Watching. Some, if the truth were known, are apprehensive. Particularly the young ones. The fact is that if you're sitting on a pony and are responsible for 'holding up' the 300 yards of thick wood in front of you, and there's nobody else in sight, you may begin to wonder what on earth you'd do if a fox suddenly leapt out of the trees. This bewilderment tends to become more pronounced after you've been waiting for 15 minutes. It gets worse after 30 minutes, and it is not unusual to be left far longer than that. In cub-hunting, for much of the time, absolutely nothing happens. Or happens anywhere perceptible to you . . .

Was that the Huntsman's horn? It was such a tiny, muffled toot that it's difficult to be certain. Actually, it *was* the horn, but the Huntsman is deep in the woods and is well-known for working quietly with his hounds. If anybody were short of a trumpeter for a fanfare at the Albert Hall, he'd be the last they'd send for. He has urged his hounds into the trees with one quick attention-getting call, and his voice. 'Leu, leu, leu . . . in-in-in-in . . . Eleuin, then . . . try-y-y-y.' Huntsmen have a traditional vocabulary in which the actual words are distorted by their own accents and manner, but which seem well understood by their hounds. It's as much the *tone* of voice that conveys the instruction. With the hounds among the trees now, the Huntsman sits on his horse and listens carefully. All he can hear for the moment is the brushing and crackling sound of hounds pushing about among bushes. One makes a noise somewhere between a yelp and a squeak, but it is meaningless, probably a young hound pricked by a bramble. The Huntsman wants to hear one really reliable old hound speak with certainty, and then the others echo the cry. With every silent minute that passes, his anxiety increases a slight notch. But years of experience have taught him patience. There are foxes somewhere in the woods. Sooner or later, his hounds will find. It's just that he'd prefer it to be sooner. The young ones must not get the idea that all they have to do is frolic in the undergrowth.

A hound lopes out of the trees, approaches the Huntsman's horse and looks up enquiringly. The Huntsman gestures with his hand. 'Yerrrt, little bitch . . .' The hound reassured, executes a U-turn and disappears. Two more emerge. 'Eleu-in . . . eu, eu, eu . . .' They do the same. Clearly they're at a loss so far. The Huntsman squeezes his horse on a few steps, stops and continues listening.

At the far edge of the woods, a 12-year-old girl on a grey pony is also listening, but with far less confidence and reason. Despite many school holidays spent with her uncle in the country, she cannot recall ever having actually seen a live fox. She's seen pictures of them, of course. And her uncle has two foxes' heads mounted on wooden plaques in his library, and bewildered her long ago by calling them masks (she wondered why or how anybody could wear them). And her mother once had a fox fur with a tortoiseshell lower jaw as a sprung clasp. You could press this to open the fox's mouth so that it bit its own tail, thus securing the fur like a scarf. She'd enjoyed playing with this when she was younger. With its jaws pressed open the fox looked realistically fierce. But the fur was undeniably dead, and lined with silk to prove it.

There now seems every possibility that the next fox she sees will be alive. And fierce? Nobody has bothered to tell her. Already lonely, with no other human in sight, she begins to experience unease.

The sound of a horse approaching from her right. She is relieved to see that it's her uncle, trotting smartly on his big handsome chestnut. 'All right, my dear?' He is clearly not going to stop, being on one of the mysteriously urgent missions that sometimes engage Masters of Hounds.

'What do I have to do, uncle?' (Oh dear — shouldn't she have said 'Master'?)

The Master is brisk: 'Make a noise, dear, make a noise. Just say aye-aye-aye. Frighten him back — don't let him get past you . . .' And he's gone. The girl is not reassured by these instructions, feeling that she's likely to be more frightened than the fox. Don't let it past you? How on earth could you stop it? She wishes fervently that she had somebody with her. And what was that about saying, 'aye-aye-aye'? Well, that was an important piece of information about fox-hunting practice.

'Aye', of course, is very old English for 'yes'. Since the 16th century, English sailors have been saying 'aye-aye, sir' in response to orders. At political meetings, those in favour of a motion are still sometimes asked to say 'aye', leading to the ayes, on occasion, having it. In a quite different and far more colloquial context, though for possibly many years, Englishmen have been murmuring 'aye-aye' to each other to indicate lascivious optimism. In these circumstances, the words are frequently accompanied by a nudge, a wink, and a leer in the direction of a desirable and possibly available woman. It should go without saying that this last use is unthinkable in the fox-hunting field, where 'aye-aye-aye' is uttered, muttered or stuttered outside coverts to indicate to foxes that they should stay inside until they're clobbered by hounds. Probably nobody could explain this esoteric custom. It may be simply that it's easier to say 'aye-aye-aye' than, for example, 'oo-oo-oo' or 'ee-ee-ee'. Anyway, 'aye-aye-aye' it is, and it's usually delivered in a gruff, barking manner to signify threat or warning. Really, though, as the Master said, it's just making a noise.

Many fox-hunters reinforce their vocal efforts by slapping their riding boots with their whips, to make a bit more racket, but since foxes have excellent hearing, this is probably not necessary. A fox would hear 'aye-aye-aye' if you whispered it. Nevertheless, the greater the volume of noise, the more convincing the barrier. It is certainly true that a line of riders strung alongside a covert striking their boots and chanting the magical no-password is usually enough to persuade a fox that that's not a good direction to take. In this way the animal is said to be 'held up'. Even when sitting alone and clearly unwitnessed by other members of the field, the really dedicated fox-hunter may occasionally contribute a few quiet solo 'aye-aye-ayes' and whip-slaps, if only to keep himself and his horse awake.

The girl on the grey pony is in no danger of falling asleep. She's far too nervous for that. Stopping foxes from getting past her seems a grave and impossible responsibility. Apprehensively, she scans the edge of the thick woods in front of her, but nothing stirs. The cup of tea she drank before leaving home makes a tiny gurgle somewhere inside her. Other than that, she hears nothing.

Not so very far away, but out of sight, other riders are similarly situated in silence. As are foot-followers. And the Huntsman. All waiting. Only the hounds are busy, but so far they are scattered, each still seeking in individual perplexity until scent unites them in common purpose.

From the outside of such a thick covert, there is almost nothing to be seen. An occasional glimpse of a pale, questing shape amid the trees; perhaps a brief sight of a hound emerging into the open, skirting the wood and then diving back into it. To an outsider, there would seem little of interest in the proceedings, but to a fox-hunter these are moments of fascinated anticipation. Hounds are working. Soon, they will speak. Listen! Listen. And watch . . .

Standing by a hedge, still thickly summer-green, is a grey-haired woman with two terriers close to her feet. For the present they are quietly obedient at the twin ends of their double lead, but, like most terriers, set to quiver. The woman is a widow who regularly rode to hounds before her husband left her with a mortgage-load of grief and an inadequate pension. For nearly twenty years now she has followed hounds on foot, and seems content so to do. She seldom misses a Meet and rarely talks to anyone. Like many foot-followers, she tramps and gazes alone, knows the country well and has an uncanny instinct for being where the action is. The Huntsman always raises his cap to her at Meets. This morning she has chosen to place herself on the right-hand side of the wood, so that hounds will draw in her direction. She can see the wood, the gateway leading to the Huntsman's track, and three sentinel riders. This is her pleasure, to be the well-placed, anticipatory spectator.

High in the pale blue sky, twin white vapour trails are being forged by a jet aircraft so far away that she can neither see the machine nor hear it. She notices the thin white lines, steadily lengthening, but they do not engage her attention. There are ripe blackberries in the hedge beside her and she is just pondering whether they can be reached without touching nettles when she hears the cry of a hidden hound, followed quickly by two or three more. The dog-lead in her hand tautens and twitches like a fishing line at a bite. The terriers tremble eagerly, even though they know they will not be unleashed.

The hound cries are augmented by others, but still lack conviction. A horse fidgets and shakes its head. The rider shortens his reins slightly and applies a fraction of knee pressure. Two couple of hounds run out of the gateway, skirt the wood to the right and find a gap to re-enter. They are eager, but not excited, as their sterns disappear into the trees.

The Huntsman's horse is standing riderless on the track now, its bridle held by the first Whipper-in, who is still mounted. The Huntsman is on his feet in undergrowth too thick to ride through, urging his hounds on. He blows a series of short, sharp notes on his horn. 'Eleu-in, then . . . Eu, en, eu . . . try y-y-y-y . . .' The hounds are still uncertain. The Huntsman stands still and quiet, the better to listen.

Outside the covert, the terrier widow is listening just as keenly. She hears the horn again, followed by a few more hounds. Moments later she sees the senior Master come from the left at a canter and turn into the gateway. She loses sight of his red coat, but it reappears shortly afterwards as he trots back through the gateway. Quickly through it, he squeezes his horse to canter towards the three horsemen lining the edge of the wood. 'Make a noise, everybody, make a noise — aye-aye-aye-aye-aye!' The riders pick up the shout. The terrier widow tightens her grip on her dog-lead. The Master rides on, beyond the horsemen and out of view. 'Aye-aye-aye-aye . . .'

The Whipper-in is still holding the Huntsman's horse on the track and wishes he were not. The horse is known to 'go up' (rear) at times and this, with nobody on its back and a feeling of excitement growing, might be just such an occasion. He jiggles its bit to keep its attention. Nobody likes to be sitting on one horse while trying to control another.

He cannot see the Huntsman, who is far into the woods. Neither can the Huntsman see his hounds, which are even further into the woods. They sound to him to be divided into at least three groups, with odd ones crashing about God knows where. He wants to get up closer to them. He looks about through the trees and chin-high ferns, and steps carefully towards a silver birch tree 20 yards ahead, lifting his spurred shiny boots high to get above brambles. The thorns snag at his breeches and red coat. He is not particularly happy.

A good distance from this activity, and quite unaware that anything is happening at all, the girl on the grey pony is wondering how long she is expected to sit about seeing nothing, hearing nothing and hoping that she'll have to do nothing.

She begins to breath a puzzled sigh.

And then stops breathing altogether. A furry gingery shape has appeared from the woods and is moving towards her. It is an animal. An animal with a sharp snout, conspicuously big pointed ears and a long and thickly bushy tail which it carries straight out parallel with the ground. It is remarkably similar to the thing that mummy used to wear round her neck.

Oh, my goodness. It is, beyond any doubt, A FOX. Furthermore, if it maintains its present direction and smooth, low trot, it could soon reach her pony. The girl is stiffened with shock. Her mouth opens, but nobody will ever know if she was going to scream for help, whimper with fear, or shout a brave 'aya-aye-aye'. For absolutely no sound comes out of her pale young lips.

The fox has nothing to say, either. Because he hasn't seen her. For all the legends and beliefs about foxes possessing senses superior to other animals, they don't see all that well, especially during daylight. They hunt brilliantly at night by smell and by sound, and can detect a mouse at 100 feet and a man at a mile. But on a perfectly still morning, with not a breath of wind to carry scent or sound, they might almost bump into a horse or a human being before they knew it was there.

This is not to say that foxes find their pathetic way round the countryside with little white sticks. Superbly equipped in the sniffing and hearing department, they don't *need* good eyesight. Their horizon is very limited anyway by their height — few are much taller than 12 inches at the shoulder — so they wouldn't be able to see very far in a field of six-inch stubble. And even if they stood on a box they would be quite unable to distinguish a stationary object 100 yards away. Even at half that distance they wouldn't be too sure, unless the object moved. They're mustard on movement. They can also bring a suspicious object into sharper focus, but only for a few moments — long enough, perhaps, to establish that it is best avoided.

The girl, of course, is not aware that foxes are so terribly shortsighted. Nor does she know that they have no appetite for young girls; they are frightened of human beings. With good reason. This time, though, a fox is moving towards a frightened human. She watches the animal getting closer until it stops, no more than five yards away from her. It must have heard or sensed *something*.

The girl stares at the fox, seeing danger. The fox stares at the girl, seeing nothing but some kind of object or obstacle. The fox appears to be weighing up the situation and, in its own way, it is, with the help of its pricked ears and black wet nose. Within three seconds it is satisfied, and with only a slight change of direction, resumes its unhurried journey, passing no more than two yards away from the girl. She could have thrown a doughnut at it. If she'd had a doughnut. And if she'd been astonishingly quick.

But the fox has gone now, its brush flowing and its belly hairs shimming over the stubble, leaving behind not only scent, but turmoil. The girl's heart-beat is returning to normal, but her mind is stunned by a jumbled mixture of shock, relief and remorse. She, the niece of an MFH, has let a fox stroll past her without so much as a single 'aye'. What will she say to Uncle Peter? What should she have done? She has never, ever, felt so bewildered and distressed.

She looks about her and is relieved to find that she is still quite alone; at least, nobody has noticed her deeply shaming behaviour. Slightly reassured, she wonders if perhaps it may not be absolutely necessary to say anything about the incident. She begins to muster some proper fox-hunting resolve. To her pony's mild astonishment, she takes a firm tug at the reins. 'Stand up properly,' she orders, 'and for goodness sake keep your eyes open.'

Just in time. Here comes her sister, cantering in the wake of a severely smart-looking woman who calls out, 'Come along, dear — they're not drawing this way.' Marvellous! Action! She kicks her pony up to follow on, but he requires no such urging. He puts in a frolicsome buck and joins the chase. Actually, it isn't much of a chase, because they soon round a jutting portion of the wood, pass the Huntsman's track and encounter the previously quite voluble riders who now seem to have nothing to 'aye-aye-aye' about. The woman eases her horse back into a trot and halts by the second rider, an elegantly bowler-hatted gentleman who, as it happens, is both her husband and one of the Joint-Masters.

The two girls, uncertain what to do, stop as well. 'Ah, darling,' says the gentleman, 'could you go right round that corner' — indicating to the right with his whip — 'and hold up on the other side? You know, by the lane —

we don't want him getting across there.' He looks at the girls, who are strangers to him, then decides. 'You two go as well, will you?' And they do, feeling the importance of a mission and the joy of a canter.

Not much joy, though, for the Huntsman in the woods. With saplings, bushes, ferns and blackberry brambles, he's lost sight of his hounds and is having a tangle-struggle to get up to them. He can hear them moving, but the cries that had given him a touch of optimism a few minutes earlier seem now to have faded out. There is just the odd voice that carries neither conviction nor message. He presses forward, shielding his face from springing twigs, and reaches a clearer patch in the trees. He pauses, shedding the noise of his own progress, and listens. A hound comes from behind him.

'Lucifer! Get on in,' he orders, and the hound plunges ahead busily. As Lucifer disappears, there is a high cry from another hound, followed at once by two deeper ones. Even muffled as they are by distance and trees, there is a keen urgency to them, and to one in particular. The Huntsman shouts immediately 'Hark to Butterfly — hark-hark-hark to Butterfly . . .' The sound of hounds swells, fills. Then dies to disappointed and disappointing silence.

But there it is again! The short silence is pierced by a baying, yelping, multi-pitched, ragged rage of voices that crescendoes into a bellingly bloodthirsty chorus. Hounds are definitely speaking, and the Huntsman moves smartly to ascertain what about, this time with rather less care for his breeches, and calling urgently 'Tally-*O* . . . tally-*O* . . . tally-*O* . . . eu-eu-eu-eu . . . push 'im up, then . . .'

'Aye-aye-aye . . . aye-aye-aye-aye-aye . . .' Outside the wood the stationary riders open up as well, echoing the hounds in a duet of death. Timpani from whips on boots embellish the rural orchestration until, finally, the solo comes in — a long clear, triumphant note on the hunting horn, sounding The Kill.

The riders stop making a noise. One calls to another, 'That *was* The Kill, wasn't it?'

'I think so, yes.'

'You haven't got the time by any chance, have you?'

The wristwatch is consulted. 'Just coming up to quarter past seven.'

'Thanks awfully.' God, still hours to go before breakfast.

The hounds have had theirs now, in a manner of speaking. The fox hasn't been so much hunted as 'chopped', that is, quickly killed before it had a chance to get up and run. That's why the whole incident was virtually over by the time the field realised it had started.

Indeed, it was over when the Huntsman reached the scene. About 10 couple of hounds seemed to have been in at the kill and were squabbling, growling, snarling and tugging at the torn body of the fox. 'Damn!' declared the Huntsman, seeing that they were all old hounds. None of them resisted as he leaned into the struggling pack and pulled the limp, ragged corpse from the jaws that were pulling at it. He held it up by the neck and could see that it was a young fox, although it looked more like an empty old satchel that had been dragged behind a bus in a rainstorm. It was damp from the slavering of the hounds, and its ripped body between tail and head looked empty, apart from some dangling entrails. One of its eyes was out of its socket but, still attached, lay on its cheek. The Huntsman pulled out what was left of its guts, threw them to the hounds, and reached for the horn tucked under the top button of his coat.

Then he blew The Kill. Curious late hounds, including two couple of the new entry, lolloped up to join the pack. He began shaking the corpse over the hounds' heads and shouting 'Tally-O-tally-O-tally-O-tally-O . . .!' His voice revived the frenzy in the older hounds, and the young ones joined in. With them all reaching up to snap and snatch at the dead fox, he pushed his way through the old hounds to reach the young ones on the fringe of the pack, and shook the body at their muzzles. 'Tally-O-tally-O-tally-O-tally-O! . . .'

After a few seconds of this, he tossed the dead quarry upwards and it disappeared as hounds, young and old, fell upon it. As further encouragement and reinforcement, he blew a succession of short notes on the horn. 'Tally-O-tally-O-tally-O . . .!' But the hounds were soon bored with worrying something so soggily slack, and abandoned it. Most of them, though, had bloodstains on their muzzles. That was the important thing.

The Huntsman tucked his horn back into his coat, picked up what was left of the fox, and began making his way back to where he'd left his horse. Not a marvellous start to the day but better, as he always said, than a clump round the ear.

And there was plenty of the morning left.

Signs of the times. After deciding definitely last night that my best cap will have to do for another season, down to the Kennels, where I authorise brand new everything for Brian, plus breeches and new caps for the others. All to be ready for the Opening Meet. An interesting bill that's going to be when it comes in. Got them to lay out their stuff like a kit inspection before agreeing, and nearly drew the line at a new coat, but Brian's two coats are not really good enough — one is terribly faded (three seasons only) and the best one's been stitched up where the lining's coming away at the back flap (the supposedly waterproof bit where mine went soggy). All right for the Master to look like a scarecrow, but not the Huntsman! If we had the money I'd renew the lot for all three of them. Like to see them looking half decent. Brian says when his father went into Hunt service (God knows when that was) all the servants were automatically given new coat, new boots and two pairs of breeches every season — bespoke, and no messing. Those were the days. I suppose the subscription was about £25 and you could buy a made hunter for £200. AGM on Friday, when subs will have to go up. £300 basic, I reckon, and hope that the Members will be generous. There'll be much moaning at the bar, but I don't suppose anybody will actually die of shock. There's gold in them there hills.

Assumptions of Wealth

People who hunt are assumed to be rich. And many of them actually are. Others, though, simply look rich or would like to be thought rich. It could be gently suggested in passing that envy of this real or apparent wealth lies at the bottom of much of the opposition to hunting. In full fig, fox-hunters are splendid-looking fellows, and some of their ladies are a bit tasty, too. How dare they canter about the countryside in careless arrogance (and on weekdays, too a lot of them!) while the less privileged can only afford to take sporting risks at darts and football matches? Perhaps it does seem a bit unfair, but there are more iniquitous examples of inequity, and the distribution of wealth is a controversial topic better disputed in the political arena than the hunting field.

But do you *have* to be rich in order to hunt? Well, of course, it certainly helps, but it isn't vital. Thousands of people keep one horse and hunt it happily with a provincial pack every Saturday for £1,000 a season, which must compare reasonably well with the costs of shooting, sailing, golf and ski-ing. That a lucky few can pursue all these outdoor sports in grandeur in between playing polo, buying racehorses, and refreshing themselves with trips to the Bahamas is a matter best referred to the Communist Party.

To hunt, you need clothing, a horse, horse transport and subscription money, and there are big variations in the prices of all these. Take clothing. The man determined to go regally bespoke in utter elegance could easily spend £2,000 on basic essential attire in fashionable establishments catering for hunting clientele: top hat £200; coat £600; boots £700; breeches £250. Then there are items like a waistcoat, hunting tie, tie-pin, shirt, gloves, spurs, whip and flask (*never* go hunting without a little drop of something). It is very easy to spend a lot of money. However, with the possible exception of breeches, shirt, tie and gloves, all this apparel and equipment can last a lifetime and longer. Quite a few men are seen out hunting in their grandfathers' boots, coats and hats. Passings-on, handings-down, borrowings and lendings of clothing are quite common in hunting families. The results are not always smart, comfortable or safe, but they get the wearers where they want to be — behind hounds.

Good hunting attire, well cared for, can be kept serviceable for ages. If you look closely at some gleaming boots, you'll see the stitching marks of many a repair and cunning restoration. For those with limited funds who fail to inherit and cannot borrow, ready-made and second-hand kit is available at a fraction of the made-to-measure prices. The huge cost differences between off-the-peg and bespoke are not confined to hunting, of course. You can buy a perfectly good pair of shoes for £40 in any high street in about six minutes; go to the best bootmaker in London and have them hand-lasted and they'll cost £400 after you've waited six months. They're probably worth it, too, if you can afford that kind of money. Hunting boots certainly are, because they should fit at foot, ankle, calf and knee, giving 700 quid's worth of comfort and elegance and a bit more security in the saddle.

However, it is possible to buy a decent pair of leather boots for £100, a black coat for £175, stretch breeches for £35 and a riding cap (safer) or bowler (more traditional) for between £25 and £100. (What you wear on your head is a highly prickly matter already dealt with.) So it is feasible to look unobtrusively presentable in the hunting field for around the £400 mark, and this is money that will not have to be spent again.

Once clad in these fetching clothes — and they can do a lot for a man — there is no point in standing about on the ground wondering if the weather is going to improve. The garments are designed to be worn in the saddle, and the saddle will need to be on a horse. Sadly, horses are not cheap. And they eat a lot. Some of them also kick, buck, rear, bite and bolt, but all these services are free. It's the bed and board that costs the money. To keep a hunter at livery can cost between £25 and £50 a week, depending on the area, the standards of the stables, and the services provided. Riders who live in the country, have stabling, and can recruit cheap amateur local labour (wives and daughters often fall into this category), have big economic advantages over their urban brethren. But, however many corners are cut, keeping horses is a highly effective way of maintaining cash-flow — outwards. They need exercising, grooming, mucking out, shoe-ing and occasional vetting. Munching, though, is their most constant and costly activity, and the charges made by professional livery stables are a reasonably accurate reflection of the true costs of maintaining the beasts.

Horse clothing and tack are not inexpensive either. Saddles cost between £200 and £300 and you'd be hard-pushed to get hold of the other basic tack — stirrups, leathers, girths, bridles, bits, reins, numnahs, sweat nets, New Zealand rugs and so on — under another £300. Again, these are long-lasting items, and savings can be made in the second-hand sphere. Just occasionally someone will sell you a horse complete with tack.

Ah, yes — your horse. Well, this could cost you anywhere from £500 to £5,000, according to its age, size, breeding, state of schooling, temperament, appearance and other factors less easy to define, such as the delicate balance between the seller's honesty and avarice. It's probably safe to say, though, that with £1,000-£1,500 to spend you could become the owner of a good hunter. You'd probably find it through the small-ads in *Horse and Hound*, the horse world's weekly Bible, and if you bought it without independent advice, you'd be mad. Horse advertisements require as much careful interpretation as house advertisements. If you are a newcomer to equestrianism, beware of such descriptions as 'not a novice ride', 'gay but not lethal', 'strong ride', 'suit experienced rider', 'bold jumper', 'loves his hunting', 'needs capable rider' and similar, all of which contain warnings that you would probably be put on the floor or run away with in your first few minutes. More encouraging phrases are 'a perfect gentleman in every way', 'goes first or last', 'kind, sensible ride', 'bombproof', '100% in traffic', 'easy to box, shoe, clip and catch', 'does not hot up', 'hunted by mother and daughter'.

People who sell horses privately are rather nicer than those selling cars, and there is no reason to suppose that dealers are rogues. But do take a knowledgeable somebody with you when you go to look at a horse, and get them to trial ride it if you doubt your own capabilities. The sale, it goes without saying, should be subject to a vet's certificate, and some sellers will let you take the horse out hunting before you decide. And you can't say fairer than that.

A horse that behaves like a pool of tranquillity in a trial ride, or out hacking, may turn out to be a storm when you take it hunting. Horses get excited in the company of their kind, and hunters *know* when they're going hunting. Do not be tempted to buy a horse out of Hunt service. If a horse has carried a Whipper-in for a couple of seasons it will be used to being out in front on its own. Asked to stay back with the field, it may be bewildered, or even resentful. It is not amusing having your arms pulled out, and the line between elation and terror is a very thin one.

Gaining possession of your horse, and needing to take it home, will remind you, if you had overlooked the fact, that you'll need some kind of transport to move the animal about. Very few Meets are close enough to hack. A trailer for about £1,000 will do, although really smart multi-horseboxes can go up to £10,000 and considerably beyond.

Now, equipped with clothing and transport for self and horse, you may address yourself to the matter of following hounds, which will mean subscribing to the Hunt that you want to join. Subscriptions vary considerably, from as little as £50 per rider per season, to as much as £1,000 for a family hunting in a smart country. It is virtually impossible to strike a true average, but between £150 and £300 is fairly common. Hunts are essentially clubs, and, as with golf, sailing and social clubs, the more fashionable they are, the more they charge. Similarly, there are Hunts that are difficult to get into because they are over-subscribed and have waiting lists. In addition, they may not particularly want you; in this rare case, the right introduction may be useful. This is not to say that Hunts are bastions of snooty, exclusive privilege. Most are welcomingly democratic. It's simply that hunting is becoming increasingly popular, and there is a limit to the size of field a Hunt's country can accommodate. If a thousand riders turned out regularly, there wouldn't be a hedge or hollyhock left standing. Even a field of 200-plus — not unusual in the fashionable countries — is an awesome body requiring Field-Masters with iron resolve and qualities of leadership and command fit to make them Field-Marshals.

Recognising that not everybody is rich, many Hunts are prepared to make concessions over payments. In some, for example, it is possible to pay half a subscription for a limited number of days, and reduced rates for teenagers are quite common. Details of all the Hunts are published once a year in *Horse and Hound*. They give the names of the Masters, Huntsmen, Whippers-in and Secretaries; which days they hunt on, the phone numbers of the kennels and what the subscription is. Where, under 'subscription', they simply say 'apply to Hon. Sec.', they are not necessarily being cagey, but want to know your requirements. You might wish to hunt only one day a week, or two, or three days a fortnight. Or you might want to pay a family subscription. The permutations can be quite bewildering but are almost invariably accommodating. Most Hunts are eager to recruit new subscribers to help meet ever-rising costs, but they are fearful of unmanageably large fields. More detailed information about every Hunt is contained in *Baily's Hunting Directory*, right down to a description of each Hunt's terrain and the most suitable kind of horse for crossing it.

Some of the descriptions might deter the timid or the merely prudent — 'stone walls and big timber, needing forward-going, strong-galloping ready jumper' sounds a bit like the Grand National. But Hunt countries are as varied as Britain's countryside itself, and the advice is sound. *Baily's* also tells you what each Hunt's evening dress is, in case this should be bothering you. Unless you are a Member, and well-breeched, as they say, black tie will suffice for most Hunt Balls, which tend to become less grand every season. Nowadays they are more likely to be a hop in the town hall than an exclusive affair in a stately home.

Hunts charge visitors a 'cap' for a day's hunting. Again, this varies considerably within from £10 to £40, and is often only ascertainable by ringing the secretary. Heavilysubscribed Hunts only allow visitors by invitation and most will only put up with them for three or four days before asking them to become subscribers.

A visit to another country — a friend's, say — is always interesting. And, if you've just moved into a new area, a day as a visitor to the nearest Hunt will give you a good idea of what their people and hounds are like and whether you'd like to join them.

Whether a visitor or a subscriber, always have a few pounds in a handy pocket. At the Meet, most Hunts charge 'field' or 'riding' money for the day, to help pay for damage to fences and so on. This can be anything from £2 to £10 and, for subscribers, can sometimes be paid as a lump sum in advance. This makes life easier for the Secretaries, who require vigilance, agility and tenacity to make sure everybody pays. Gathering pound notes from people wearing gloves and sitting on restless horses in half a gale can be amusing for the spectator but trying for the collector. The Secretary is also the person to whom a visitor should pay the cap. He will often wear an armband bearing the legend 'cap'.

Capping visitors is a fairly recent practice. In long-ago days when autocratic rich country gentlemen maintained packs of hounds at their own expense and for their own amusement, allowing the field to follow for nothing, it was the Huntsman who capped the followers, at the kill. It was quite usual for them to dangle the dead body of the fox in the branches of a tree in the belief — possibly true — that it made hounds keener if they were only permitted to gaze and growl at the corpse for a while before being allowed to break it up. In fact, this delay also allowed time for the stragglers in the field to catch up and swell the contributions to the Huntsman's reward for the kill. This was what would be called today one of his 'perks'.

'Woo-ooop,' the Huntsman would cry, holding out his cap for golden sovereigns to chink into it. Today's Hunt secretaries are rather more restrained, but their zeal for capping is undiminished.

At the enviably intensive, grand, top end of hunting, the sport can be formidably expensive. Just having the *time* to hunt four days a week implies that you're not pushed to make a living. There are high-living, hard-riding individuals in crack countries who are able to keep half-a-dozen Thoroughbred hunters and change to their second horses — ridden gently by their grooms until required — half-way through the day. One set of costly clothing is insufficient for these privileged few, because it is quite impossible to hunt without getting frequently soaked and mud-spattered. And to such, one would suppose, it is fairly unthinkable to go to the Hunt Ball in anything but a chauffeur-driven car, having been assisted by a valet into the proper evening dress.

The stable back-up and transport for such riders is also a considerable item. If anyone were to ask these lofty beings how much it cost to hunt, the answer could well echo the millionaire's famous reply when he was asked how much it cost to run a yacht: 'If you need to ask, you can't afford it.'

But don't be put off. Many people who hunt regularly and happily can't afford a second car, let alone a second horse.

20 September

Quite a lot out this morning (six brave souls on foot). Absolutely poured down non-stop from start to finish. Never seen so many utterly bedraggled people so early in the morning. I'd have stayed in bed if I'd had the option. Terrible. Met at the Star, Brock Green, then round the back of the College (where the caretaker reckons there's a litter near his beehives). Stay clear of that little lot! Down the ride to Butler's. Very squelchy. Drew up the slope towards the big barn, and hounds were in covert for ever without so much as a murmur. Very strange. On to the Bottom and better luck, but the pack divided, a cub killed before the other half knew what was going on, pity. No way to escape the rain, bowler dripping like a gutter. Old Bert Tring made me laugh, said you're not properly wet till the rain gets through to your skin and then starts working its way out again. Didn't work its way out of me —everything soaked when I got back, right down to underpants. Utter misery and barely time to have a shower and get off to the solicitor's. Not a nice day, but at least not cold, which really gives me the downs. Brian's going to ring the College and ask about the beehives. Diana says they want me for a 'Brains Trust' in the community centre. I'll tell them about cub-hunting!

Early One Morning

Peter Lasham wished he were back warm in bed. Instead, he was alone in the kitchen of his country cottage, the only member of his household not asleep at half-past five in the morning, rubbing hard at his rubber riding boots in an attempt to give them a leather-like sheen. In an hour he was going fox-hunting for the first time in his life.

The prospect so worried him that he felt a loose, trembling sickness in his stomach, a sensation not improved by the quantity of alcohol he had drunk the night before.

It had been a shade too much and was the direct cause of his present predicament. The pints had come up rather fast, and gone down similarly. The saloon bar of the local had seemed a satisfying, jolly place to be. The companionship good. Real men. Warm men. Convivial men. Country men. Hunting men. Come with me in the morning, one of them had said — you can have my daughter's horse. And he had accepted.

Such expansive invitations are often extended in pubs, but are not always meant to be taken seriously. You must come and have dinner with us one night . . . come over for a swim . . . I'll take you out in the boat one of these Sundays . . . you should try a spot of fishing with us . . .

Thank-you-very-much-I'd-love-to . . . now, come on, this is my round . . .

The moment passes, and is forgotten before closing-time. But the invitation to hunt had focussed up to the specific. He was being lent a horse. And that made the matter definite. He was to be at his host's house not a minute later than 6.30 a.m. Six-thirty! He must have been mad.

Peter was not a countryman. He was a musician who worked mostly in London and retreated, as they say, to the country at weekends. He had had the cottage a couple of years and become a Friday night and Sunday lunch-time regular at the Fox and Hounds. He had also, feeling vaguely that he ought to acquire some rural accomplishment, and certainly that he should lose some weight, been taking riding lessons in London.

In the Fox and Hounds, he had not described them as riding lessons. Although not normally an untruthful man, he had found it easier to say, instead, that while in London during the week, he 'went riding' when he could. Which gave his humble equestrian activities a slightly enhanced, not to say misleading, flavour. In fact, they could not even be properly described as lessons. After only six sessions of rudimentary tuition in a class of eight, he had opted to go out in a park on 'instructional accompanied rides'. This meant that he and about a dozen other novices followed each other in single file on sleepy old hacks.

They were accompanied by a healthily attractive girl who, in this and other ways, paid the riding establishment for the lessons she was having herself. She was about 17, an age at which many girls will willingly muck-out horses for 23 hours a day for the joy of being on top one of them for the 24th. Riding at the head of her somewhat somnolent cavalcade, the amount of instruction she was able to impart to her charges was limited. At geographical points well-known to all the horses, the class would automatically trot; at other points, they would canter. The girl had learned, after one alarming experience, never to canter on the homeward-bound leg of the ride. The one occasion on which she had been rash enough to do so had demonstrated that some of the horses could be quite agile; the ensuing impromptu cavalry charge had also shown that very few of her pupils were ready to gallop.

Peter, although 35 and married with two children, always rode immediately behind her when he could, the better to silently lust after her. The manufacturers of girls' stretch riding breeches are responsible for a great deal of male frustration. Peter had now been on about a dozen of these trips, and was sufficiently enthusiastic to have bought breeches, boots and velvet riding cap. He had overcome his initial stiffness, could rise fairly confidently to the trot, and found cantering exhilarating. The girl knew his name, tried always to allocate him his favourite horse, and sometimes dropped back to give him little bits of advice. Heels down, hands down; that sort of thing. He always looked forward to his weekly hour in the park, felt pretty good up there in the saddle, and was under the impression that what he did while thus mounted was riding a horse. In this he was profoundly mistaken. On those happy Thursday afternoons he was no more than a passenger on horseback, the amount of influence he could bring to bear on the animal's pace or direction being no more than nominal. The horse simply followed and copied the one in front, without regard to the person on its back.

Peter was not yet horseman enough to go hunting, and

the suspicion that this might be the case grew stronger with every stroke of his boot-brush. Ignorance, he reflected, might not turn out to be bliss. Didn't hunting people go flying over five-bar gates? He had never even left the ground on horseback. Why hadn't he kept his silly mouth shut about riding?

Why, indeed. If Peter had known a little more about his pastime, he would have been in a far greater state of anxiety. Jack Sutton, the man who had offered to take him hunting, was a prosperous local builder who had ridden all his life. He was not a polished horseman and did not aspire to be. He liked hunting, and the way to follow hounds was on horseback. He had seldom ridden his daughter's horse, but it was similar to his own — an unremarkable animal, and a safe ride in knowledgeable hands. His wife rode it, so did one or two of his daughter's friends. He would have put anybody up on it without hesitation.

Anybody, that is, who knew what they were doing. Into which category, as far as Jack could tell, Peter fell. It was a good and considerate arrangement. The Londoner — which Peter would remain if he stayed in the village till his dying day — had implied that he rode quite a bit, and shown interest when hunting was spoken of in the pub. It would have been madness for him to buy a horse and hunting clothes and then find that he had neither the time nor the inclination to hunt regularly. So he would have a quiet morning's cub-hunting, and see how he liked it — a gentle introduction to the delights of the chase.

It really was very nice of Jack to make the offer, but exceptionally ill-advised of Peter to accept. It's true that he had asked if hunting wasn't a bit hairy but, his confidence reinforced by the pint in his hand, he had been reassured by Jack's reply. Proper hunting, he had said, could be a bit quick at times — that was the idea of the sport. But cub-hunting was really only culling. Most of the time you had nothing to do but sit and wait. As for riding, you'd be lucky to get out of a trot. He would OK it with the Master, cub-hunting being, by tradition, at his invitation.

Peter hadn't liked to confess that the word 'cub' in front of 'hunting' made him feel rather uneasy. Like many people, he regarded any kind of cub as a candidate for cuddling rather than culling, but it might have seemed cissy to say so.

Oh well, he certainly couldn't back out. Presumably Jack would be getting the horses ready by now. In the silence of the kitchen, under the harsh glare of the fluorescent strip light, the sound of the central heating switching itself on seemed unusually loud. He stopped rubbing his boots. However much he shone them, they would never look like leather.

Quick wash and shave. Then, so as not to awaken his wife, he left their bedroom light off as he tried to get his breeches on, but, with one leg in, lost his balance in the darkness and fell against the bed. His wife stirred and murmured sleepily. 'What's the time, darling?' He whispered back, 'Just gone six.' 'What?!' She shrugged herself deeper into the quilt. No comfort here for the fox-hunter.

With only one leg in his breeches, he limped downstairs to complete his wardrobe in the kitchen, where he could see what he was doing. Into the boots. Polo-neck sweater. Jacket. Gloves? Yes, might as well.

Finally, while electric kettle and toaster hummed their breakfast duet, he put on his riding cap and looked at his reflection in the mirror in the lounge. When attired thus, ready for his rides in London, he had often thought himself quite a fellow — the dashing horseman, ready to mount. This morning, unaccountably, he felt like an absurdly-clad idiot.

The sound of the pop-up toaster popping up took him back into the kitchen. As sometimes happened with this gadget, it had worked over-energetically, and launched the slice of toast half-way across the kitchen and on to the floor. Which is how he came to tread on it. Drinking his tea and munching an unusually thin piece of toast he did not, he felt certain, have the demeanour of a dashing horseman.

It was still dark outside and — oh God, no! — it was raining. Quite lightly. But definitely. Peter hadn't been up this early in the morning since the last time he'd had to catch an aeroplane.

As his car entered Jack's drive and he switched off the headlights and windscreen wipers, Peter had a sudden surge of hope that hunting did not take place in the rain. He plodded towards the house, his footsteps muffled into rubbery silence. It was distinctly chilly, too.

Jack, it turned out, was not a talkative man in the early morning, and was brisk almost to the edge of impatience. Peter had not been to his house before, and began to be aware that he really hardly knew the man. It did not improve his confidence. The darkness was lifting, but the rain was not. Jack, though, did not seem to notice the drizzle.

'You'll have to move your car — I'm bringing the horsebox through here. Stick it outside the gates, there.' Peter did as he was told, feeling that he had started off by doing something wrong. As he reversed back down the drive, he was strongly tempted just to keep on driving — go home, get these silly breeches off and slip back into bed with his wife, who was never brisk, seldom impatient, and a lot better-looking than Jack. He pushed the thought away and walked back up the drive.

'You fit, then?'

'Yes, fine thanks.'

'Where's your stick?'

'Stick?' Peter had no idea what was meant.

'Riding stick.' Jack held up the whip in his own hand, the long thong looped like a lion-tamer's.

'I, er . . . I haven't got one.'

'Hang on, there'll be one in the hall, here.' Jack stepped through his front door and swiftly emerged with a riding stick. Clearly, the idea of mounting a horse without carrying the means to clout it was unthinkable. 'Here you are. You may need to wake your old bugger up a bit. He isn't properly fit yet. I'd wear spurs with him, myself.'

Peter gripped the stick uncertainly. He had never even

held one before, and had no idea how it was employed. Pupils at his London riding establishment were not armed with such weapons. And as for spurs — he couldn't recall ever having seen a pair, except on cowboys in films. Jack though, he now observed, was wearing them. And very business-like they looked, too, jutting out from the heels of boots that were unmistakably leather. Good, old, and properly wrinkled leather.

His clothing was perfect ratcatcher. His breeches were far from new, but were of still serviceably thick twill, buttoned, evidently bespoke, at the knee. The weathered tweed coat was generously long and skirted to protect the thighs, its high-cut lapels just allowing the edges of a yellow waistcoat to peep above them. Tightly at his throat was a blue polka-dot stock, pierced positively by a plain gold pin. The final statement of equestrian familiarity and readiness was his bowler hat, squarely set and tilted forward slightly. Nobody looking at the two men would have had any difficulty discerning which was the horse-man, and which not. A horse could certainly have told the difference.

Peter felt conspicuously amateur-looking in his rubber boots, nylon stretch breeches and 'sports jacket', which was already beginning to absorb the rain. The stick in his hand was a meaningless emblem of equestrian authority he knew he did not possess. This was not the happiest morning of his life.

'Hop in, then. We don't want to be late.'

Not accustomed to lorries, Peter had difficulty getting his body into the cab, which seemed excessively high up. His rubberised foot slipped on the wet metal step, he hit his knee sharply, and dropped the riding stick. In some pain, he fumbled on the ground to recover the stick, which had fallen slightly under one of the horsebox wheels. Jack revved up the engine noisily.

'All set, then?'

Peter suppressed a curse and managed to mutter, 'Yep — half a tick.'

Up in the passenger seat, he rubbed his knee, which

was hurting quite badly. In doing so, he became aware that he had also scraped his knuckles. He tried to examine his wound, but could see little in the gloom.

The lorry started to move. Peter could have wished it were an ambulance. The noise of the engine, which seemed to be under a steel casing separating the two men, was so loud that conversation, had either of them attempted it, would have been practically impossible. This gave Peter no concern, but it increased his feeling of isolation, of not belonging. And of wishing that he were somewhere else.

After twenty minutes of loud travel and noisy double de-clutching, they passed a parked horse-trailer and, a few moments later, a rider. Jack and the rider exchanged waves in what would have been broad daylight, had the sky not been so dark. Peter's growing sense of apprehension worsened. Obviously they had nearly reached wherever they were going and he would soon meet his horse, which presumably was in the back. Jack pulled over on to the grass verge.

'This'll do — right, out you get.' Peter's attempt at alighting from the vehicle was as clumsy as his effort to get into it, but he managed to slither down to the ground without further injury. Jack strode briskly to the back of the horsebox and unbolted the ramp. As he reached up to let it down, Peter stepped forward in a gesture of help, but he was too late, and wasn't certain, anyway, what was required. Jack, in fact, needed no help. He had un-boxed by himself on thousands of occasions. It was a routine he could have managed in his sleep.

He stepped up the ramp, then came down it holding a rope, at the end of which was what looked to Peter like a very large horse indeed. The animal hesitated, then rattled down the ramp in a sudden rush that quite frightened him. Jack handed the rope to Peter and went back up the ramp for the other horse.

Peter clutched the rope tightly and nervously, not knowing what he was supposed to do, other than ensure that the horse did not run away. When Jack brought the other horse down he tied it to a ring-bolt on one side of the box. He nodded, 'There's another ring on the other side,' and started unbuckling his horse's rug. Peter remained standing helplessly, holding his rope as though it were a bomb-fuse.

Jack removed the surcingle that was holding the rug, left the rug in place to keep the rain off his saddle, and pulled off his mount's tail-bandage. It was only then that he perceived that Peter was doing nothing. This puzzled him. 'The ring's round the other side — here,' and he took the rope, led Peter's horse round and tied it to the ring himself. Then, since he was there anyway, and the action was almost automatic, he whipped off its tail-bandage and rug. He didn't want to be late and was not over-concerned if someone else got a wet backside.

Putting the rug and bandages in the horsebox, he re-emerged with two bridles, handed one to Peter, and went to the other side of the box to fix his. Peter was now in total, lonely perplexity. He had a riding stick in one hand, a bridle in the other, and a big horse on the end of a piece of rope. Evidently he was expected to put the bridle on the horse, but he had no idea how to do this. When he went riding in London, his horse was brought to him already dressed.

He looked at the horse, but the animal was offering no help. He looked at the bridle, and then at the horse's head, but this increased his bewilderment. The horse was wearing a head-collar. Did a bridle go over this or under it? Or through it, or round it? Or what? There was no way he could devise a plan of even starting. He was still in this damp dilemma when Jack appeared round the back of the box — already mounted and ready to go. He looked down at Peter in some surprise. 'What's the matter?' Peter felt wretchedly uncomfortable, but could see no solution to his problem except confession.

'I, er . . . I don't . . .' He gave the bridle a little shake. 'I'm not quite sure how you do this.'

Since this might well have been the first time Jack had met anyone who didn't know how to tack up a horse, he overcame his surprise remarkably well.

'How do you manage when you ride up in London, then? All grooms to look after you, is it?'

'Well, no. It's just that where I go, you just go, and er . . . well, you just go . . .' He realised this sounded a bit lame.

'Ah,' said Jack, 'and when you've finished riding you just chuck your reins at the groom, eh? Very nice, too.' He slid off his horse, pulled the reins over its head and handed them to Peter. 'Here — hold this horse.' Jack now knew his saddle was going to get wet, and that he would almost certainly be late for the Meet. He was not pleased, but when he said he was going to do something, he usually did it. And he had said he was going to take Peter hunting.

If Peter had had a good memory and been able to take it all in, what followed was an excellent lesson in how to get a bridle on a horse with little waste of time. The removal of the head-collar and slipping the reins over the horse's head were accomplished smoothly in two virtually simultaneous movements that looked like one. The horse had now lost the restraint of the head-collar but was secured by the reins. No horse was likely to take off while Jack was attending to it. The bit was in the horse's mouth almost before the horse or Peter was aware of it; bridle over head; ears through; forelock pulled over browband; throatlash buckled; a bit of a fiddle to get the drop noseband tight enough — and that, as they say, was that. Continuing this flow of efficient activity, Jack pulled the girth up a couple of holes on the nearside, slid the stirrups down with two loud snaps and took his horse's reins from Peter's hand.

'There you are, your lordship.' This was meant to be jokey, although Peter felt it might have been sarcasm. But he was less bothered about that than he was by the problem of getting up on a horse that seemed bigger than anything he had encountered previously.

He tried to remember what little he had picked up at his riding school, and managed to get his left foot in the stirrup. Fortunately, the horse ignored being prodded sturdily with the riding stick as, with four or five ungainly hops of his right foot, Peter succeeded in swinging his leg over.

It was anything but a smooth, fluent mounting. His breeches would not slide into the saddle because it was wet. He was uncomfortable physically and ill at ease. But he was up. Jack witnessed the scramble with misgivings and doubt, but could think of nothing helpful to say.

'Right, let's try to find hounds. Christ knows where they are by now.' Jack squeezed his horse into a sharp trot, and Peter's horse, receiving no signal to the contrary, followed along the road out of a mixture of instinct and habit. The two horses were regularly exercised together.

Whoever had last used Peter's saddle must have been much taller, for his feet were barely in the stirrups. It was the leathers being so long that had made it relatively easy for him to mount; that same length now made it impossible for him to reach the stirrups sufficiently to help him rise to the trot, and he had never been taught to sit to it. Losing both stirrups almost immediately, he clung on frantically with his heels. The feel of this pressure, plus being tapped by the loose, dangling stirrups, gave the horse the impression that greater effort was required and, since there was no contrary influence on the bit, the animal began to lengthen its stride to catch up with his stable companion. Some fortuitously adhesive inter-action between nylon and damp leather kept Peter roughly in place, but as soon as his horse drew level with the other, it slowed abruptly, pitching Peter forward on to its neck.

'OK?' asked Jack, still trotting effortlessly. It could be argued that he might have checked the stirrup length for Peter, but people who presume to ride are presumed to be capable of attending to such matters for themselves. Peter said, 'Fine, thanks,' and resumed a more upright posture, but he was being bounced in a manner that would have lost him a lot of marks in a dressage competition.

'I should come up a few holes on those leathers,' advised Jack. 'They look a bit long.' He brought his horse back to a walk, to wait, but Peter didn't know how to

make the adjustment on the move. So, fumbling ineffect-
ually at one strap, he continued being towed along in the
wake of the other horse.

His relief was considerable when Jack spotted another
rider, realised they were not late, after all, and pulled his
horse up. Peter's horse did the same, giving him a chance
to attend to his stirrups. With practice, pulling up a leather
while in the saddle becomes a simple operation, even on
the move. With almost no experience, Peter found it
hideously difficult. He knew the principle: take the free
end of the strap in the hand and pull up against the weight
of the foot; pull up past the chosen hole, then let the
leather slip back until, with the forefinger to guide it, the
pin of the buckle slides neatly into the hole.

He did this adequately, but in moving his hand found
that he had left his glove trapped in the buckle. In some
circumstances, this might have been moderately humorous.
In drizzle, with hounds still not in view, Jack missed the
funny side. To Peter, at that particular moment, nothing
would have seemed amusing. He recovered his glove and
eventually adjusted both stirrups more or less to his
liking. Only more or less, because he had not yet been
riding long enough to learn what was his most suitable
length.

Jack stifled a sigh of impatience. 'All set?'

'Right,' Peter replied, and they set off again, this time
in slightly better order, and with Peter occasionally finding
that synchronisation between horse and rider which so
satisfied him when he achieved it riding in London.

They arrived outside a small country pub, unyieldingly
closed at seven o'clock on a wet Saturday morning. The
rider they had seen earlier appeared from the gateway to
a field. 'Come on, Jack, they're up in Barley Wood.' Jack
did not introduce the man to Peter, and all three rode
along the edge of the field in silent single file, Jack second
and Peter third.

For a few minutes, it was not unlike being back in the
park, although more potentially perilous and lacking the
attention of the young instructress's rear aspect. At the

edge of some scrubby thick wood, they halted by four horsemen, one of them wearing a scarlet coat. He was the Huntsman. Another, in bowler-hatted ratcatcher, greeted Jack quite affably. 'Too early for you, were we?' He was the Master, and seemed not to notice Peter, except by implication. 'You and your friend get up towards the corner, there. I wanted to line that side but all the idle sods are in bed.'

Peter thought the more likely explanation might be that the idle sods had got more sense than to come out in the rain, but he found himself following Jack. Again, simply because his horse did so.

Jack explained. 'Now, you get the idea? Hounds are in the covert and they'll be drawing this way. We've got to see Charlie doesn't get out.' He didn't elaborate on how this was to be achieved, and Peter didn't ask. After a hundred yards, Jack drew up. 'I'll stop and watch this bit. You go on to about half-way to that corner.' Peter pressed his heels into the side of the horse in the manner he had been taught, but this apparently conveyed nothing to the horse. He tried again, with the same lack of response.

'Kick him on, then,' urged Jack. Peter pushed his heels right away from the horse's sides and brought them back in with a thud. 'That's the idea — give him a couple more.' Peter did so and, to his surprise, this assault worked. The horse, albeit somewhat sluggishly, began to walk in the required direction away from its friend.

'Keep on kicking him,' Jack called out, 'he's going to sleep.' Peter slammed his heels in again, provoking the horse into a semblance of a trot. As this occurred, although slightly startled, Peter was also rather pleased. Without realising the fact, he was beginning to grasp an essential principle of equestrianism — that the rider is boss.

However, since he had not learned yet how to continue with leg persuasion while trotting, as experienced riders can, the trot soon deteriorated into a walk and, not long afterwards, a halt. By then, though, he had evidently travelled far enough. He heard a cry of 'That'll do!'

So, here he was sitting on a horse in the rain, wondering

what would happen next, and what was expected of him. He had learned in the pub that 'Charlie' meant the fox, but what, if one appeared from the wood, was he to do to stop it?

Fifteen minutes later, tangibly wetter and colder, he remained unenlightened. He hadn't had a glimpse of a fox, or even a hound. Luckily his horse (unlike some) was content to remain inactive, but (like all) it could have done with a snack. Unless gravely ill, horses are always ready to eat, but they soon learn to do so only when permitted and, while out hunting, this is never. Children on ponies may allow their mounts to treat hedgerows like cafeterias, nibbling self-service leaves as they go, but fox-hunting riders disapprove of such indulgences. Their horses are fed at home.

Peter's horse knew this well enough, but he had spent the summer in a field, browsing constantly, and since he was in a field now, and nothing much seemed to be going on, it was worth a try. He lowered his head towards the tempting grass and found, to his gratification, that he was not promptly jerked in the mouth and cursed as his rider pulled at the reins to get his head back where it belonged.

Peter was alarmed as the reins slid through his sodden gloves and he was left, feeling rather exposed, with no horse's neck in front of him, and no reins in his hands. His sudden fear soon subsided, though, as he saw that the horse was simply grazing, and he was happily ignorant that to let it do so was an equestrian solecism. Were it not for the incessant rain and its attendant discomforts, he would have been quite content to sit thus for as long as the horse cared. After a while, there was a brief distant tooting sound which might have been a hunting horn, but since Peter had never heard one before, he couldn't be certain, and wouldn't have known, anyway, if it had any significance.

Evidently it had. Jack came up towards him at a vigorous canter, brandishing his whip in a manner that could have been interpreted as menacing, or beckoning.

He may have been angry at seeing his horse enjoying an alfresco breakfast; he may simply have been in a hurry. What is certain is that he shot past Peter with great urgency, shouting 'They've gone on! Follow me, follow me!' Peter might have thought about this instruction for a moment, before acting on it. But not Peter's horse. Excited by the flurry, it obeyed at once. In one lightning movement it threw up its head, whirled, and took off after the other animal.

It did so, unhappily, without Peter on its back. He was dislodged instantly, performing a kind of half backward flip that planted him on his shoulders, with his feet pointed upwards, in the wet grass. It was not a particularly painful landing, as riding upsets go. As he lay on his back, the rain falling gently on his face soon became the greatest discomfort he had to endure.

When he got to his feet, he found he was quite alone in the field. He picked up his velvet riding cap, and the stick, and tried to consider what he ought to do next. What would have been uppermost in a fox-hunter's mind would have been to become reunited with his horse as soon as possible, but, as he was not yet a fox-hunter, this was the furthest from Peter's thoughts. He had no wish to see the horse, or perhaps any other, ever again. That, for him, was the end of his first day's hunting.

And, as it transpired, the last.

Still cubbing, but it's more like hunting now, with the Meets so late. Loads of people out. I have the same feeling every year, looking forward to the season but a bit sorry that cubbing's over. I like the friendship, just a few people you know, the ones who understand about hounds and what's going on. The Hoorays are starting now, but we can't do without them. There'll be a mob out on Saturday in their riding caps, neither one thing or the other, all impatient for a run. No idea about cub-hunting, but I'll push one out if I can — the new entry still don't really know what it's about so it'll do them good. Actually a fox did break on Tuesday and gave us a bit of a jolly round Palmerstone, so we might have a half decent pack yet! Apparently the antis have started already. On TV last night but we missed it. Somebody's hounds rioted on to deer and killed one right in front of the cameras. According to Nigel (who always knows everything) the antis laid a drag, put the hounds on to a deer and then waited to film it, gore galore. Then they took the film to the BBC and a woman anti was interviewed and said this proved how many animals were killed by hounds every day — including hundreds of cats! God, that'll get the old ladies going, and they'll believe it because it was on the telly. 'Ware pussy!

Down with Hunting

From the blinkered viewpoint of the old-time fox-hunter there used to be two kinds of people — those who hunted, and those who did not. The former were probably good fellows, and the latter didn't matter.

Today there's a new kind of chap — the 'anti'. Antis are people who, while perhaps accepting that foxes may have to be controlled, cannot tolerate the concept of people actually hunting them for pleasure.

Anyone opposed to the sport for any reason is disliked by the fox-hunting fraternity, but the ones who irritate them most obviously are the 'sabs' — members of the Hunt Saboteurs Association, who occasionally turn up at Meets carrying anti-hunting placards and subsequently try to spoil the day's hunting by distracting hounds and frightening foxes out of the Hunt's range.

They spray foul-smelling substances to mask scent, lay false trails, shout confusing holloas, and blow hunting horns, although not usually very well. However, they are sometimes skilled enough to bewilder hounds and can succeed in ruining the day. More militantly, they sometimes explode firecrackers and make rude remarks to followers.

The explosions of the firecrackers frighten horses, a fact which seems strangely at odds with the aims of people who claim to be opposed to cruelty to animals. But presumably they feel that, since an upset horse may well imperil its rider — and the rider is the enemy — they are justified.

Most fox-hunters are either sufficiently well-mannered to ignore the insults, or articulate enough to deal with them. Two actual verbatim examples:

Anti: (to elderly lady riding side-saddle) How can you sit there with an ugly face like that, you old cow?

Lady: With dignity.

Anti: (to a Master) What do you do with the hounds when they're too old to hunt?

Master: Shoot them, like we ought to shoot you.

All fox-hunters are aware of the hunt saboteurs, but not all have encountered them because their numbers are not great enough to visit all the countries with significant frequency. To be anything more than the sporadic nuisance they are, they would need an army. On a typical 'strike' upwards of a dozen sabs turn out, usually in three or four cars, often equipped with CB radios. The cars tend to be old, either because they can't afford new ones or are fearful of retaliatory damage by irate fox-hunters.

Nearly all sabs are young — university students are common— with a few leaders perhaps in their thirties. Oddly enough, many fox-hunters respect the views of the 'real' sabs, but suspect that the majority are rent-a-mob hooligans recruited (and paid) by the day and out for a lark. On occasion, the larks escalate to the ugly. Bones, as well as Her Majesty's Peace, have been broken, and court appearances have ensued.

What is overlooked, or simply not seen or understood by the non-hunting portion of the population, is that fox-hunting is not enjoyed exclusively by people on horses. Where insults, threats and jostling blows are exchanged between the pro-hunt and the anti-hunt, the action takes place on the ground. Mounted followers may *feel* like lashing out with their hunting whips — and the urge might be experienced by anyone who'd just had a firecracker let off behind his horse — but it's the foot-followers who are most likely to be actively upset by demonstrators, and respond violently.

Every Hunt has regular foot-people and a fair few of them are young farm workers who regard hunting as a good day out on a day off. They enjoy their sport, and will not have it ruined by a handful of their urban contemporaries . Given this knowledge, and accepting that young men who do manual work in the open air are probably fitter and tougher than the average university student, the sabs must be saluted for bravery.

Some of them are girls, too. When foot-followers try to grab a sab's hunting-horn, he'll pass it to a female demonstrator if he can. She can then stick it down her cleavage and rely on rural chivalry to keep it safe, thus saving the sabs the £50 it probably cost to buy. Some sabs carry a cheap dummy horn to yield in emergency, for the same reason.

It has become usual for one or two policemen to attend Meets, and sometimes to follow hounds on motorcycles for part of the day. Some of them seem rather to enjoy it.

The real threat to fox-hunting in the 1980s comes not

from the hunt saboteurs, but from the political far Left, where its enemies have long lain. In 1979 the Labour Party accepted a donation of £80,000 from the League Against Cruel Sports and in its 1983 General Election Manifesto promised (or threatened) to make 'all forms of hunting with dogs' illegal. By then, nearly twenty Socialist-controlled local authorities had banned hunting on council-owned land, and the Co-op had done the same on its farming land.

The hunting case was put by the British Fields Sports Society, to which fox-hunters subscribe, but it needed greater unity and strength to resist the General Election danger. Out of this need grew the Campaign for Country Sports, which was established early in 1983 and represented the British Field Sports Society, the British Association for Shooting and Conservation, the National Anglers' Council and many others, including prominent horsemen and trade unionists. Subsequently the Country Sports Appeal Fund was launched to finance the fight up to and beyond the General Election.

That the anglers joined the Campaign was particularly interesting. The Labour Party Manifesto specifically excluded fishing, mindful, no doubt, that the sport has over three million adherents and that all those dangling rods represented not just floating voters, but a great many traditional or even habitual Socialist votes. The fishermen were sure, however, that if the League Against Cruel Sports succeeded in getting fox-hunting banned, it would direct its efforts next against shooting (also excluded from the Manifesto) and fishing. The logic was clear: if it is cruel to kill a fox, is it not cruel to shoot a bird or catch a fish?

The support of the anglers went a long way towards demonstrating that the Campaign for Country Sports was not formed simply to preserve privileges for chinless toffs, that field sports are enjoyed by a far wider section of the population — politically as well as socially — than was generally supposed, and that their adherents are not solely country-dwellers.

Fox-hunters, whose ranks contain a growing number of urbanites, were delighted at the Tory victory in 1983, but they know that the abolitionists will not give up. If the sport is to survive, its followers will have to remain alert.

Like the fox itself.

31 October

On the very eve of the Opening Meet (my, my, doesn't time fly) and I have to put up with a lecture from an anti. Very pleasant dinner (here) with Jeremy and Sarah and their frightfully brilliant Sussex University niece, who is anti-everything except bigger grants for students. Sat listening to us talking about the new season and then interrupted (I always love that) the conversation to inform us all that (a) we'd better enjoy hunting while we may, because it will soon be banned and (b) all her friends go drag-hunting, which is far more dangerous and doesn't 'murder' innocent wild animals. Jeremy looked a bit awkward, as well he might, but she'd got the bit between her teeth. All sensible and sensitive people in Britain, of all political persuasions, are disgusted by fox-hunting. Their combined horror will make the ban inevitable. Why do we need to go out slaughtering when we can enjoy good clean sport galloping and jumping drag-lines, etc., etc.? When I'd climbed back off the mantelpiece (she must know I'm an MFH and the attack was sheer cheek) I was pretty good. Very cool, but the claret was working a bit. I agreed that fox-hunting had become increasingly restricted and admitted I feared it might come to an end one day. Ah! She loved that, winning already. While she was swooning with delight at her victory, I bit her with the next part. However, I purred, the threat to fox-hunting lies in intensive farming making less land available, not in political action by half-baked ignoramuses who know nothing whatever about the sport. Ouch!!! Collapse of students' union. But I hadn't finished. I explained that drag-hunting is a joke in which some athletic idiot dangling a tin of cat-food is given a 10-minute start over a carefully prepared line of jumps so that a mob of mongrels can pursue the smell while being chased by a load of idiots on horses. The last bit was the claret talking, and I was feeling extremely shirty. I've been to some very good Meets of Draghounds, and they go like hell. Terrifying. But it isn't hunting. They don't really need hounds and are constantly in danger of over-running them, so they could easily just settle for what they want — a rattle across country. But I wouldn't dream of trying to ban them. Live and let live and leave us to our hunting with hounds and the element of chance we all love. Diana is still furious. She says I was rude, sarcastic, and took unfair advantage of a child. Child? I say to hell with that. Children should be seen and not heard — and I'm going hunting in the morning. Hope she doesn't hide my boots.

Image of War

Jim Carter turned the hot and cold bath taps until they flowed in encouraging unison to produce just the right temperature and volume of water. Then, sitting on the edge of the bath with the steam rising behind him, he began removing his riding breeches. Or unpeeling them, since they were still sodden from a day's hunting in relentless rain and were clammily clamped to his knees. These, when revealed, were white with a touch of chill purple. With weary grunts and sighs, he rubbed his kneecaps and calves to revive the circulation, and took off the remainder of his clothing. His saturated boots, coat, cap, gloves and waistcoat were already discarded downstairs in the kitchen utility room, where the central heating boiler was. Coat and waistcoat on hangers, to dry slowly back to shape; trees in boots.

Briefly, contemplating his belly, which bore pink indentations from the waistband pressure of the breeches, he once again resolved to lose some weight one of these days, and reached out for the generous tumbler of whisky he had placed on the top of the shaving cabinet. Ice cubes tinkled festively as he carefully lowered himself into the water, avoiding the double perils of scalding his lower regions and diluting the whisky with medicated bath foam. This action safely accomplished, he breathed a sigh of great content.

It had been a good day. As his exhaustion began to dissipate in the warm water and the whisky spread its pleasing glow through his aching body, he indulged himself in what may well be the greatest pleasure of fox-hunting — savouring it afterwards.

It has been famously said of the sport that it bears the image of war, without the guilt, and only twenty-five per cent of the danger. The analogy with war can be taken further than Somerville asserted in the eighteenth century and Surtees echoed in the nineteenth. Hunting could be said to resemble war because its whole is made up of ninety-nine per cent boredom and one per cent terror. You pays your subscription and you takes your choice.

The winter's day that Jim Carter now re-lived with satisfied relish would have struck any non-fox-hunter as truly appalling. It had rained remorselessly at the Meet, and had seldom stopped all day; at times the rain had given way to hail, driven practically horizontally by gusting wind. No sensible person would have been out in such weather by choice, even in a motor car. To be out on horseback voluntarily was a fair indication of incipient insanity; or of addiction to fox-hunting. In some circumstances, the two afflictions are virtually indistinguishable.

But even fox-hunters have discomfort thresholds, and by 2 p.m. the field that had ridden out bravely 70-strong was reduced to fewer than 30. By 3 p.m. even more people had said 'goodnight' and disappeared. When there was little more than half an hour of dim, damp and cold daylight left, even the remaining chilled and soaked diehards were furtively praying for the Huntsman to blow his horn for home.

Jim had stayed on because be was a true fox-hunting farmer, a stalwart who seldom missed a Meet and shared the other regulars' contempt for fair-weather hunters. He went home when hounds went home. But he could have wished, today, that there had been good sport to mitigate the severity of the weather. Huntsman and hounds had persevered, but conditions — particularly the wind — were against them. The field had endured a series of uncomfortable vigils while hounds drew, interspersed with splashily but sporadically warming dashes to the next covert, as hounds were put in to draw yet again. Some of the horses, bored with standing about being rained and hailed on, had been fractious. To anyone considering giving up fox-hunting altogether, this would have been the day to do it.

Hounds had unkennelled one fox, but it was quickly marked to ground without adventure, and the dismal digging-out was only persisted with because the Hunt had been specifically asked to deal with a local poultry killer. There was no way of knowing, as the cartridge of the humane killer exploded, whether the dead fox was the guilty party.

At about half-past three, Jim was one of perhaps a dozen soggy riders waiting with the Master by a field of not very abundant winter cabbages while hounds drew a big patch of gorse far to the left. Beyond and to the right was a steep and unevenly wooded railway embankment about 40 feet high, like a long dam. The railway was disused, as all the party knew, and the rails and sleepers had been taken up long since at the behest of the once notorious but now forgotten Dr. Beeching. The track was used nowadays as a bridle way by hikers and leisure riders enterprising enough to find the few gateways giving access. The bottom of the embankment was protected against trespass by a shoulder-high wire mesh fence topped by two strands of barbed wire that would have deterred even the most rashly bold fox-hunter from attempting to jump it.

Like all good fox-hunters, Jim sat listening for hounds and studying the terrain, working out how best to get to them, whatever way they took. He paid little attention to the embankment, because hounds were working away from it in the opposite direction.

Now and again the stationary group could hear the Huntsman's horn as he pushed hounds through the gorse, but the gusty wind smothered and fragmented the sound. In this cold and wind it was a marvel he could manage to blow it at all. The Master, sitting next to Jim, said with a rich chuckle, 'He'll have that horn blown straight back down his throat if he doesn't watch out.' It was an old joke, but they were old friends. The Master was a farmer, too. Either man would have been hard pushed to say how many times they had hunted together. Rain dropped like a leaky tap from the ribbons dangling wetly from the back of the Master's cap.

'Had enough yet, Jim?'

'Oh, I'm all right, Master. Can't get any wetter.'

Jim, a traditionalist, adhered to the convention. At the cattle market on Tuesday it would be John again. Out hunting, it was Master.

'If we don't find here in a minute, we'll call it a day.'

Jim nodded and considered whether, at last, he might change his soaked string gloves for the spare dry pair he had tucked under his horse's girth. He decided no, it wasn't worth it. They'd be wet before he'd got them on.

A young woman in the group spoke to her horse quietly but firmly. 'Stand *still*!' The animal was trying to move backwards in its frustration at not being allowed to go forwards. It was a Thoroughbred, a once middling useful point-to-pointer, and had been 'nappy' (unpredictably nervous, disobedient, or downright dangerous) all day.

A good rider, she was holding the horse nicely between hand and leg — strong but subtle restraint from the reins prevented the horse going ahead, while her spurred heels stopped it stepping backwards. The horse chose another option. It swung its quarters sideways and tried to buck, but she didn't allow it to lower its head sufficiently to make the manoeuvre effective.

So it reared.

This is one of a horse's most terrifying tactics. Confirmed rearers stand straight up on their hind legs, and there are even those that will fall backwards onto their riders. The horse's forelegs pedalled the air; the woman stuck tight and leant forward as far as she could, her head at the side of the horse's neck. A few seconds of this balancing act, and the horse dropped its front feet back to the ground. The rider had won another little argument.

The Master said, 'You can take that horse home if you want, Betty.'

'No thank you, Master. He's got to learn some manners.'

There are women of daunting courage and determination in the hunting field. Calmly, she made the horse walk steadily in a wide circle, to distract it from further unruly endeavour.

As the rest of the group watched, a thin distant sound slipped shakily through the wind. It might have been a shout.

'Hark holloa!' cried the Master with quick authority. They all listened.

And there it was again. Everybody looked for the source of the holloa. Then came the sound of the horn, its piercing quality made wavery by the wind.

'Up on the embankment, Master!' shouted one of the party, pointing. 'It's the Whip!'

And it was. And galloping, with his cap held in front of him.

'God almighty,' muttered the Master, 'what the hell's he doing up there?' But, when a Whip holloas, it's taken seriously. 'For'ard on!' the Master cried, putting spurs to his horse as he swung it left, skirting the cabbage field, with the rest of the group tucking themselves behind him in single file. Only the Master, out in front and quickening his pace, avoided the clumps of mud which each horse scooped up and flicked behind it. For the last few of the riders, it was like a cavalry charge through a bombardment of clods.

At the corner of the cabbage field the Master turned his horse neatly to the right and kicked up into a gallop for the corner of the gorse, about half a mile away. The next rider, over-excited, tried to turn his horse to follow, but he asked too soon when the animal was going too fast. Its legs slithered helplessly from beneath it. Horse and rider hit the ground with an audible thump and slithered two yards before coming to a surprised halt. The horse wriggled quickly to its feet and the rider, his black coat now rather less smart-looking than when he'd set out, re-mounted with commendable if confused alacrity.

'You all right?' shouted Jim, who was next.

'Yes thanks,' replied the man, 'for'ard on!'

With no cabbage crop to impede them, the riders spread out and galloped to catch up with the Master. In the relief of action, the weather was forgotten. It was almost as though the sun was shining.

Jim shortened rein, too experienced to allow his horse to get carried away in a mad rush. He could hear hounds now, and meant to get to them, but under control. The Master's red coat was still in sight, going straight for the gorse. Jim followed, trying to guess what was happening. The last place they wanted hounds was up on the embankment, going away from home and on the wrong side of a fence that would have dismayed a kamikaze pilot, but that was where the Whip was last seen. Jim knew there was a bridge a little way down that had once carried the railway over a lane, and presumed that the Whip had got in by a pedestrian gate there.

Ah! — there was the Huntsman. He emerged from the far side of the gorse, riding fast and directly towards the path of the Master and following field. As the Huntsman saw the riders he shouted 'Gone away!' and spun his horse to his left; now, he was leading the field and apparently making for the bridge. Would he, Jim wondered, go under the bridge, into the lane, and follow hounds on the far side of the embankment?

No, he would not. As the bridge came into sight, Jim saw the Huntsman kick hard and swing purposefully towards the pedestrian gate, although it was made of four-foot pointed palings and far from inviting. And dammit if he didn't jump it in a daringly graceful arc and plunge on up into the trees on the slope.

'Hell's bells,' Jim swore to himself. A well-mounted professional might risk such a jump to get up to his hounds, but he wasn't too keen on putting his old faithful at it. It was a relief to see the Master slowing up and looking back to see who was with him. One was Betty, on the point-to-point horse, which was pulling fiercely. She saw the situation and shouted, 'Can I go on, Master?'

'If you want, Betty.'

She sawed at the horse's bit to check it. It pranced on the spot in frothy impatience. After a moment to summon the horse's attention, she eased the reins, allowing it to go forward, but stifling its urge to rush. Then she sat down hard and went for the gate. One stride . . . two . . . three . . . and UP! Like a top show-jumper, it made nothing of the four feet, and as it landed cleanly on the other side of the gate, attempted to gallop off. But not with Betty aboard. She checked it again and began picking her way upwards through the trees.

The Master's reaction was immediate. 'Ha!' he yelled, 'come on!' and popped his own horse over the gate with a bold flourish. Given such a lead, Jim took a deep breath and pointed his horse at the jump — and the 12-year-old flew it with disdain. The horse now wanted to catch up with the others, and tackled the slope vigorously, with Jim crouching forward in the saddle to counteract the gradient and avoid tree branches whipping him in the face. 'Steady, my man,' he urged, 'steady!'

A loud crash of splintering wood and a shriek came from below him. Some emboldened soul had evidently taken the shorter way — straight through the gate. Oh well, he thought, there were plenty of people behind to deal with any casualties. And hounds were somewhere ahead.

Stones loosened by the Master's horse scrabbling above rolled down at him, and it looked for a few seconds as though they might be followed by the animal, and the Master, as well. But, with a last convulsive heave, the horse pulled itself up on to the level track, where Jim rapidly caught up. He was breathing heavily but happily. 'We going hunting then, Master?'

'I'm not too sure, but I want to see those hounds before it gets dark — kick on!' And they did — high up on the embankment on a straight and level track, galloping abreast like two excited schoolboys having a race. Their two horses pushed their heads forward in well-muscled willing effort. The rain stung their faces, but they didn't care. If there was any exhilaration left in the world, then this was it.

'How far's this track go?' shouted the Master above the wind and thudding hooves.

'No idea, Master.'

It was a rare sensation riding fast and high up in the air. Jim pointed down to the left with his whip, where they both saw the second Whipper-in and four members of the field, all galloping flat-out. It was like a Western movie, with bandits trying to keep up with a speeding train.

Train?

Suddenly they were passing between the platforms of what had once been a station, but had been converted into a private house. Had the owners looked out of the window, they couldn't have been more surprised than if they'd seen the Flying Scotsman go through.

But even greater surprise lay before the two galloping horsemen. With their heads ducked against the rain, and only squinting uncertainly from beneath their caps, they were a fraction late seeing the old level-crossing gate that permanently blocked the track in front of them.

The Master screamed, 'Hold hard! Hold hard!' and made to rein back. But the moment to stop had passed. Both horses were in hot overdrive, and too close to the barrier to pause. Fear fell into Jim's stomach like a dropped anchor as, without any guidance from him or the Master, the two animals found their own strides, rose at the gate — and soared over it.

On the other side, the riders pulled the horses back to something like a sedate canter. 'That came up a bit quick, didn't it?' said the Master. Jim, all his pulses throbbing, could only agree. He had taken some jumps in his time but had never, in his dreams, his nightmares, or his imagination, leapt a level-crossing gate before. He did not intend doing so again.

The dark day was darkening to its end as they covered another mile of the track at an easier, but useful pace, both standing in their stirrups to save the horses. The Master was slightly in front when he called back, 'There's the horn!' They pulled up, the better to listen.

'What did you make of that?' asked the Master.

'Can't be sure, Master. Didn't hear properly.'

'Let's get on, then.' And they trotted on.

In a few moments they came across the stationary figures of Betty and the Huntsman.

'I've blown for home, Master.'

'Good man. Where are hounds?'

'Just below, sir.' Jim and the Master moved up to the other two horses and saw that 'just below' meant a dark, awesome abyss — a gap where a 40-foot-wide bridge, long demolished, had once taken the railway line over a road that lay at least 30 feet below. Hounds were assembled down there under the eye of Fred, the Whipper-in, whose holloa had set everybody off.

'That'd have made a fair old jump, wouldn't it, sir?' the Huntsman joked to Jim. 'Hounds come along the track here and that stopped them dead, so while they was scrambling down, like, Fred managed to stop 'em. Otherwise they'd have been down in the road and off God knows where, and it was getting a bit late, like.'

'Well done,' said the Master. 'Anybody see the fox?'

'I did at the start, Master. Then Fred did. But he's long gone — traveller, I reckon.'

They all dismounted and lead their horses gingerly down the slippery slope where the bridge had been. Then they mounted up for the long hack back, with muddied hounds at their horses' feet.

'All on, Fred?' asked the Huntsman.

'All on.'

Jim rode alongside the Huntsman and the Master, to the rear of the pack. Rain and darkness were merging into a totality of discomfort, but they were content.

'Wet old day it's been, Master,' observed the Huntsman.

The Master and Jim muttered agreement.

'Still — they can't all be good. I 'eard there was a bit of

grief at that little gate on the railway.'

'Anybody hurt?' asked the Master.

'Nah — don't think so. But you've got to get that one just right.'

'How do you know?' asked Jim in surprise. 'We've never hunted on the railway track before, have we?'

'No, sir, but I had hounds up there in the summer on exercise, and that old gate was the devil to open. Got a chain on it.'

'What did you do about that level-crossing gate, then?'

'What — by the old station?'

'Yes.'

'Went round it, sir — there's a gap at the side.'

'Is that what you did today?'

'I should say so — wouldn't catch me trying to jump that, not when I knew there was a way round.'

'We did,' declared the Master, somewhat heavily.

'Did you now, sir — any bother?'

'No,' answered the Master nonchalantly, 'flew it like birds, didn't we, Jim?'

'Yes, Master.'

Jim unscrewed his whisky flask and handed it to his old friend. Tiredness was oozing into them both now, and their horses' heads were drooping. The Master swigged gratefully and returned the flask. Jim handed it to the Huntsman, who had his swallow and gave it back. 'Ah,' said the Huntsman, 'that makes it all seem worthwhile, sir, and no mistake.' Jim put the flask to his own lips . . .

. . . just as later, in his bath, he emptied his glass of whisky, smiled in recollection, and shook his head in near disbelief at the memory of jumping the level-crossing gate. The quick stab of fright that had changed so magic-ally into the elation of a brave chance safely taken. Like so many other hunting incidents, he'd go on talking about that jump for many seasons to come. He chuckled to himself with profound satisfaction, and slid dozily deeper into the welcoming warmth and caressing comfort of the water . . .

   . . . hunting . . . image of war . . . no guilt . . . danger . . .
He was almost falling asleep in his bath.
It was time to say . . .
Goodnight.